Breaking & Entering

Breaking & Entering

THE EDUCATION OF A FILM PRODUCER

Steve Starkey

Sand Point Press

Copyright © 2022 by Steve Starkey
ALL RIGHTS RESERVED

ISBN 978-0-578-27470-6 (SOFTCOVER)
ISBN 978-0-578-27471-3 (HARDCOVER)
ISBN 978-0-578-27027-2 (EBOOK)

PRINTED IN THE
United States of America.

Grateful acknowledgement is made to the following for use of the photographs that appear in the art insert: courtesy of the author: pages 1-4, 12, bottom page 15, 17, top page 18; courtesy of Lucasfilm: page 5; courtesy of Universal Studios: pages 13, 14, top of 15, 16, bottom page 18; courtesy of Disney: pages 6, 7, bottom page 9, bottom page 10; courtesy of Disney and Amblin Entertainment, Inc.: top of pages 8, 9, 10, page 11; courtesy of Touchstone and Amblin Entertainment, Inc.: bottom page 8, pages 19-23.

BOOK DESIGN BY
John Balkwill, Lumino Press

COVER ART BY
Doug Chiang

to Liv

So you want to be a rock and roll star
Then listen now to what I say
Just get an electric guitar
Then take some time
And learn how to play

Roger McGuinn & Chris Hillman

Contents

Prologue
1

CHAPTER 1
I Never Heard of Film School
9

CHAPTER 2
Breaking In
27

CHAPTER 3
Day of the Locust
35

CHAPTER 4
Starting Over at Lucasfilm
51

CHAPTER 5
The Empire Strikes Back
75

CHAPTER 6
Behind the Scenes
93

CHAPTER 7
Return of the Jedi
103

CHAPTER 8
Behind the Scenes at Amblin
119

CHAPTER 9
Amazing Stories
129

CHAPTER 10
My Amazing Story with Steven Spielberg
155

CHAPTER 11
Shooting the Rabbit
193

CHAPTER 12
Bringing the Rabbit to Life
219

CHAPTER 13
A Solo Performance
247

CHAPTER 14
Back to the Future II
253

CHAPTER 15
Back to the Future III
275

CHAPTER 16
Jurassic Park
293

CHAPTER 17
Noises Off
305

CHAPTER 18
A Meeting with Bob
311

Epilogue
317

Acknowledgments
319

About the Author
323

Prologue

WHEN I OPENED the stage door, I had no reason to think that on this particular day of shooting on *Death Becomes Her*, I would learn what it means to be lonely at the top. We were filming on an interior set, and it was raining outside the windows. Rainbirds had been strategically placed overhead. When turned on, they would simulate the pouring rain. Troughs had been built around the perimeter of the set to collect the massive amounts of water, which was then pumped outside the stage into drains to prevent flooding. After a few takes, the troughs couldn't hold the water, overflowed their banks, and started to flood the stage floor. The effects technicians had wellies, knee-high boots, on their truck for working around rain. None of the rest of the cast or crew were prepared with any kind of water gear. Take by take, the flooding got worse. I went to the supervisor of the effects crew, Michael Lantieri, and said that this was becoming a serious problem.

The water was now creeping toward the entrance to the set. Michael said they were trying to fix it, but that he didn't think that the troughs could handle this amount of rain. He couldn't lighten the rain because that's what the scene called for, and it's what director Bob Zemeckis wanted. I went to Bob and brought the problem to his attention. I wanted to see if he had a solution I had not considered. Could there be less rain or no rain? I hesitated to ask, because, dramatically, what we were doing was appropriate for the scene. Bob did not offer up any solutions, so I went back to Michael. If the flooding is going to persist, I told him, we are going to have to take longer breaks between takes to let the draining system do its job. We tried that, but adding minutes between takes wouldn't solve the problem. And if we didn't solve the problem, the water would damage the stage floor and the production would have to pay for it. I dreaded calling in those cost overages to the studio.

With Bob not having the patience to slow down shooting and Michael without an immediate solution, the crew started to gather outside the set, staring at the rising water. Bob joined us, and all eyes landed on the me, the producer, when Bob said, "Steve, what are we going to do?" At that moment, I knew that I alone would be making the decision. It was the job I chose to do, aspired to do, and was finally doing. I looked at Michael. I knew he and his effects guys needed a day to fix the problem. To buy him time, we would have to stop shooting the scene and try to salvage the day somehow. I looked over at Rick Carter, the production designer. He and I had just walked through the set we were scheduled to move into next. It was dressed and ready. I thought about the cast. The same actors were already here, at the studio. I asked the costumers if the wardrobe was on hand and available if I moved to the other set. They nodded, yes. In my mind I quickly ran through the props needed, and nothing seemed to be missing. I knew I would lose a few hours to make the film company move from one stage to the other; wrapping the camera and sound and all the other departments would take time. And time is money. I ran through all these considerations in less than a minute, like the character in the Ambrose Bierce story, "An Occurrence at Owl Creek Bridge." All the preparations that were needed to go to Plan B played out in my mind before I said, "Let's wrap it up here on this scene for today. Let Michael take the time he needs to fix the problem. We will make a company move to the other stage to begin shooting a new scene."

Prologue

There was a moment of silence, then everyone turned and went about their business. Bob said he was going to his motor home to prepare for what he was about to shoot and to call him when we were ready. Standing alone for a moment, with everyone gone, looking at the pools of water, Michael asked, "Are you okay?" "Yes, I'm fine. I think we made the right decision." He turned and walked away and left me alone with my thoughts. In those moments, I understood the role I was playing.

MY EDUCATION in the film industry lasted for fifteen years before I became a producer. One year as a production assistant. Two years as a lighting technician. Six years in the editing room. Five years as an associate producer. One year as a co-producer. All before I was asked to produce my first film. At that time, I did not realize exactly what the job of a producer entailed or what it would be like. It is a position that is hard to define until you actually do it.

Some days later on the set, a crew member wandered over and asked me how I got the job as the producer of the film. It was a good question. I still ask myself the same question. How did I get the job? The question fed into my insecurities. I was trying to get comfortable in my new role, and I didn't know if I was up to the task. Maybe the crew member sensed that as well. But before I answered the question, it got me thinking. Did they really want to know my life's story? Some of it, perhaps. But where would I start?

The truth is, I never set out to become a producer. As my career progressed, it became the goal, then the final step, but it was not what I had in mind in the first place. At the beginning of my career, when I pounded the pavement in Los Angeles, I really had no idea what I was looking for. For me, as a transient of sorts, certainly a child of the '60s, film work offered adventure with loose commitments. Traveling from place to place on one show to the next might satisfy my wanderlust and lifestyle. Beyond that, I had no idea what to expect or what I would find.

But rather than my life's story, what most people really wish to know is how I broke into the business, which door I knocked on first. My answer always takes them by surprise. You really wandered the backlot of Universal Studios asking around for work? No one does that. Isn't that illegal? Now they're intrigued. Maybe they see a door slowly opening, revealing a way into producing. Maybe they could climb the same ladder I did and reach their own goal. When I look back on it, even I wonder what I was thinking, hopping that bus that took me onto the studio lot. I was breaking and entering. I guess it *was* illegal…

It could be that they were amazed that someone with no actual producing experience had been given this opportunity. In other words, with a little luck, they might get a job producing too. We all hope for that. Or, since they had no other reasonable explanation, what if it was someone I knew, or some "connections" that had gotten me the job, in which case I had not really earned the position. And since I had no real qualifications, maybe there was an easy way to get the job without any credentials. After all, it was not like I had a framed diploma, as you might see on the wall of a doctor's office, displaying my degree in film producing alongside one from my alma mater. How did it happen, then? As it turns out, there was a perfectly good reason for how I finally ended up where I did. It just didn't happen overnight or in any conventional way. On the set of *Death Becomes Her* that day, my answer to the inquisitive crew member was quite simply, "I was hired by Bob Zemeckis."

Prologue

YEARS LATER, as the stages continued to flood on *Forrest Gump, Cast Away, The Polar Express,* and numerous other films, the original curiosity question remained: How did you get your first job producing? Even now, friends or new acquaintances continue to ask me how I got started in the film industry and how that led me to producing. Because Hollywood work seems glamorous, they think my story will be equally fascinating. And while some find my journey captivating, everyone finds it surprising and unique. In fact, there is no other story quite like mine.

I did not keep a journal or a diary of those years. I must rely on my memory, and we all know the pitfalls of that. But many of these stories seem fresh in my mind. Some cause me grief, some make me cringe in disbelief, other times I laugh, but they all remind me what kept me going: I loved every step along the way.

Breaking & Entering

CHAPTER 1

I Never Heard of Film School

THERE ARE THOSE who, at a young age, know exactly what they want to do for the rest of their lives. Many filmmakers are like this, in particular, Steven Spielberg and Robert Zemeckis, two of the filmmakers I worked with throughout my career. They made home movies when they were young boys. They dreamed of making films when they grew up, and the dream never let go of them.

Not me. I never had that dream. Even though I grew up in Los Angeles, in the heart of the film industry, the dream never entered my mind. In 1961, when I was nine years old, I went to see *The Absent-Minded Professor*. I was spellbound. My dream was to buy some flubber, that magic goo, and fly through the air on the basketball court, as they did in the film. That same year, I went to a birthday party with a group of boys to see *West Side Story* at the Bruin Theater in Westwood Village. We loved the film and came out of the theater snapping our fingers, trying to be cool. But I didn't get the urge to go home and pick up our 8mm camera and make a film. The camera was for home movies made by my dad on our family holidays in Lake Arrowhead.

As I grew older, movies continued to have an effect on me. In 1967, when I saw *Cool Hand Luke*, I was profoundly moved. One line of dialogue really resonated: "What we have here... is a failure... to communicate." That's how I felt. With the war going on and the divide between myself and the older generation growing wider and crooked politicians making insane decisions, I could identify with Luke. He was a true nonconformist, resisting all authority. The film really stuck with me. Later, as a form of protest, I considered not registering for the draft, but I still gave them my name. I was scared of the war and scared of the consequences of not registering. At that time *Easy Rider* and *Midnight Cowboy* were playing across the street from each other in Westwood Village. I went to one, then the other. Then I went back again. When Steppenwolf, featured on the *Easy Rider* soundtrack, came to play a concert in my high school auditorium, it was the first rock band I heard play live. I thought I was born to be wild. Or, as it turned out, maybe a bit reckless.

If you opened my high school locker in those days, you were likely to find four or five ounces of marijuana. Not many people knew I was selling, but I always sold out rather quickly—10 dollars a lid, or 3 for 25. I would buy a kilo of pot, spread it out on my bedroom floor, remove all the seeds and stems, then fill beautiful baggies for my consumers. By selling 24 ounces of clean pot, I made my money back, then I had 4 or 5 ounces in profit for myself. Even after giving away half of that to friends, I could feed my recreational habit for a while until I needed more.

One morning I showed up for print shop, and the teacher looked out at the class and said that if anyone was not able to safely go to work—implying we were stoned—he asked that we stay in our seat and not get near the machines. It could be dangerous. Then he said. "Go to work." Everyone, joking or not, stayed in their seats. Our high school had its share of stoners. In health class, the teacher instructed us on the detrimental effects of using drugs. She passed around a sample joint and got two in return.

I stopped dealing drugs when I nearly got arrested. I had considered growing my business and was planning to buy five kilos of pot. The transaction would take place in the parking lot of the University Synagogue on Sunset Boulevard in Brentwood. I used to go there on Friday nights to hang with friends. It was a safe haven for pot smokers. Late that afternoon, though, as we approached the lot in my friend's car, I saw a half a dozen police cars with their lights flashing. I suddenly said, "Don't pull in there. Keep driving." I never sold pot again.

It didn't stop me from smoking, though. My dad never came into my bedroom to speak with me, until one day, he did. "Are you smoking marijuana?" he asked. I admitted I was. "How often?" he wanted to know. A few days a week, which most weeks was slightly less than the truth. "You know how I feel about drugs." He gave me a long look. He had said his piece. I looked down at the carpeted floor, hoping there were no seeds or stems hidden between us. He left me with that.

I did know how he felt about drugs and doctors in general. He never took an aspirin. When I fell off my skateboard onto some asphalt and had a deep gash in my hip, he just gave me a bandage rather than suggesting that I get it sewn up by a doctor. It left a pretty good scar. His seriousness sometimes scared me. After work you could usually find him in his library reading the mail or a book. When friends came over to pick me up to go out, they had to pass by my intimidating dad, sitting in his den chair, just inside the front door. He was quite a buzz kill. He did have a fun-loving side and was even quite artistic, though that was not what I saw most of the time. When he showed me his love, it was in quiet ways.

My mom, on the other hand, was a delight to be around. Her spirits ran high, and my friends enjoyed spending time with her. If I was upstairs in my room, waiting for them to pick me up, I often found they had already arrived and were downstairs laughing and chatting with my mom.

In my last year of high school, I went to see *Five Easy Pieces*. I had smoked a bit before the movie. Afterward, my friend Robert Pacht and I came back to my house—I didn't have a car, so I relied on friends to drive me everywhere—and we sat out on our deck on the hillside. The movie struck a chord in me. I told Robert that sometimes I just felt like heading out on the road and leaving all the craziness behind me, just like Jack Nicholson in the movie.

I FINALLY DID hit the road when I went off to college at the University of California, Berkeley. Many producers, writers, and directors I came to know in the business, including Robert Zemeckis and George Lucas, went to the USC film school. Despite the fact that I liked movies, I never thought of going to film school. I had never even heard of film school. In fact, at UC Berkeley, no film classes were offered.

The year was 1970. As the Vietnam War raged on, so did the protests across America. From Berkeley to Ohio State, demonstrations turned violent. During a rare visit, my dad wanted to witness a protest up close. My mom stayed back at the hotel. As we approached the battle line between the Blue Meanies (riot police) and the demonstrators, I suddenly stopped and screamed at my dad to start running. We ran for our lives as a surge of protesters fled toward us, chased by tear gas.

At People's Park, a square block on the south side of Berkeley, confrontations continued to erupt over use of the space for speaking and recreation. Angry orators could also be heard every day on the Berkeley campus, their voices echoing off the buildings that sur-

I Never Heard of Film School

rounded Sproul Plaza, where the Free Speech movement began. The walk from my dorm to class took me to the corner of Bancroft and Telegraph, the epicenter of political activity. If it weren't for the freshly baked donut holes that I liked to pick up along the way, I could have taken an alternate route to avoid the assault on my peace of mind. As I entered Sather Gate, the southern entrance to the campus, Hare Krishnas clinked their little cymbals and moaned, ignoring all around them as they sang. Nascent political organizations and ROTC set up tables just inside the gate, with volunteers keeping their eyes out for vulnerable new recruits to bolster their flock. The rumbling of conga drums could be heard most days from the lower plaza, reverberating through my body as I walked.

Weaving through this sea of disparate souls, I felt lost. If I were looking for an identity crisis, I had come to the right place. The passions of those around me intensified my anxiety. I had my allegiances to the counterculture but not to the extremists that surrounded me. Sometimes I had to wonder where I fit in to all this? What was I thinking when I chose this school?

I had to scramble to be admitted to Berkeley from my public high school. My grades didn't quite meet the minimum requirements. To get the mark I needed in history, my teacher forced me to write a paper on the effect of computers on industry between 1950 and 1960. The essay had to be 20 pages long, single spaced, with a bibliography annotating the periodicals I had referenced. I had been a lazy underachieving student, and I think the teacher enjoyed making me work hard.

My entrance exam scores were above average, but my deficits in English became very clear when I took the English achievement test before graduation. My dismal result forced me to take dumbbell English in my first quarter. The $50 fee for the course would be waived if you took the class through the Humanities Department. The catch was you had to enroll in the Humanities for two years. For an independent spirit like myself, it turned out to be the best decision I made at college. The Humanities program gave me, under the protection of a free environment, the ability to explore literature and, eventually, film, in a way I would never have had the courage or the chance to do.

Professor Alain Renoir, who founded the Department of Comparative Literature at Cal, was one of two professors who led the Humanities program. He could have been an actor. A spirited, French actor. While performing his lecture on the *Canterbury Tales*, he cast himself as a young rogue. With his leg propped up on the desk, bare skin exposed, and his hair disheveled, he gave an animated performance. His bright blue eyes darted from side to side and with a gleeful smile, he delightfully reenacted the cavorting of the young couples hidden in the bushes. The lecture was like theater.

His cohort, Professor Jim Larson, was a tall, slender, handsome dandy from Scandinavia. Except for a carefully cropped beard, he looked like a young Max Von Sydow. He had piercing eyes that were wickedly amused while focused on his small audience of philosophy students. Larson leaned forward, resting his elbows on the lectern, closing the distance between us until he broke the spell and jolted his audience, as he stood upright to pace the floor. He had recently taken a sabbatical, renting a cabin in the woods in Sweden to do some writing. He said he woke up each day wondering what he was doing there. Instead of writing, he pored over every book on the women's movement he could get his hands on. Frustrated with it all, he returned home to Berkeley earlier than planned to resume his teaching of Kierkegaard (an eye-opener for me on existentialism), which he found much more pleasing.

A group of graduate students filled out the staff. One of them, Peter, was an actor and offered a beginning acting course. I thought it was worth a look. He mostly led exercises that had the students improvising with one another. None of us could act. Peter was in the San Francisco production of *One Flew Over the Cuckoo's Nest*. He played Billy Bibbit, a weak stuttering character who is demonized by the tyrannical Nurse Ratched. Peter was so convincing in the role that I came away from the play thinking he had the same problems as the character he portrayed. The next day I called him up and asked if he was OK. How naïve is that? He reassured me that his problems were all acting.

My second year at Berkeley started out with me sleeping on the floor. Housing was tight, and without a permanent place of my own, I went from one friend's house to another, usually unrolling my sleeping bag in their living room. I'd stay for a few weeks to a month, until I thought it best to move on. While crashing at the house of my friend Eloise, an exotic Mediterranean-looking girl, I met another student friend of hers, John Ross, who also found a space on her floor when he wasn't sharing her bed.

Eventually John and I moved into a small, one-bedroom place near Telegraph Avenue. John got the bedroom while I slept on the couch in the living room, straightening up daily to make room for drinking beer and playing guitar. John became tired of school and decided to join the working class doing construction. He was a Socialist at heart, attempting to break away from his upbringing in upscale Connecticut. I stayed in school, but I shared his beliefs to a lesser degree. Wishing to assert my independence from my parents by refusing their paltry financial support, I started to work construction alongside John to pay my living expenses. My initial enthusiasm for my classes was starting to fade.

At the end of my second year I dropped out of school. That meant I gave up my student deferment, so I was now eligible for the military draft. Birth dates were assigned numbers by lottery, and mine—March 31, 1952—was given number 161. I nervously waited to see which numbers would be called. The last one required to report for duty was 95. I was out. Forever. I wouldn't have to go to Canada.

WITH THE DRAFT behind us, John and I decided to take our guitars and construction skills on the road. We packed up his Chevy wagon and drove to Mammoth Lakes, California, which was experiencing a building boom. We spent the summer, fall, and winter there doing foundation work and carpentry and finally working for a drywall and painting company. I grew my beard during those months, ridiculed every morning by the work crew for not washing my face as the beard slowly grew in. I have not shaved since.

When spring came along and the work in Mammoth finally dried up, we headed east to John's hometown, Wilton, Connecticut, where we resumed pounding nails for a local hot tub and sauna company. When I got tired of the work, I took a break and spent days on the couch, watching the Watergate hearings, then reporting the day's events to John and his family during the evening cocktail hour. I fell into a relationship with John's high school girlfriend, who was in town for the summer. The relationship ended when we were scolded for making too much noise one night while frolicking together. John was amazed, less at my indiscretion than by the fact that I got caught, since he had quietly survived numerous high

I Never Heard of Film School

school dalliances without any problem.

Lazing around on the couch of John's parent's home, I got the crazy notion that I might want to go into landscape architecture. I'm not sure where the idea came from. I did enjoy a drafting class I took in junior high school, and I loved the outdoors, so I thought doing landscape design might be a better fit for me in the construction world.

While thinking about going back to school, I jumped into construction again. John told me we were invited to help the owner of the hot tub company finish his home in the Adirondacks for three dollars an hour and an open charge account at the local store. We drank a lot of Genesee beer. From there we continued to the Ross family summer home on the Island of Islesboro in Maine. For our keep, John and I refurbished and painted the barn on their property. I think we were happy to show off our newly acquired skills. Next we used our talents for the Barlows. Mr. Barlow was a friend of the family and an executive with The Harford insurance company who also had a summer home on the island. While John was chasing after the Barlows' daughter, I stayed behind after work to dig clams and enjoy evening cocktails in their fine home. Mr. Barlow ventured to ask if I might come to work with him at his company. An interesting and kind offer to a long-haired transient. I still wonder what he saw in me that he thought might fit into his line of work. I politely refused. When I was ready to leave the island, both the Ross and Barlow families asked that I arrive early for my ferry. They had put up a table with a pitcher of Bloody Marys and a croquet set on the adjacent green. But not even a Bloody Mary could sway me. I wanted to head west to Mammoth Lakes before the snow started to fall.

When I got back into town, most of the guys I knew from my

first trip were packing up and leaving. They didn't want to work through another winter. That left openings at the company for John and me. We were promoted to positions as painters and started to make pretty good money. On one of the new condo projects, I fell to the floor from a second-story balcony without railings and hit my head. I lost my short-term memory. I think it knocked some sense into me. When I finally regained consciousness, I decided I had done enough construction work and chose to return to school at Berkeley. John's mind-set had not been altered. He planned to rough it through the winter. That would be the last time we worked together. In fact, John bought the painting company and spent the rest of his life in Mammoth Lakes.

I WAS NAÏVE in thinking I could simply show up at Cal and pick up where I left off. That was not the case. I needed to reapply. I am not sure if it was my innocence or my pleading that caused the administrator to cut me some slack and open the door for me. This time around I immersed myself in school with much more passion. When I reentered the Humanities Department, I felt invigorated. I was allowed to invent some Independent Study courses. One I called Literature of My Childhood Conditioning involved rereading a selection of books that had left a mark on me since I was young. I read the first few chapters of the Bible, *The Adventures of Huckleberry Finn*, and *One Flew Over the Cuckoo's Nest*, to name a few. I was intrigued to see how my perspective and feelings may have changed. Another class I designed, Young Charlatans and Classic Losers, I modeled on myself—a wayward soul, trying to make sense of the world. *The Stranger* by Camus and John Fowles's *The Magus* were included. I had no idea where this course of study

I Never Heard of Film School

was going, but that didn't stop me.

During this time my love of film grew. I became a regular at the Pacific Film Archive, a screening room with a daily film program in the basement of the Berkeley Art Museum. Tom Luddy, who went on to co-direct the Telluride Film Festival, was the director. The screenings were presented by filmmakers from all over the world, who not only introduced their films, they stayed behind to discuss them. I remember Howard Hawks talking about *Red River*. Martin Scorsese came, as did Nicholas Ray. There were also retrospective film series, which showcased Kurosawa, Bergman, and Antonioni. Listening to these directors, writers, and producers, I was mesmerized, always wanting to hear more about the places they filmed, how they did it, and what their movies were about. I think a seed was planted. I started to think that working in film was something I might want to do. I could travel the world, tell stories, and learn a new trade all at the same time.

In addition to the PFA, Berkeley was a very active film town. There were small repertory theaters that programmed wonderful retrospectives and showcased independent films. One time a scholar from Rome screened all of Federico Fellini's films and discussed them afterward, giving insights into the films and also telling amusing stories. He recounted, for example, how Fellini met his wife and muse, Giulietta Masina: Fellini spied Masina in a coffee shop, went up to her, and said that he had to meet her for coffee; if she refused, he would kill himself. Happily for movie lovers, she agreed. I was so excited by this series that I created an Independent Study on the films of Fellini.

My interest in Fellini led me to study Italian. I was not only taken by the beauty of the language and culture, but I was smitten by my Italian teacher. As luck would have it, one of the professors in the Italian department decided to teach a class on the History of Italian Cinema. The course began in the silent era, then surveyed the epics of the early 1900s, followed by the lavish films of the 1930s, made during the oppressive Mussolini era. Finally came the neorealist works made following World War II. The passion, beauty, and immediacy of these films took hold of me. When I saw *Roma, Città Aperta*, I could not imagine how Roberto Rossellini made the film on the streets of Rome amid the devastation brought on by the war, with mostly nonprofessional actors. Suddenly I found myself immersed in Italian films, primarily neorealist cinema. Rossellini, Vittorio De Sica, and Luchino Visconti all caught me by surprise. I was getting a bit closer to considering film work as something I might want to pursue when I graduated.

I mentioned this idea to Alain Renoir. Although he was an Old English scholar, he knew his way around movies. He was the son of the legendary Jean Renoir, who made, among other films, *Grand Illusion* and *The Rules of the Game*. I was not thinking specifically of that connection at the time. I thought of him as a professor I admired and who had given me a home in the Humanities program. I valued his opinion. Alain tried to discourage me. He said he had spent time on his dad's film sets and that it was dreadfully boring. He tried to convince me to pursue a career in academia, in particular, studying the classics. He made me reconsider my options.

As I was nearing the end of my undergraduate studies, I was summoned by my counselor in the Humanities to discuss my major, which I had still not declared. She reviewed the classes I had taken: philosophy, psychology, sociology, English literature, Greek studies, Italian, music. There was no real focus. Then she reviewed the various Independent Studies I had created. Those did not add up to a major either. But she saw that I had focused a number of these on film, notably the class on Fellini. That, plus the yearlong class on Italian cinema, suggested that film had become a major interest to me. Was there anything else? I said that I enjoyed philosophy and particularly loved the class on Kierkegaard and existentialism taught by Jim Larson. What about—she was really stretching it—an Independent Study combining my interests in philosophy and film. We could call it Existentialism in Literature and Film. She told me to see if I could come up with a proposal for a thesis. A thesis? It sounded so grown up. Isn't that what they do in graduate school? I didn't know this was even possible. By writing a thesis, I would graduate with a degree in the Humanities called Existentialism in Literature and Film. Anything goes at Berkeley, I suppose.

I came back with an idea that grew out of my love for Italian neorealist films. I would compare an early Visconti film, *La Terra Trema*, made in 1948, with a novel by Giovanni Verga called *I Malavoglia*, written some 65 years earlier, upon which the film was loosely based. Both were about the political struggle and desire for independence of an exploited fisherman in a small Sicilian village, and both were created in the wake of oppressive eras when authors or filmmakers returned home and told heartfelt, realistic, personal stories. I think I saw a parallel in my own era, which had recently emerged from the cloud of the Nixon Era. I felt a sense of rebirth all around me. I was hoping that Alain Renoir and Jim Larson would find the subject equally engaging and, since they were part of the Comparative Literature Department, that they would accept an Independent Study that spanned literature and film. They both blessed the idea. I wrote a thesis and graduated with a degree in Humanities from Berkeley.

I DID NOT ATTEND my graduation. I was playing tennis. Being on the court with my girlfriend was much more important. During my final year in college, I lived with a new roommate, Kevin Caldwell, in a two-bedroom basement apartment in a redwood-shingled house a few doors down from Live Oak Park on the north side of Berkeley. I was able to help the upstairs neighbor/landlord with his house remodel in exchange for rent. I was also collecting unemployment and had a small grant from the university. I was living on easy street. There were markets for fresh food close by, a cheese shop, wine merchants, coffee shops, and restaurants, including Chez Panisse, which would become our favorite restaurant in the world. It was a good life.

I passed Live Oak Park every day as I walked to school and noticed that the tennis courts were always full. Tennis was extremely popular at the time. Players of all ages and abilities sat on the courtside benches, waiting for their turn to play. I had played the sport growing up and had even been on my high school tennis team. I quit when they told me to cut my hair. I said, "What about Torben Ulrich, the great pro from Holland? He has long hair." The coach replied, "When you are as good as Torben Ulrich, you can have your hair as long as you want." I was recruited for the tennis teams of a few colleges, but when I arrived at Berkeley, my interest had quickly faded. Seeing the courts each day, I got the urge to give it a try again. It would be fun, not competitive.

On one of my first days on the court, I met Liv, my future wife. Not only did her long, flowing blond hair, blue eyes, and radiant smile catch my attention, but she also could hit the ball better than most of the men playing at the park. Following a game one afternoon, I asked if anyone would be open to playing some morning.

I Never Heard of Film School

Liv expressed interest, and our first date was set. I was hoping that would happen, since I had been attracted to her from the moment we met. Following one of our morning dates Liv mentioned she had to get to work. Since I lived nearby, I offered her the use of the shower in our house. It was more innocent than it sounds. I don't recall if she accepted, but we started seeing more and more of each other. At the time Liv was living with a doctor, who happened to be off on a trip with some of his pals. We took our blooming relationship slowly, mostly because of my shyness, but we were becoming more serious by the day. I had fallen in love.

I was at a crossroads. While committed to Liv, I don't think I was ready to move in with her and start our life together. She also needed to sort out her relationship to her boyfriend. And although I had developed a love of film, I was still not ready to jump into filmmaking. In fact, I didn't know what kind of work to pursue. I needed a break and time to think. With my future unclear, the phone rang. My close high school friend, Robert Pacht, was up in Alaska working on the pipeline, and he was calling from the bush. His room in a two-bedroom house in Anchorage was available, along with his Toyota pickup truck. If I had nothing else on my plate, I should come up and check it out. It was a once-in-a-lifetime opportunity. There were tons of jobs, if not on the pipeline, certainly in Anchorage. All I had to do to get ready was say good-bye to Liv and find a home for Robert's dog, Felina, whom I had been taking care of since he left the Lower 48.

I cut my hair—something I hadn't done since high school—and took off for Alaska. Sure enough, I got work in construction in Anchorage. Even without any experience, you could get hired in just about any trade. I moved around from job to job, first as a plumber then as an electrician. I got my first paycheck, well, cash, in a strip club. It was the Wild West. The first night I arrived, my new housemate took me to a bar to meet her group of friends. I remember going into the bar as the sun was setting, sometime before midnight, and leaving when the sun was coming up, only a few hours later. It never seemed to get dark in the summer in Anchorage. Since I had reluctantly left my sweetheart behind in Berkeley, I had arranged for a triangle ticket that allowed me to fly round trip from San Francisco to Anchorage, with a free stop in Hawaii on the way back. I also provided Liv with a round-trip ticket from San Francisco to Hawaii before I left. After working through the summer in Alaska, we set a date and met each other in Hawaii.

Our weeks together in a simple one-room shack in a Filipino community on Maui solidified our relationship. The place was owned by a mutual friend in Berkeley, who not only let us stay in his rustic home but also gave us the use of his VW truck. The place was down a dirt track off the winding road that led to Hana. The shack had no warm running water. The single bulb above the mattress on the floor was the only light source. There was no stove or refrigerator. We cooked on a propane camp stove and stored our food in a cooler. The toilet was outdoors—a raised toilet seat over a hole in the ground, surrounded by a white picket fence for a bit of privacy. We were in paradise. The only time that our bliss was disrupted was when I was bitten in the ear by a centipede in the middle of the night. Liv could see the pincer holes. I picked up my pillow and saw it quickly wiggle away and vanish through the floorboards. The lone book on the bookshelf was about insects and reptiles of the tropics. It noted that centipede bites can be fatal. I tore open the cooler and drank a beer without breathing, then went to the clinic in Paia early the next morning. "If you have lived this long, you have nothing to worry about," they told me. "It must have been the

I Never Heard of Film School

harmless type." That was a relief.

Upon my return to Berkeley, I set out to find a job and a place to live. Every rental I found, some quite nice, Liv rejected. She wanted me to move in with her. It was time, she told me, and I agreed. With my house-painting experience, I was hired by the Karl Kardel Company, painting houses and commercial buildings. As the weeks wore on, I became frustrated with the work. The idea of film crept back into my consciousness. The seed that had been planted in college was nagging at me. I had been doing construction work for many years, and I was starting to see that it was a dead end for me.

I began networking, asking everyone if they knew anyone who had worked in the film business or knew someone who had. The only lead came from Liv. She recalled a client, Jim Bloom, that she had met while working at the Vorpal Gallery in San Francisco. Jim was an assistant director who had cut his teeth working on the TV show *The Streets of San Francisco*. I contacted him, and he was happy to meet with me. It was an easy walk to his house in the Berkeley Hills. Jim, as it turned out, had recently worked as an assistant director on *Bound for Glory*. He asked me what I wanted to do. I said I had no idea, but that I wanted to learn and assist someone doing anything involving film. I am not sure what planted this sudden desire in me, but the desire never wavered, and I never questioned it.

Jim got me in touch with Bill Malley, who worked as a supervising grip, electrician, and stagehand on commercials and industrial films. I did a few jobs with him—a commercial at a winery in Napa, an industrial film at a hospital in Palo Alto. Not much really. All I was doing was following orders. Get that piece of equipment and bring it here. Put a light over there, turn it on, and shine it on that wall. I remember I even went to apply for a job with the Mitchell Brothers in San Francisco, the leading makers of porn films at the time. There was no job there either. I reached out to Jim again and told him it was tough to get any kind of steady work. He said that if I really wanted to work in the film industry, I was going to have to go to Los Angeles. I figured that was coming. I had already applied to graduate school in film at San Francisco State University and was accepted. Ultimately, I decided that the best option would be to go down to LA, spend the summer, and see if I could get a job. If I did not succeed, I would return and go to school. After talking it over with Liv, I decided to follow Jim's advice and give it a shot. I went to LA in the summer of 1976 with no connections in the industry, just the desire to break into the film business.

CHAPTER 2

Breaking In

I GREW UP in Beverly Hills surrounded by many actors and actresses. I knew none of them, except my next-door neighbor. Jayne Mansfield had lived next door before she moved to the famous Pink Palace on Sunset Boulevard. By the time we arrived on Wanda Park Drive in Benedict Canyon, Spencer Segura, who was my age, lived in her former house. We became friends, and he showed me the tile portait of Jayne in a bikini in the deep end of his swimming pool. Spencer lived with his stepfather, Ed Gilbert, an actor who appeared in quite a few TV shows. He had a deep, gravelly voice that sounded like he belonged on the radio. I never got to know him very well. I was better acquainted with Spencer's dad, Pancho Segura, who was a tennis pro and gave me my first tennis racquet.

Wanda Park Drive was a small, dead-end street, almost like an alley, where it was difficult for one car to pass another without stopping and pulling over. Ann-Margret lived up the street. Occasionally I would see her ride down Wanda Park on her small motorcycle. All I remember is the color red. I think the scooter was chrome and red. Maybe her bandanna was red. Or her lipstick. Sometimes I would take our dog on a walk up the street and pass by her house, hoping to get a closer look or say hello or something. I am not sure what I was hoping for. I was quite an innocent boy at the time.

At the top of our street, one of my neighborhood friends lived in a caretaker's house behind a Spanish villa. His dad, Lionel Siegel, was a writer on the show *Peyton Place*. He owned a Lincoln Town Car and would occasionally drive me and his son, Conner, to school. The car was large and spacious and had a leather interior. Lee was avuncular, much more outgoing than my dad, so I enjoyed the ride. They were always late.

I could ride my Sting-Ray bicycle up the street, pedal past the Spanish villa and Conner's house, ride through a backyard to Oak Pass Road, then have a great downhill ride all the way home. Usually, I went through that backyard undetected. One day, though, I came skidding to a halt in front of a large cat. It was an ocelot. The sliding glass door opened, and an attractive woman in a bathrobe stepped out. She told me not to worry, the cat was chained to a tree, and its claws were cut short. I discovered this was Yvette Mimieux, although I did not know it at the time. On my downhill ride, I would pass by both Gene Barry's house and Janet Leigh's estate, but the closest I came to them was a wave or a brief hello.

When I arrived in LA for my job search in the summer of 1976, I realized how few people in the film business I knew from growing up in LA. I did try to contact Lionel Siegel, my neighbor up the street, but I was unsuccessful. The family had moved away. My mom and dad were on holiday in Europe, so I was able to stay at their home. My sisters must have been on vacation or at camp, since they were not at home either. Liv had remained in Berkeley, so I was on my own.

My older sister, Michele, had given me my first car, a 1967 VW Bug, so I had wheels. Although only a year older than me, she always seemed much farther ahead in life. She had a steady boyfriend long before I met Liv. She always had a car. She knew what she was doing. I never did. Even though Michele hung out with guys who had souped-up cars, and I sat on the grass with the longhairs, we cared for one another.

My other sister, Danielle, was four years younger. Those four years separated us more than one can imagine. When she entered high school, I was just leaving. We were like two ships passing in the night, but we were both heavily influenced by the same high school English teacher, Mr. Holtby. I had not appreciated reading until I took his class. Each of us had to choose a book to read and then evaluate it. I chose *One Flew Over the Cuckoo's Nest*. After turning in their paper, each student came to the back of the room, one at a time, and sat at a table. The table had a tape recorder on it, nothing else. After placing headphones over your ears, you punched play and listened to Mr. Holtby read your paper out loud. I heard him read my opening words: "In the book *One Flew Over the Cuckoo's Nest*, the author, Ken Kesey, asks the reader to decide, 'What is insanity?'" Mr. Holtby then stopped reading and said, "Congratulations, Steve. Well done. You may go back to your seat." After I set down the headphones, Mr. Holtby gave me a smile as I passed his desk.

NOW, YEARS LATER, I could define what insanity is: coming to Los Angeles to look for a job in the film business without knowing a soul. The first day there, I drove to the Larry Edmunds Bookshop on Hollywood Boulevard. I looked through the film book section and ended up buying a directory of production companies in and around Hollywood. I went home and came up with a game plan. I would organize each day around a number of production companies in a given area and go knock on doors. I was entirely indiscriminate. Whether the company was involved in movies, television, commercials, industrial films, it did not matter to me. Most people I met were pleasant, but I never got even a remotely promising response. Quite a few companies had their offices on film-studio lots, so I was unable to easily access them. I am not sure how I persisted in this daily ritual. I was hungry, and I guess I figured it was the only way to get a job.

I did learn that the major studios had human resource departments where you could apply for a job. There was little or no chance of anything coming of this, but I had to try it. No other jobs had presented themselves. My first stop was Universal Studios.

The HR office at Universal reminded me of a dentist's waiting room. Generally, no one spoke. You couldn't help but look around at all the hopeful candidates and compare yourself to them. What on this application is going to make me a more favorable candidate than any of them? That must be what actors feel like going on auditions. It was agonizing, like having your teeth pulled. But it was here that I got my first break. While filling out the application, in the quiet of the room, I overheard an applicant say what a useless waste of time it was to submit an application. He then described how he had snuck onto the lot at Warner Bros. and started asking around for a job. Now that was bold, I thought to myself. And suddenly, I had an epiphany. I decided then and there I was going to sneak on the lot at Universal and look for work.

The next morning I drove around to the back of the studio and found the employees' parking lot off Barham Boulevard. I parked and sat in my car and carefully watched the arriving employees. I discovered that they would cluster at the end of each row and be picked up by a bus that would take them into the studio. I hopped on board the next bus, said polite hellos to those around me, and nervously rode onto the lot. No one asked me for any ID or, in fact, asked me anything. I watched with amazement as we drove past the back-lot sets at the studio. Then, as we approached the first stop, I wondered where should I get off? The first few places did not look promising. After a few more stops, the bus riders started to thin out, so at the next stop I made my way to the front of the bus, thanked the driver, and stepped out onto Main Street. There was no security anywhere to be seen. How great is that, I thought, but I still had no idea where to go.

I wandered up to the first sound stage where I saw some activity and pulled open the heavy, soundproof door. Once inside, I drifted around to each department and quizzed people about their job and how one got started doing what they did. The people in the sound department were the friendliest. I spoke with the sound mixer who was recording the dialogue from the set. In between setups, he had plenty of time to talk. He described the other members of his department, beginning with the boom man, who was standing on a cart with a microphone extended over the set. He pointed out the cable person, guiding a cable between his mixing console and the boom man. Now this looked like something I could quickly catch on to.

The mixer suggested that I go to the sound department on the lot and see if there might be an opening. He told me that when someone was needed to fill out a crew, the first place they would call was their department at the studio. I was told the same thing at the camera department. The lowest person on the totem pole in the camera department was the loader. They went into a darkened tent and loaded film into magazines when needed. They also took the used magazines from the assistant cameraman, labeled them, and prepared them to be sent to the lab for processing. Loaders were also general camera department assistants, getting coffee or doing whatever for the higher-ups. Each department seemed to have a strict hierarchy. In less than an hour I had learned more than I ever knew about the crew on a film set. After making my way around for a while, someone asked me what business I had on the set. I told him I was just visiting with people, and he said I had to leave.

Back on Main Street, I looked around for the various departments. I found the sound department and the camera department, but they had nothing to offer. In fact, they were neither helpful nor optimistic. Not sure where to go next, I came upon the electrical department, which supplied the gaffer—the head electrician—and all the lighting technicians on the set. I walked into a small covered alleyway, at the end of which was a pegboard behind glass, with the title of each show on a tab. Under each title was the name of the gaffer, followed by the best boy and each electrician. At the side of the board was a sliding window looking into the office. It happened to be open. I rapped on the window, introduced myself, and said I was looking for a job. A lanky man with a bit of a Texan drawl said he had nothing at the moment but to keep in touch, since it was pretty busy in town. That was the first positive word anyone had said to me since I had arrived in Los Angeles. I couldn't believe it. There was a possibility of a job.

Before I turned to leave, I saw a sign with his name—Ray Shackelford. I knew of a tall, graceful, sharpshooting basketball player at UCLA called Lynn Shackelford. He had played there on championship teams with Lew Alcindor (later Kareem Abdul-Jabbar) while I was in high school. I asked if he might be a relation. He said Lynn was his son. We talked about UCLA basketball for some time. Mr. Shackelford then said to call him the next afternoon in case he needed someone to fill out a crew. He explained that if he called the local electrician's union, and the members were all working, he could hire me as a permit, which allowed me to work on a union show without being a union member. I did not call the next day; I showed up again in person. I did the same the following day. This was the chance I had been looking for.

Finally, after about a week of repeated visits, he told me to show up at the shop the following morning at 8 a.m. with pliers, a screwdriver, and a pair of gloves. He offered me a job. If I knew how to jump in the air and click my heels I would have done so, but instead I called Liv, gave her the news, and ran off to the hardware store to get ready for the morning.

CHAPTER 3

Day of the Locust

I TURNED INTO the crew parking lot at Universal Studios plenty early for my first day of work. This time, boarding the bus, I had a job to go to, and I even knew where to get off. A small group of guys were huddled around the electric shop. I stood out from the others with my brand-new leather tool pouch and unused tools. My gloves were stuffed into the back pocket of my jeans. The call times—the time you are required to report to your job—are different for each show. Ours was 8 a.m. A few of the electricians from my show were there waiting, so they led me to the stage. The gaffer and the rest of the permanent crew reported directly to the stage. The show was a TV series, *Baa Baa Black Sheep*, a World War II drama based on the exploits of a Marine Corps aviator, Greg "Pappy" Boyington. Pappy was played by Robert Conrad, who seemed to fit the part of an older pilot who liked to drink and fight a lot.

I was introduced to my boss, the gaffer, who said, "So you're the permit." It was no different than getting called an FNG (F… ing New Guy) or a grunt in the military, something that was meant to humiliate you and put you in your place. "Yes, sir, I am." He gave me my marching orders. In fact, I took orders from everyone, since I was lowest on the food chain. Particularly on my first day. I was sent up a wooden ladder onto the scaffold, a kind of gangplank about four feet wide, overlooking the film set, just above the set's ceiling height. The more experienced electricians stayed by the gaffer and the camera, where they could move quickly to light from the floor of the set. Lights of varying sizes were strategically pinned into holes on the scaffold, facing down, into the set. Electric cable was laced along the gangplank to each of the lamps. Heavier electrical cable went higher up to who knows where. The source of the electrical power, I presumed.

The gaffer barked up to me, "Go over to that baby junior, put on a set of barn doors, and drop in a double and point it at my hand." I glanced over at the electrician on the opposite side of the scaffolding who gave me a slight smile, then nodded to the smaller of the lights nearby. I got to the light without any problem and looked around for the barn doors. "It's the black metal square with flaps. It fixes on the front of the light. And don't forget to safety it off." This was taking too long, I knew. I thought that everyone on the set was looking up at me. I got the doors on, thankfully, without dropping them to the floor. I quickly safetied them off, hooking the doors to the lamp with the chain that was attached on one side. I moved in the flaps on the sides and the top and bottom of the barn doors, framing the light.

"Turn the lamp on, point it down, and center it on my hand and make it full flood," the gaffer yelled. Rotating and tilting the light and pointing it correctly was not so easy. As you fuddled around, you didn't want to point the light into someone's eyes. Once you found the spot, you had to use the butterfly knob on the side of the lamp to lock it in place. And the light was getting hot. As the light quickly heated up, the gloves helped. Finally, I got it centered right, and the gaffer reminded me about the double. "It's the red one." In a bag by the light were a variety of scrims, color coded for quick access and for those who couldn't tell them apart, like me. I found the double, which had a tighter wire mesh to limit the amount of light emitted, and I dropped it in the slot in the front of the lamp. "And make it full flood." The light fixture inside the lamp is on a track; slide it back, and the light becomes more focused. Sliding it forward makes it full flood. I slid it forward and back until I got it right. "Thanks, he said." That was my first light. They could have shot the scene in the amount of time it took me to square away one light. It got better as the day went on. Leaving work that day I was elated. I had a job. A real job. And I wasn't fired. I was given a call to return the following morning.

I WAS A DAILY employee at this point. Actually, as I learned, most electricians are daily employees. Very few have weekly guarantees. There was a seniority roster in the union, so someone with more seniority than I could not be laid off before I was. Since I was a permit, or a temporary employee, I would be the first to go. If the next day's work called for fewer technicians, they would scale back the crew, always trying to keep the core group together. The best boy on the show would let you know if you had a call for the next day. After a few days I was laid off. I was told that when the Universal electrical department was notified of my layoff, they might switch me over to another show that needed extra help. I got back to the shop and checked the board. My name was missing. I checked in with Shackelford to see if there was anything available for the following day. Nothing. After a few days of work on my first show, I was unemployed.

Shackelford said to keep checking in with him. For some reason, I did not go looking around for another job elsewhere. I put all my eggs in this one basket, and, sure enough, after calling diligently every afternoon, I was hired again. This time I went to a TV show called *Switch*, a detective series starring Robert Wagner and Eddie Albert. The call was for noon on a Friday, and with the usual shooting day lasting 12 hours, I knew I would be working until at least midnight. It was common on TV shows to end the week shooting late into Friday night, so the cast and crew had the required turnaround time before reporting back to work on Monday morning.

We were shooting at the Van Nuys Airport that night, and I recall that when we wrapped shooting in the early hours of Saturday morning, most of the electrical crew was either asleep or drunk. I was pretty much by myself, wrapping up the electrical cable. Some of the guys would intentionally work slowly on a Friday night, because the pay increased after 12 hours of work, and a premium was added on after midnight. Not to mention meal penalties if they did not feed you within six hours of the last meal. I was young and just starting out and didn't know that being lazy and drinking were common on Friday nights among my electric crew brothers.

After a few days or a week, I was laid off again. As I came and went from one Universal TV show to another, I discovered I needed 30 days of work in order to join IA Local 728, the electrician's union. I desperately wanted to get into the union. Although I would have less seniority than others, as a member, I would be eligible to work on all the union shows based in Hollywood. If I didn't drink on the job, hide from the work, and stayed awake until wrap, I would probably continue to be hired. Sure enough, I was. At the end of the following week, I was working on an episode of *McCloud*, starring Dennis Weaver, that was part of the *NBC Mystery Movie* series, rotating with *Columbo* and *McMillan & Wife*. We shot on the Universal back lot. All I can remember is how cold it was working late into the night, despite the fact it was summertime. I learned that many of the more seasoned workers turned down Friday night calls, knowing they would be freezing or working into the early hours of Saturday morning, destroying what remained of their weekend. I didn't have a choice. I couldn't turn down a chance to work. Not at this point. Also, If I did refuse a job, especially an unappealing job, Shackelford or the union steward might not call me the next time something more favorable came up.

The most pleasurable TV series I worked on during this time was *The Rockford Files*. James Garner was a great guy to work for and called the shots on the show. Most importantly, he liked working eight-hour days, a novelty for me so far. I could not believe he did his own stunts. One time we shot in a parking garage where he drove the car at high speed, chased down from floor to floor by a stunt man. I was impressed. The work on *Rockford Files* was short-lived, but it showed me how it could be done right.

Everything impressed me. I was so happy to have nearly continuous work. I was excited to do what I was doing and proud to tell my friends stories about my job. I took set lighting seriously. I started studying photography. I looked at the art of Vermeer and other great painters. I read books on lighting techniques for film. Of course, I was working in TV, where most lighting was done in as short a time as possible. I would never know if the director of photography or gaffer could light artfully because they were never given the chance.

With all this bouncing around from show to show, I got my 30 days in that summer and joined the union. Of course, I had the least amount of seniority on the roster, but I was in. It turned out that the reason the union was hiring so many new permits was that *Close Encounters of the Third Kind*, which was filming in Alabama, employed countless electricians. I guess I can thank Spielberg's show for helping me get started.

I HAD A GOOD relationship with Shackelford, who seemed to be trying to keep me employed. One afternoon he actually called me into his office and told me I was selected to start work on a new three-camera show called *Sirota's Court* that was going to film at Hollywood General Studios. He had handpicked a group of guys he thought might be appropriate for the work. We would begin by rigging the stage for the show, then stay on to work as the on-set lighting technicians during the taping. This was not usually done. Generally there were two separate crews. I had never worked on the rigging crew, the guys who rigged the electric cables and put the lights in place around the scaffolds. I had only worked while shows were filming. In fact, I had never even been up high, as they called it, on the permanent catwalks, the wooden platforms close to the ceiling of the sound stage. This is where the source of the power came from for the lights on the scaffolding. So far, I just turned on the lights. If a light didn't work and could not be fixed by replacing the light bulb, I would not have known what to do.

I was about to learn. I reported to Hollywood General and met the rigging gaffer, Paul Bushey. Paul was the most colorful guy I met while working as an electrician. He was a bit crazy, and if you encountered him on the street, you might have thought he was a vagrant. He was short, had a head of wild hair, and usually a few days' growth of facial hair, and not for reasons of fashion. He showered and changed his clothes irregularly. He was hunched over and walked with purpose, always expecting that his minions would be following close behind. He had a staccato cackle, laughing at his own thoughts, observations, or jokes. He was not well educated, but he was the best rigger I ever met. He had served in the navy. Somewhere along the way, he became adept at rigging a sound stage. He was very methodical and neat. All the heavy cable on the up-high permanents was laid down with precision and labeled perfectly. When the electric cable was then dropped to the scaffold where the lights were positioned, it was tied off tightly to upright supports. Each cable then followed the most expeditious path to the light it served and was labeled appropriately. The rope ties keeping the cable taut and neat were also bound tightly and finished off with perfect knots.

Strangely, I loved all this attention to detail. It not only made me feel safe, but I also appreciated the order that was created. I really worked hard for Paul. I felt confident that when we finished rigging and setting up the lights on the stage, I knew what was going on behind the scenes. This was how I imagined basic training would be in the military. I often teased Paul by answering his orders with, "Yes, Sir!" When the rigging was complete, Paul got a bit antsy. In fact, he didn't show up for days at a time. Once, when Paul went AWOL, the gaffer asked me if I had checked in with the county jail. I thought he was serious, so I called. No Paul. He eventually showed up, looking as if he had not showered and with a growth of beard.

Since this was a three-camera show and was taped live, all the lights were fed to a dimmer board, where a lighting technician could control the lights from a platform with a clear view of the set. The lighting came on cue, following the camera and the action as the scenes progressed. On most movies, you position the lights in a permanent place for each shot. In this case, the lights were all choreographed in advance for the live taping. In a sense, this made working on the show a bit boring; usually, the prelighting for an episode was done in a day or two. Then there wasn't much to do until the rehearsal, when you ironed out which lights came on when and made detailed notes for the taping.

During slow periods on the show, the other electrician, also named Steve, often sat huddled beneath the bleachers that were set up for the live audience. He listened intently to a small transistor radio airing the horse races live. One day he said, "If you give me $358, I will double your money in a week's time." "How are you going to do that?" I asked. "I have a formula for winning at the races."

Steve was a very affable guy but a bit looney. He once asked me to have lunch with him at a place nearby his apartment. Tired of the same routine, I went along. It turned out his apartment was above a strip club. We ate lunch in the club. I thought about his financial proposal and decided to go ahead. He drew up a contract that looked like it was written by a first-grader. When I told Liv about Steve's offer, she said, "You didn't do it, did you?" She really thought I was nuts when I showed her the contract. In a week's time he had doubled my money. I did not ask what his secret was, nor did I wager again.

I often found myself playing catch on one of the studio backstreets with Fred Willard, a very funny guy and part of the *Sirota's Court* cast. He came armed with two baseball gloves and a ball. When Fred was called back into work, the guys asked if I wanted to go check out the generator room. Why not? After we rapped on the door, John, the chief engineer on the lot, invited us in. Inside was a large diesel generator providing power to the studio. Between the door and the generator was an open space that had a couch, a few easy chairs, and some director's chairs. Separating the generator from the rest of the room was a large wooden cutout of a few palm trees. There were also some standing plants in pots and a few other discarded props and bits of set dressing. To one side was a refrigerator. John opened it up and offered me a beer. I could tell he had already had a few. I shared a beer or two, and John invited me to stop by anytime, so I came back every now and then, when my work was a bit slow. While I was lucky to be working on a very nice TV show, I was also getting exposed to the seamier side of Hollywood. I felt like I was mingling with the characters I read about in *The Day of the Locust*. In fact, I had to admit to myself, I was one of them.

When Liv and a friend came to visit the set on one of our taping days, I took them over to see my secret hideaway. Somehow, the generator room with its kitschy props, sagging couches, and an old fridge full of beer suddenly seemed much less appealing. My excitement at just working in the business had kept me from really thinking about what I was doing or the shady characters surrounding me.

WITH ALL THIS steady work, Liv and I decided to rent a charming little cabin in Beverly Glen Canyon that proved to be central to most of the studios around town. Liv had been a cook at Patricia Unterman's restaurant, the Beggar's Banquet in Berkeley, before we moved, and once we got settled, Liv quickly found work at a variety of restaurants, including Chef Gregoire in Sherman Oaks and the Brownstone in West LA. Liv's love had always been pastry, and her drive led her to an internship at L'Ermitage, the best French restaurant in Los Angeles. In her job interview, she faced a line of questioning that only a woman would have to endure. "What would you do if your car broke down on the way to work?" "I would call AAA." "We don't have a changing room for women." "In that case, I would arrive at work in my chef's uniform." From the start, the chef/owner, Jean Bertranou, took a liking to her and recognized her talent for pastry. She quickly worked her way up to become the pastry chef, something unheard of in an upscale French kitchen at the time. I felt the irony in the fact that while I was struggling with getting film jobs, Liv's career was taking off, especially since she hadn't planned to come to LA in the first place.

AROUND THIS TIME the producers had signed a new agreement with the IA. The most immediate significance of the deal was that I was elevated to Group 1 status on the seniority roster. This meant that no one in the local had greater seniority over me when I applied for a job, nor would I be laid off from a job because I had less seniority than another guy. Since I really had no affiliation yet with any particular gaffer, I had to rely on the local for getting work, and they still had their favorites. Although I could now work on any show in town, I was not offered the good ones. Whenever I met with the shop steward, he made sure to remind me of the power he had. I was still hungry, so I reluctantly had to kiss his ass. My first job offer from the local was at Paramount Studios, working on the rigging crew.

Coincidentally, Paul Bushey, from *Sirota's Court*, was heading up the crew. The start time was 6 a.m., generally 8-hour days. This was tough work. Hundreds of pounds of coiled cable had to be pulled up by hand to the highest reaches of the sound stage. The cable was hooked up to the main power source, then strung along the walkways and attached to intermediary feeder boards. Smaller cable was dropped down to the scaffolding and fed to the lights, which were also hoisted up from the stage floor. All this was in preparation for an incoming show. Rather than neatly keeping the cable in place once a show wrapped, all the cable was coiled up and dropped down to the floor along with the lights, loaded on a cart, and brought back to the electrical shop, unloaded, and stored for the next show. Then, often the next day, it was taken back and rerigged. It made no sense to me to clear the stage and then immediately rig it up again. I felt like Paul Newman in *Cool Hand Luke*. Rig that stage. Strike that stage. Rig that stage again. When I asked about the crazy derigging and rerigging, the boss reminded me that it was job security. I thought it was a waste of time and money.

I bounced around from studio to studio, eventually working at every place in town. While at MGM, I landed on a show called *The Other Side of Midnight*. I was sent up high to operate a group of arc lights. The arcs created a very bright source of light, which was needed for the large exterior scene they were filming on the sound stage. In order to activate an arc light, two carbon rods, one negative and one positive, were quickly brought together, then drawn apart, leaving a flame ignited between the two. The distance between the rods was regularly adjusted by control knobs on the outside of the lamp, maintaining a consistent, flicker-free flame and source of light. You had to constantly stand vigil by your lamp. After climbing up the long ladder to the permanents, I was greeted by a friendly older electrician who had been doing electrical work his whole life. His motto was two, two, and two: Two aspirin followed by two shots of whiskey in the morning, then two beers at lunch. Before I left him to go to my light station, he offered up a tip based on his years of experience, "When you sit down on the wooden chair next to your arc, tie a rope around your waist, and secure it to the guardrail. That way, if you fall asleep, you won't fall to the floor." I thanked him for the advice. Later he did fall asleep, and I had to run over to tend to his flickering arc, which I managed to do without waking him up.

During a lunch break one day, while wandering around the MGM lot, I noticed the name Franco Zeffirelli on an office door. Although well known for his film, opera, and theater work, early in his career Zeffirelli had worked as an assistant director on *La*

Terra Trema, the film that I had written about for my college thesis. Looking at his name on the door, I thought it was an amazing coincidence. Up to then, I had not consciously thought of making a career change, but at that moment something moved me forward. I sheepishly rapped on the door to his office, and his friendly assistant greeted me. She must have been a bit startled by the dirty technician standing in her doorway. I told her that I was looking for a job as an assistant. She probably did not take me seriously. I then mentioned that I had written a college paper about a film that Zeffirelli had worked on as a young man. She told me to drop it off, and she would pass it along to him and mention that I was looking for a job.

I came back the following day and dropped it off, never really expecting to hear from her. I was shocked when the call came. Franco Zeffirelli agreed to meet with me. Over lunch he said he enjoyed the paper and told me war stories of his days working with Visconti, De Sica, and Rossellini. The meeting made writing my thesis worthwhile. It aroused a passion for film that I had not felt since I had watched Italian movies while in school. The work I was doing had buried the reason I had pursued film in the first place, and I started to dream about getting into this other world. Suddenly it seemed possible. Zeffirelli told me he would see what he could do about hiring me on the show he was prepping, called *The Champ*. Not long after, he called to tell me that since his show was filming in Florida, the producers wanted to hire someone locally as his assistant. Although deflated, I was grateful for the meeting and thankful that Zeffirelli went to bat for me. I had worked very hard to get to where I was, but I could not let go of the feelings that were stirring inside me. I was awakened to the fact there were more options in the film world than what I was doing.

Day of the Locust

My hopes for a change were heightened when I ran into my old neighbor, Lee Siegel, who was now a writer and executive producer on *The Bionic Woman*. I told him I was working as an electrician in town but had started to look around for something different or more challenging. He said they did hire associate producers on his TV show, and he would check to see if a position might be available. I gave him my number, and he said he would call. I got excited that I finally had a personal connection to the business that might lead to something new. I never heard from him.

I RETURNED to steady work, now mostly at 20th Century-Fox studios. The Spelling/Goldberg company was making countless TV shows at the time, including *Charlie's Angels*, *Starsky & Hutch*, and *Fantasy Island*, and I worked on all of them, going from one to the other. When I first arrived on the lot and went to the electrical department, I found myself gazing at the framed black-and-white photos on the walls of the waiting area. What struck me was the dress of the crews in the old days. The electricians often wore coats and ties, which reminded me what a privilege it was to be working in this industry. Usually, you had to know someone to get a job. Quite often, nepotism played a role, as jobs were handed down from generation to generation. I worked with three different generations of the Dahlquist family. Though I was starting to feel I was not cut out for life as an electrician, I still felt fortunate to have a job at all.

In all this time I never read the script for a show I was working on. Usually only the gaffer was given the script. Electricians didn't read scripts. It just did not happen. Even if I asked, the script was never given to me. In addition, if I ever asked about the lighting scheme or how the gaffer intended to light a scene, I got the brush-off. Everyone was very protective of their positions. They did not want to impart any information to me. I wondered if the gaffers were concerned that I was overstepping my bounds as an electrician in my desire to get involved in the more creative or supervisory aspects of the job.

One day on *Starsky & Hutch*, the gaffer was late for work. The cameraman asked me to step in, follow his directions, and give orders to the other guys to light the scene. When the gaffer arrived, the scene was ready to go. I expected the gaffer would thank me for covering for him. Instead I was not invited back to the show the following day. I was starting to see the writing on the wall. Advancement was going to be difficult to come by. Any interest in learning lighting or taking an interest in the script was off-limits. I became more restless.

As it turned out, Liv was getting restless in her work at L'Ermitage. Although she was excited working as the head pastry chef and learning new recipes daily from Bertranou, her assistant was using every means he could to get her job. She needed to get away from the jealousies in the kitchen that were conspiring against her. We *both* needed a break.

We went to visit friends in Marin County who were getting married. They asked Liv to sit in on a meeting about the menu for their wedding reception. Liv not only made suggestions but shaped the entire menu. After the meeting, the head of the catering company, Nancy Van Wyck, asked Liv if she might consider managing the business for her. On our drive back to LA, we gave the job offer serious thought.

When I returned, I got a call from Tommy Hayes, a gaffer I had worked with on and off for the past few years, offering me a job on a TV movie called *Bud and Lou*, with Harvey Korman and Buddy Hackett. Tommy was teamed with a cameraman, Richard Glouner, and I enjoyed them both. The shoot was only a few weeks long, so I took the show. While sitting by the set at a car-wash location on Sunset Boulevard, Tommy and Richard asked me why I was an electrician. I said it was the first job I got, and I was reasonably happy and grateful for the work. But they went further. I was too smart for the job, they told me. Too smart? What the hell did that mean? "It's a dead end. You should be looking for better work than this." They were not negative. They were simply offering advice and encouragement. I was a bit stunned, since this came out of nowhere. As it turned out, they gave me the kick in the ass that I was looking for.

Circumstances, conversations, and feelings started converging, all pushing me to make a change. Then my dad called. He said he was at lunch with a lawyer whose brother-in-law was a film producer, and he was willing to speak to me. His name was Howard Kazanjian. When I reached Howard on the phone, I quickly brought him up to speed with my work and said I would be willing to do anything, help him in any way, if he had a position available. He said he would love to hire me, but he was moving to Northern California to produce a film for George Lucas, *More American Graffiti*. George Lucas? I loved *American Graffiti*, and *Star Wars* was a phenomenon. I suddenly became desperately excited.

I had read somewhere that Lucas was working in the Bay Area, and I had fantasized about moving back north and getting a job with his company. Like Zeffirelli, Howard said that he would have to hire a local assistant. I offered to move so they would not have to pay my living expenses. I was even familiar with the area, since I had gone to school at Berkeley. Howard told me to give him a call if I relocated, and he would see if there was a position for me. That was enough. It was time to go. I was ready. Liv was ready. We made the move. Liv took the job at the Nancy Van Wyck Catering Company, and I was unemployed but hopeful.

CHAPTER 4

Starting Over at Lucasfilm

WHEN I SET out for Northern California on Highway 101, I felt like I was born to be wild once again. If I had a car with a convertible, I would have taken the top down. The wide-open spaces reminded me of the broad horizons that lay ahead. I had read about Coppola and Lucas and how they were making Hollywood films outside the system. As a product of the '60s, I thought that made sense. We also had a nice group of friends waiting for our arrival, mostly from Liv's early days living and working in the Bay Area. Many of them had settled in Marin County, north of San Francisco. We rented a caretaker's cabin nestled in the backyards of several rather large estates in the town of Ross, a wealthy enclave there.

The neighborhood was within earshot of a Presbyterian seminary whose church bells would ring out the hours. To get to our redwood cabin from the street, you went up a gravel driveway between two homes to an open, sunny, and very private piece of property. The grounds were spare except for the few towering acacia and pine trees that dotted the perimeter. In front of the cabin was a worn-out tennis court missing its net, with cracks in the concrete that exposed the lack of care. The cabin was in similar condition, but we loved it. The cabin was empty, save for a few built-ins. I constructed a crude platform bed that was firm and comfortable.

STEVE STARKEY

We put a couch in front of the fireplace and got a chopping block for the kitchen. It felt like home. After I waved to Liv as she went off to her catering job, I turned to consider my future. While I had gained some experience as an electrician on movie sets, it felt like I was starting all over again.

I called Howard Kazanjian, the producer of *More American Graffiti*, whom I had spoken to in LA. I thought that since I had taken the initiative to move to Marin, he would probably sense my seriousness and have some kind of work for me. "Nothing at this time," he reported. "We are just setting up the offices. But maybe once we line up the crew, something will open up. Locations or the production office may need production assistants." I had really thought that a job would be waiting for me. Trying not to appear too desperate, I reminded him that I was willing to do anything. Howard said to keep in touch. Suddenly I felt at loose ends.

I then reached out to Jim Bloom, my Bay Area contact from the Berkeley days. He was the only other person in the film business I knew. I told him that I had spent the last two years, as he had suggested, working in LA. I was back, living in Marin, looking for a job. He asked me to join him for lunch. In my absence, Jim had been busy, working as an assistant director with Steven Spielberg, Hal Ashby, Matthew Robbins, and Philip Kaufman, among others. He was wrapping up his work at Lucasfilm in San Anselmo, which, amazingly, was just a short bike ride away from our cabin. I rode my bike across town and found my way to Park Way, a rough-and-tumble potholed street that ended at a security gate. After announcing myself, I was let into a beautiful compound, at the center of which was a sprawling Victorian house, the offices of Lucasfilm. Off to one side, on a dirt patch, a dozen or so bohemian-looking, artistic types were engaged in a furious game of volleyball. Like summer camp for slightly aging hippies. It turned out they were mostly the editorial crew of Carroll Ballard's film *The Black Stallion*.

I crossed the stately front porch of the house and entered a spacious lobby, where I was greeted by the affable receptionist, Chrissie England. She pointed me to Jim's office. He greeted me warmly and took me around to meet a few employees. I hoped my hand didn't feel clammy, revealing my quickly mounting insecurity among this group of talented professionals. I first met Jane Bay, George Lucas's assistant. Jane presented herself impeccably. Her hair was neatly pulled back in a ponytail. She dressed casually with an artistic flair. Jim mentioned that I was looking for work. She was attentive, carefully writing down my contact information. Leaving her office, Jim told me that Jane was the gatekeeper to jobs at George's company, whereas films produced by Lucasfilm hired their own employees.

Jim then introduced me to Gary Kurtz, the producer of *Star Wars*, and his assistant, Bunny Alsup. Lastly, in an atrium off the lobby, we said hello to Lucy Wilson, the Lucasfilm accountant. I saw George's office, but I didn't meet him. I had just been introduced to more people in an hour than I had ever met while looking for an assistant's job in LA. As we parted, Jim said he would put in a word for me and keep me in mind as he moved onto his next job. As I looked back, riding my bike out the gate, I said to myself, this was where I wanted to work. I just didn't know how to get in the door.

EVEN THOUGH I had a few balls in the air, I still needed some kind of work. It seemed like years went by as I waited to hear back from either Howard Kazanjian, Jane Bay, or Jim Bloom. I became anxious. What if they never called? I should have knocked on the doors of some of the other talented and successful filmmakers who were in the Bay Area. Instead, I suppose out of impatient desperation, I ended up falling back on what I had done in LA. I drove over to Local 16, the stagehands' local based in San Francisco, to see if I might land something to tide me over until I found, well, whatever it was that I was looking for. Since I was a member of Local 728 in LA, I was able to join Local 16. Unlike in LA, where each of the crafts—electrical, grip, set dressing, props, and set construction—were all segregated, here they fell under one roof. In addition, the work was not just limited to film. Local 16 had jurisdiction over the opera and some theater as well. I got a few calls: the opera for a day or two and a few commercials. I realized it was going to be tough to get established with any kind of steady work, particularly since there was already a very hungry and talented labor pool in San Francisco. It was not a pretty picture.

Then Lucasfilm called. Actually, it was Jim Scaife, who was the Lucasfilm production assistant, working under Jane Bay. He wondered if I was available to help him set up the housing and offices for some out-of-town people coming to work on an upcoming Lucasfilm movie. I knew he was speaking of *More American Graffiti*. Now why hadn't Howard called me to do this kind of work? I would be moving in furniture and setting up the phones. It meant a foot in the door, so I jumped at the opportunity. A day or two later I was called in again for similar work. In the course of doing this, I frequently ran into Jane Bay at the Park Way house. She was always polite, asking how it was going and if the work was to my liking. I told her I was happy to be doing it. Meanwhile, Jim Scaife told me he was thinking of leaving the job and going back to LA. It was too slow for him in Marin, and he missed city life. "Maybe you could take over when I leave," he said. "When are you thinking of leaving?" "Pretty soon."

Starting Over at Lucasfilm

Jane called me a few days later and offered me the position of production assistant. I could not have been more excited. Just like that, I had a job at Lucasfilm. I guess I had made a good impression moving in furniture. In my new job, I would be reporting to Jane, although I would be answering to or helping out George and all the employees of Lucasfilm, some of whom I had yet to meet. My salary was $150 a week.

Day 1. Good morning, Jane. What did you have in mind for today? We need some groceries for the house. Anything in particular? Food for lunches and snacks. What do people eat? What do you eat? Peanut butter mostly. Speak to Chrissie; she'll help you make a list. You can use the company van. That's great, I thought, since I had ridden my bike to work. After making a list with Chrissie, she said she needed a few keys made. We use Transbay, down the Miracle Mile. OK. I got some petty cash from Lucy. She gave me a few things to take to the post office. Chrissie was very helpful from the start. She knew I didn't know anything about the town nor how to handle all the work orders I was getting from everyone. That afternoon I was sent to the stationary store for paper, envelopes, and pens. They seemed to be out of everything, just waiting for me to start.

Day 3. Hello, Jane. Steve, would you mind cleaning out the rain gutters on the roof. I had never even cleared out the gutters on my own house. I said sure. You have an extension ladder? I was comfortable on tall ladders, having done a lot of construction work. While up on the ladder, I met George for the first time. How's it going up there? Just fine. The gutters need some cleaning out—a lot of leaves. I'm sure, he said, and continued into the house. He seemed easygoing. He was dressed much like me. Jeans, a simple shirt, and tennis shoes.

Day 6. My first paycheck. Lucy, the accountant, asked that I please cash the check. Well, of course I will cash the check, I need the money. She said some people don't. They think that George's signature is more valuable. Like I said, I need the money, not an autograph.

Day 8. I finally sat down to organize my desk, which was tucked in a corner of the main room. I could see all the comings and goings. A handsome, nicely dressed man a bit older than me walked in the front door and went straight to see Jane. He had come in unannounced to see if George was around. Later, as they headed toward the front door, Jane led him over to me and introduced us. "Howard, I would like you to meet Steve Starkey." Jane was always respectful, never attaching my lowly job description to my name. Without thinking, he extended his hand to me, "Howard Kazanjian." Then, after a pause and a double take, he said, "What are you doing here?" A bit nervously, I replied, "I just started working here." Howard quickly shifted gears and enthusiastically added, "Well, that's great!" I know he recognized my name. I imagine he was surprised to see me, but he didn't show it. He didn't even ask how I got the job. "Nice to meet you. Looks like we'll be seeing more of each other," he said pleasantly, as he turned to go. I went out to get some keys duplicated.

MY OFFICE SPACE was getting dwarfed by *Star Wars* merchandise. Wookie plush dolls, R2D2 cookie jars, Luke Skywalker and Princess Leia action figures, they were all coming in by the boxful. Chrissie asked me, "What are you going to do with all this stuff?" I was about to ask her the same question. And then UPS arrived with another truckload. I needed a lot of storage space, and I needed it fast. I scouted around and found a warehouse. I secured reasonably priced shelving that assembled with simple rivets and slots that I could put together by myself. I went with 4x8 sheets of particle board, which was cheap and required no cuts, since the width and the length of the shelves would be standardized. I went to Lucy for a purchase order. She always questioned the cost and the purpose of my expenditures. She was firm yet pleasant. I liked her. She helped with the lease for the warehouse space, and I opened my toy store.

When I had everything well organized, I mentioned to Jane that the space was ready for George to take a look. I doubted this was high on his list. Surprisingly, a few days later he asked me to meet him at the warehouse. Only a few of us knew the security code. George tried it and it worked. George loved the space and the layout of the merchandise. "That's great," he said, characteristically. "Who helped you?" I did it myself, I told him. I found shelving I could handle alone, and I'll keep adding to the supply as it comes in. "Great," he said again. George offered that I could take a sample of any items that looked appealing. He picked a few items for his family and some friends. "Thanks for stopping in," I said, as he left. I had not just turned in a draft of a screenplay or secured financing for *The Empire Strikes Back*, but I had completed my first task for George, and he had approved of my work. I took an R2D2 cookie jar, locked the door, and set the alarm.

The warehouse was strategically located across the street from the newly transplanted special-effects company Industrial Light & Magic on Kerner Boulevard in San Rafael. It was convenient for me if I had something to drop off or pick up at ILM, and easy for George if he was visiting the facility. Many of the warehouses in the area were empty. Some had small businesses; others, like The Kerner Co., as ILM was deceptively called to maintain a low profile, were buzzing with activity. ILM had been in the San Fernando Valley

Steve Starkey

in Los Angeles for the production of *Star Wars*. On *Empire Strikes Back*, though, George intended to do all the post production—the editing, sound editing, final mixing, and the visual effects—in Marin County. Only the music would be recorded out of town. He planned to set up his editing rooms in San Anselmo, close to his house, and have the sound-mixing stage next door to ILM.

Since I was now a permanent fixture in the company, I could stop in at ILM at any time. I did not want to appear to be aimlessly wandering the halls, but brief visits seemed to be welcome. I started to know my way around the place and became acquainted with quite a few of the employees. ILM was an artist's playpen. In fact, it felt a bit like a nuthouse, with the inmates fueling one another's creative juices. They fueled my imagination as well. Entering each department and asking questions of the artists was like going to film school. Starting in the art department, I could see how a special-effects shot was conceptualized. Stepping into the model shop or the creature shop, I witnessed the artists sculpting the characters or shaping, gluing, and painting a spacecraft in exacting detail. I would stand and watch the filming that took place on the blue-screen stages, where all the elements were photographed. Finally, the individual elements were rephotographed and assembled in the optical printer. Each shot was a mini movie, composed of the work of the many artists I had recently met.

I USUALLY TRIED to time my day so I could take part in the lunchtime volleyball game at the Park Way house. In addition to the editorial staff of *The Black Stallion*, the players included a number of Lucasfilm employees. They were an eclectic, energetic group, not serious competitors. One athletic standout was Duwayne Dunham,

Starting Over at Lucasfilm

a fit, handsome guy, who could have been a lifeguard on the TV show *Baywatch*. He was an experienced assistant editor and knew his way around film and the editing room. He was set to be an assistant editor on *More American Graffiti* and asked me to help him set up the editing rooms. George had just purchased a Victorian-style building in downtown San Anselmo. The upstairs would be for picture editing, the downstairs for sound.

The first time I entered an editing room I was carrying equipment. Like Paul Bushey on the electrical rigging crew, Duwayne was a perfectionist. Once again, a guy who suited my sensibilities. We began by lugging editing benches up the stairs and into the rooms, then mounted storage racks on the back of each bench, attached a desk lamp, and outfitted each workstation with rewinds, a splicer, and a synchronizer. I learned the names of the equipment as we unloaded it and put it in place, even though I had no idea how any of it was used. Film racks found a home on empty walls. Movers came with the KEM flatbed editing machines and Moviolas for the editors to cut on. After the initial setup, I made time to assist Duwayne any way I could. There was a palpable excitement in the editing room that had gotten under my skin.

Deep in the basement of the Park Way house, all by himself, was sound designer Ben Burtt. In his private space he was unaware of the sounds of life all around him. No birds were chirping, no dogs barking; there was no idle chitchat. He was wearing a headset, listening to sounds that were created on reel-to-reel tape machines in his subterranean office. Walking in to speak with Ben came with the risk that I might disturb his train of thought, thereby derailing a blend of unique sounds that might never be retrieved. Very focused, he would cock his head as he tried to bend his ear around the nuance of his latest gunshot, growl, or beep.

Ben was an extraordinary sound designer, brought onto *Star Wars* by George to create otherworldly sounds that would accompany the freshly imagined imagery. Ben had made films while attending USC film school, then started to focus on sound. His technique was organic; he used found sounds that he would combine in unique ways, creating something that had never been heard before. Think of the lightsaber hum or the laser-gun blast or the voice of R2D2, from *Star Wars*. Those are Ben Burtt creations. After snapping out of his dreamlike state of mind, Ben was always happy to play his latest creation and solicit an opinion. I never listened to film the same way again after spending time with Ben, and I heard the world differently as well. The birds were singing more loudly and distinctly after I spent time with him.

I rode into work on a one-speed Schwinn Cruiser. One day I was stopped by Howie Hammerman, who declared, "That bike just won't make it." He was the in-house technician and audio engineer and an avid mountain biker. Howie had been a roadie for numerous Bay Area bands before joining Lucasfilm. He said he was going to take me to the shop where Tom Ritchey and Gary Fisher put together their handcrafted mountain bikes. "They aren't cheap, but they'll outlast you on the dirt." Getting to work became a lot more fun. Howie was a maniac while riding his bike, and he had a crazed look and demeanor as he went about his work. He found ironic humor in everything. He wired whatever needed to be wired, he fixed whatever piece of equipment broke down, and he was the in-house projectionist. He taught me how to patch one piece of equipment to another and how to thread and run a film projector. When he explained something to me, it was plain and simple. I just didn't know what he was talking about. I would nod my head with understanding, hoping I wouldn't be alone when asked to perform

Starting Over at Lucasfilm

in his absence.

I could not have been more surprised when I ran into my neighbor, Hal Barwood, at the Park Way house. We must both have said, "What are you doing here?" and simultaneously answered, "I work here." Hal lived in the house at the head of the driveway leading to our cabin. We had become friendly, but we had never asked each other about our lines of work. Hal, and his partner, Matthew Robbins, were writing a script for a film called *Dragonslayer* that Hal would produce and Matthew would direct. They had met each other at the USC Film School, where they also met George.

The Bay Area, and particularly Lucasfilm, was filled with USC graduates. Sometimes I got the feeling that everyone except Howie and me had gone to the USC film school. In addition to George, Mathew, Hal, and Ben Burtt, other alumni included Robert Dalva, who was editing *The Black Stallion*; Howard Kazanjian, who was producing *More American Graffiti* (and who would produce *The Empire Strikes Back* and *Return of the Jedi*), and Caleb Deschanel, who was the director of photography on both *The Black Stallion* and *More American Graffiti*. I felt at a real disadvantage. I envied the camaraderie of this group and their continued loyalty to one another. Also they came out of film school with a broad sense of film history and a good overview of filmmaking. So far, the two years in LA as an electrician is all the film school I had. Now, as a production assistant, I would be in a sort of professional film school, learning as I went.

The Park Way house was a thriving film community. The filmmakers and their invited friends would cross paths each day, sharing ideas and production plans and even watching cuts of their movies. Work at the Park Way house was a grown-up version of George's experience at film school. His idea for a refuge for filmmakers did not stop there. He wanted to create a retreat for professional filmmakers on a much larger scale. A place with screening rooms to watch films and talk about them. A research library and offices for writers and art directors. Production offices for producers and their staff. Editing suites and state-of-the-art sound-mixing stages. A scoring stage able to handle a large orchestra for recording music. With the dream of making movies with fellow filmmakers in a ranch-style setting, George bought Bulltail Ranch.

BULLTAIL RANCH was deep in the ranch lands of West Marin, where the cattle roamed and hippies found secret hideaways. The entrance to the ranch was off Lucas Valley Road, coincidentally named before its latest landowner arrived. Passing over a steel-tubed cattle grate, you bounced along a dirt road to several farmhouses and a small barn. A short distance beyond, the ranch opened up into a large valley completely surrounded by wheat-covered hills, occasional oaks, and clusters of pine trees.

Soon after my first visit to the ranch, I was told to meet George and the design group with pointed six-foot stakes, a small sledgehammer, and some twine and helium balloons to attach to the stakes. It felt like my first day as an electrician, when I showed up with my pliers and gloves. Trying to keep the cow pies off our shoes, George and I looked over the shoulders of the land planners and architects as they unrolled the plans for his moviemaking compound. At the far eastern end of the largest valley was the entrance to a small glen, where the ranch's previous owners had a hunting cabin. Now the shack would be shuttered. At this end of the valley was where the architects positioned the main house, for George's office and the administrative branch of the company. It would also include a research library and a screening room and, of course, a dining room and kitchen, similar to the Park Way house but on a much grander scale. A carriage house next door would hold offices for writers and concept artists.

The perimeter of the main house was carefully marked out, and I drove in stakes at strategic points to mark the corners of the building. Helium balloons were attached to the stakes so the group could stand back in the field and imagine the size, location, and height of the building. On this particular day, the potential view from the main house was from the top of stepladders. You could look out over the entire property and imagine the future buildings carefully camouflaged to preserve the natural beauty of the ranch. In the middle of the pasture would be a lake, fed by some of the many springs that naturally existed on the property. Hidden behind a hill on the north side of the valley would be the technical building, designed to resemble a winery and housing the editorial and sound suites and the mixing and scoring facilities. The recreation center was set in the south end of the valley. Over time, I insisted that the recreational facility include a tennis court, which George finally agreed to. While mountains were moved, lakes dug, and buildings erected, how would they preserve the look of the pristine ridgetops and insure privacy for the ranch? I had an idea. I offered to walk the ridgeline of the entire property and identify the landowners who could conceivably build a structure that could be seen from the ranch or that might have a view down into it. I was equipped to do this exercise because Liv and I had done something similar in recent weeks.

We spent much of our free time roaming the fire roads and trails of West Marin, either on foot or on our mountain bikes. We had started to think we might want to live farther out in the countryside. In an attempt to find some land to build a house, we decided to walk the entire length of Nicasio Valley Road. In those days, barely a car passed us on our walk. Armed with maps of all the land along the road, which I had printed at a local title company in San Rafael, we could identify the lots that looked attractive and contact the owners.

I did much the same thing for Bulltail Ranch. With an understanding of the borders of the property, I was able to identify which parcels crept up over the ridge. Back in the office, I printed a blowup of the ranch and mounted it with pushpins on a corkboard wall. Then I printed and mounted outlines of all the adjoining properties, one right next to each other, fanning around the borders of the ranch. I identified and color coded each property that I thought George should consider acquiring. He passed that information onto his lawyer and accountant, who took it to the next step. There were days when George would stop and just stare at the map, deep in thought.

It was here, in 1978, on his newly acquired ranch, that George decided to have the first annual companywide Fourth of July picnic. There were not many of us to shoulder the burden of organizing the event; it mostly fell to Jane and me and, to some extent, Howie and Duwayne. We brainstormed the food, sanitation, and activities that would be included. Jane wanted hot dogs and ice cream catered. The remainder of the food would be potluck. I arranged for tents and picnic tables to be rented and had portable toilets brought in. Beer and water and soft drinks were provided in big tubs of ice. We had to have a baseball field, so I rented a gas-powered lawn mower and cleared enough space in the middle of the meadow. I erected a plywood backstop behind home plate and spray painted "Watch out for Poison Oak" as a warning. I even painted lines for the base paths. Howie Hammerman helped me mark out a volleyball court and set up a net. We created a bocce ball court for George so he could play with his USC cronies. We had contests ranging from a classic egg toss to three-legged races. With the sun setting on a glorious day, George thanked me for putting on a successful party. We both realized that with construction set to begin, Bulltail Ranch would never be the same. It was soon to become Skywalker Ranch.

WHILE RUNNING errands to the various postproduction companies around the Bay Area, I kept wishing for a way to get more involved in the films themselves. My desire was heightened when I was invited to watch a director's cut of *The Black Stallion* in the Park Way screening room. George and Francis Ford Coppola were in attendance, along with the director, Carroll Ballard, and the editing staff. The fact that I was allowed to attend made me feel a part of the filmmaking community. I respectfully listened as the group around me applauded the film and made suggestions to improve the version they had just seen. I was never nervous around these filmmakers, but when it came to joining the discussion of the film, I felt a bit intimidated. I was an unschooled novice and felt I would not have anything constructive to add to the conversation. The film was clearly too long, but I had no idea how to start cutting it down. Others in the room did. Often Carroll would dig in his heels, even though he knew he had to make some cuts. Eventually he did, but he rarely agreed to anything in the room. He would go back into the editing room and think about it. During these discussions, I was getting a glimpse into the complex process of reshaping a film during editing.

The more time I spent with Duwayne in the editing room, the more the idea of learning about film editing began to take hold. I came to the realization that most Bay Area shows, like *More American Graffiti* and *The Black Stallion*, went out of town on location to film but would return to town following the shoot to both edit and complete the sound work. In the case of *Apocalypse Now*, in addition to picture and sound editing, the final mix was done at Zoetrope in San Francisco. Fantasy Studios in Berkeley was expanding to accommodate editing and sound mixing as well. In order to get steady and exciting film work in the Bay Area, I would have to get into the editing room.

THANKSGIVING was a family affair at Lucasfilm. All the employees were invited to a delicious feast at the Park Way house, along with husbands, wives, girlfriends, or boyfriends. Some other filmmakers and their wives attended, including Francis Coppola and Hal Barwood. After the meal Liv drove home, while I stayed behind to clean up. George offered to give me a lift home. As I got in the car, I felt really thankful for the meal and the fact that I had found this warm family to share my life and work with. As we turned toward my house, a thought suddenly came to me. I was a little uncomfortable, but I mustered up the courage to ask George if there might be a position for an apprentice editor on *More American Graffiti*. He said he would check and see. It was a nervy thing to do, but the idea had been boiling inside of me for weeks. The next afternoon, George told me he had worked something out and said to meet him after work at the editing rooms in San Anselmo.

As I climbed up the wooden stairs in the back of the editing room, I didn't know what to expect. Just inside the door, like magic, George appeared. He introduced me to the assistants as the new apprentice editor on the film and announced that I would be coming to work at 6 p.m. on weekdays, following my day job at Park Way, and all day on Saturdays. And just like that, I had my first job in the editing room. After George left, I was a little embarrassed standing with the crew, though I am sure that Duwayne had been forewarned, and quite likely, the other assistant, Gloria Gunn, as well. I had been running errands for the group, so they knew me, and since I was not replacing anyone, they must have welcomed the additional set of hands. Unlike most apprentices who get a job in a cutting room, I didn't know the first thing about editing.

When I sat down at one of the editing benches that Duwayne and I had brought in weeks earlier, I did not have a clue how to work the splicer or synchronizer we had so neatly set up. It was like seeking out the baby junior and looking for a set of barn doors on my first day as an electrician. I had no idea what I was doing. A trim bin, overflowing with film, was rolled to my bench. Gloria told me to file the trims back into the rolls they came from. I wondered why some strips were smaller than rest. It turned out that some of the film was shot in 16 mm and other parts in 35mm. Why both formats? Who knows? This was the first time I had laid eyes on film, except when I mistakenly opened the back of my still film camera. And where were the rolls that these little cut-up strips of film came from? The strips, or trims, had been cut out of rolls of film that were stored in 12-inch-square boxes, all placed on racks and organized carefully by scene number.

Since I had not read the script, the scene numbers were a mystery to me. But no matter. The scene numbers had been printed alongside the film sprockets, stamped, one foot at a time, as the roll of film was fed through a coding machine. OK, got that. Look at the cut trim of film hanging on a hook in the bin, identify the code or scene number, then retrieve the matching box of film from the rack. Mount the roll on the rewinds. Wind down to the number indicated on the side of the film, and splice in the missing piece where it came from. Apply the splicing tape to the base side of the film, not the emulsion. Why? When removing the tape from the emulsion, it could peel away the emulsion if you weren't careful. This blemish could be visible when viewed on an editing machine or projector.

I had the damnedest time distinguishing between the base and emulsion side of the film, especially in 16mm, where the film was so small. "Can't you see how the light reflects on the base side differently than on the emulsion side?" "No, not really…" "Well, you can always touch the film to your lip, and the emulsion will stick to your lip, unlike the base side." "Thanks. I'll try that." Who knew there was so much involved with filing trims? There was an art to it, only without the art. It was simple after you did it hundreds of times, as I did. As an apprentice, when no coffee was ordered or dishes needed to be cleaned, I filed trims.

Many evenings when I could have been home having a nice meal, I filed trims. Saturdays, too. But Saturdays were different. The director, B.W.L. Norton, always went home to LA for the weekend, often bidding us farewell with, "Ta-ta, suckers." I often wondered what George thought of that, since he never stopped working. Saturdays were a little looser. A little quieter. Fewer people. George often sat down to cut something with Duwayne at his side. I was allowed to sit in and watch a scene being assembled, piece by piece. I had so many questions. Faced with so many choices, how do you know which angle to use—a wide or medium shot or a close-up? How do you choose the best reading of a line of dialogue? Or the best bit of action? How do you know where to cut? What a painstaking process. Duwayne always seemed to have the next piece of film that George was looking for in his hand or the next film roll ready to be reviewed. It was all a mystery. Strangely, the more I watched, the more mysterious it became.

When the editing of a scene was completed, the assistants often were left to add additional sound effects to embellish what existed in the track at the time of shooting. Duwayne asked me to help him out. The first effect I cut in was a van hitting some garbage cans on a steep hill in San Francisco. For the life of me I could not get the sync right. It took forever. Good thing no one was watching. In my defense, it was my first time working on a flatbed editing machine. The KEM Junior required some know-how to thread it properly and sync up the film, first the picture, then the sound. Then you had to learn to hit the control buttons that made the film go forward, reverse, and stop, all while watching the screen, hoping a sudden jerking action did not break the film. It was like learning to play the piano by looking at the music and not your hands.

I rolled down to the spot where the van hit the garbage cans. Usually, filler leader on the sound roll ran along with the picture until the bit of sound arrived that corresponded to the image. I had a recording of the crash on a piece of film. I made a mark on the leader, pulled the leader out, and spliced in my crash to the leader to sync up with the garbage-can hit. It was out of sync. How could that be? What did I do wrong? I stopped the film on the first frame of the truck hitting the cans, marked the sound leader again, and cut in the sound on the mark. It was still out of sync. I tried to delay the sound. I tried to advance the sound, but I could not get it right. Over and over I tried. I finally got it, although I was not sure what I did. I was particularly obsessed with this sound effect because Ben Burtt and I had recorded it together.

A few days earlier, Ben had mentioned he wanted to record

some loud crash sounds. I told him I knew just the place: the old barn at George's ranch. It was about to be torn down. I just hoped it wouldn't collapse while we were inside. Armed with a Nagra portable audio recorder and some microphones, Ben followed me into the decaying wooden structure. I revealed what looked like a garbage dump. Plenty of things to smash to bits. An old tractor engine was lying in the dirt. We found a bit of rope and slung it over one of the crossbeams in the ceiling. Tying one end to the engine, we hoisted it up off the ground and tied off the other end of the rope. We then stacked anything breakable we could find against an old refrigerator—panes of broken glass, discarded aluminum, and a bucket full of loose debris. Ben set a microphone next to the impact zone. We untied the engine, which was still hanging from the rope, and pulled it back as far as we could. We then shoved it at the stack of breakables and got a pretty good crash. We did it a few times to get additional recordings, which could be layered on our first recording to make an even bigger crash sound. This mixed recording became the sound of the van hitting the garbage cans that I desperately tried to sync up in the editing room.

My skills as an assistant were improving. When there were no more trims to be filed and picture editing started winding down, Ben asked me to come help in the sound department. Richard Anderson, a sound-effects editor who could only come up from LA on weekends, needed an assistant. Richard was a supervisor in his own right, but he had agreed to help out Ben in a pinch. Since I had already committed to working weekends, helping out Richard in the sound department was a great opportunity to increase my skills. I became familiar with the vast library of effects that Ben was amassing and could locate them and make a copy for Richard to cut in. I watched as Ben premixed the layers of sounds that Richard edited, blending them together in preparation for the final mix in LA.

When the final mix began and work slowed down, I split my time between working with Duwayne in the editing room and tending to my day job at the Park Way house, taking care of those I affectionately called the Park Way Princesses, Jane, Lucy, and Chrissie. The editing room was a great escape from my work at the Park Way house. George had given notes to Duwayne about recutting his documentary from 1968, *Filmmaker*, which followed Francis Ford Coppola around the country during the making of *The Rain People*. *Filmmaker* was going to be screened again, and George wanted to change a few things and cut it down a bit. I pored through George's basement storage boxes and uncovered the original picture and sound elements for the film. At the same time, I uncovered some student films that George had hidden away. When I mentioned them, he asked that we catalogue and properly store the films from his early days.

I had only seen his student film *THX 1138*, and I was struck by the diversity and artistic spectrum of his other short films. For the documentary *Bald*, he filmed the reactions of the actors getting their hair cut before performing in *THX*. George had tapped into a very sensitive emotional place for these actors, revealing their vulnerability and the attachment they had to their appearance. He had an uncanny ability to uncover these truths. On *Herbie*, a mesmerizing short, George artfully photographed reflections of light on chrome dancing to the music of Herbie Hancock. This very cinematic and impressionistic approach to film was similar to what he would bring to his future work.

Steve Starkey

TWO MAJOR BIRTHDAYS were celebrated in the spring of 1979, mine and Francis Ford Coppola's. Mine was special because it marked my first birthday in the editing room. The entire staff gathered around the KEM in the room of editor Tina Hirsch. Ben Burtt threaded up the track without any picture and hit play. It was R2D2 beeping the Happy Birthday song to me. They all assured me there would be many more. When they unthreaded the 35mm sound roll from the KEM and handed it to me, they said to unspool it. I saw that the whole crew had scribbled birthday wishes to me with a Sharpie, right on the film. I still treasure that birthday gift.

The other birthday, at Coppola's beautiful Victorian home in the Napa Valley, was a bit more elaborate. Everyone from Lucasfilm was invited, along with all of Francis's family and friends from the Bay Area. Carmine Coppola and a group of musicians were playing music from *The Godfather* when Liv and I arrived. Elaborate trays of food and drinks were passed around. Everyone was dressed for an outdoor picnic. A hang glider wearing a full tuxedo swept down from the sky onto the circular drive, popped a bottle of Champagne, and brought it to Francis. Soon after, the San Francisco Lesbian/Gay Freedom Band marched up the tree-lined drive to the house, sending everyone's spirits soaring. Happy 40th, Francis!

AROUND THIS TIME, Lucasfilm moved to new offices located behind the Park Way house on a street called Ancho Vista. George planned to rebuild and restore the house to the two-story structure it had been before a fire burned the top floor long ago. He and his wife, Marcia, were planning to start a family, and Park Way would become their new home. Marcia was a talented editor in her own right. She had not only edited films with George on *American Graffiti* and *Star Wars* but had also worked as an editor with Martin Scorsese on movies ranging from *Taxi Driver* to *Alice Doesn't Live Here Anymore*. She was not cutting any films at the time and had become the interior decorator of both the house and new offices.

I cleared out the editing rooms in the basement of Park Way and moved the equipment and furniture into storage or took what was necessary to the editing room to get ready for *The Empire Strikes Back*. George had bigger plans, though. He wanted to build a temporary mixing stage next door to ILM, to use until the mixing stages at the ranch were ready. It seemed the more he did his work up north, the less he wanted to do anything in LA.

Lucasfilm was growing as a company. A president was brought on board, and Howard Kazanjian was made head of the motion-picture division. They both realized that a general manager was needed to head up a newly formed division called Sprocket Systems, to oversee all post-production facilities, personnel, and equipment. And they had me in their sights. I was well suited to take on the challenge. I knew George well. I was familiar with all things editorial. Taking on the oversight of the company was something I could easily handle. This would be good, steady work for me. But what about *The Empire Strikes Back?* After my apprenticeship on *More American Graffiti*, I imagined myself following in Duwayne's footsteps, becoming an assistant editor on *Empire* as he moved up to become the first assistant editor on the show. I was at a crossroads. Which job would be best for my career? Which would I enjoy most? Which job should I try to get?

Facing this uncertainty, I prepared to drive to South San Francisco to pick up some carpet for the new offices. I would have plenty of time to think on the road. As I was leaving, Marcia said she wanted to come along for the ride. This was a first. No one, let alone Marcia, ever went on errands with me. But off we went. I remember her sitting shotgun, feet up on the dashboard, talking and laughing as I drove. Then the conversation took a turn. She must have sensed that I was thinking of pursuing work in the editing room and reminisced about those years of her life. The hours. The commitment. The toll it takes on a relationship. She was worried for me. Did I know what I was getting into? But wait, hadn't she and George made it work? I thought they did. But the exchange was sobering and unsettling.

For days I went back and forth over the job possibilities. Sure enough, I was offered the role of general manager of Sprocket Systems. Lucasfilm wanted me, and I was very thankful. I asked Duwayne about *Empire*. He assured me it was very likely I would get a job as an assistant editor on the show when they finished shooting in England and moved to Marin. I would have to meet the editor, Paul Hirsch, but Duwayne said I was the best candidate by far, particularly with his recommendation. There it was. What I had been thinking about became real.

I shared my thoughts with Liv. She said to follow my heart. But my heart was split in two.

Turning into the driveway of our house, I stopped to say hello to Hal Barwood. I told him about my dilemma. He said you are making this more difficult than it needs to be. The decision is very simple. Do you want to work on movies, or do you want to work for a company that services people who make movies? I said I wanted to make movies. Done. Take the assistant editing job on *Empire Strikes Back*. I did. And I hoped that George would understand and embrace my decision.

CHAPTER 5

The Empire Strikes Back

"Do or do not, there is no try." Yoda

SITTING AT MY editing bench in the back room I felt like a child listening. From there, I could hear words and conversations I could only vaguely understand. The words were clear, while the ideas were unfamiliar. It was like sitting in the backseat of a car as a youngster, half asleep, overhearing the voices of the grown-ups speaking up front. Paul Hirsch, the film editor, and Irvin Kershner, the director, were in the dining room, now converted to Paul's editing room, talking over a scene that Paul was cutting. The back and forth between the two was a discussion I was keenly interested in, and I was trying to eavesdrop from my workspace a few rooms away.

I had been hired as an assistant editor on *The Empire Strikes Back*, the sequel to *Star Wars*. When I had the job interview with Paul, I had been nervous, since I was still pretty green. My apprenticeship on *More American Graffiti* was the only experience I had to offer. George and Duwayne must have convinced him to give me a shot.

Mirroring the floor space on *More American Graffiti*, the editing rooms in San Anselmo were laid out in what had been a two-bedroom apartment. Paul took over the dining room for his editing suite. To get to the room I shared with Barbara Ellis, known as B.J., Paul would pass through the kitchen, head toward the back of the apartment, and cross a short hallway. Typically Paul wished B.J. and me a good morning and asked, "How is everything?" "All is fine in here," we would reassure him.

Paul was a kind man, interested in our well-being but probably also looking for a break and a chance to take a little walk in order to consider what he and Kersh had been talking about. He was trying to get the picture locked, or in a finished state for its first screening. Considering that the film had gone over schedule in shooting, the pressure was on. Sometimes Paul would share his cutting dilemma with us, but more often than not, he would simply make light conversation until a thought crossed his mind, and he was ready to go at it again. Paul had worked with George on *Star Wars*, and he brought a seasoned perspective to his work. Not just because he was familiar with *Star Wars*, but because he was an intelligent editor. B.J., his assistant editor, was an African American woman from the East Coast. It was good that our worktables were not facing one another, because her laugh was extremely contagious and looking at each other would have made working together nearly impossible. I offered a hand to B.J. or Paul if the need arose.

Most of my time was spent assisting Duwayne, who was the first assistant editor on the show. He held court in a converted bedroom at the front of the building. There was a KEM editing machine there for George Lucas to use. When George was editing, Duwayne was always present, taking notes and keeping track of the film. Duwayne also played the role of post-production supervisor. In this capacity, he coordinated the completion of the entire show. Duwayne was the point person dealing with the sound department and ILM in Marin County, and all the various optical houses, the negative cutter, and Deluxe lab in LA. With a shortened schedule, the process for the delivery of the film had been accelerated. Duwayne needed a second pair of hands. That was me. He expected me to pick up wherever he needed the help. I was not familiar with any of the duties he passed along to me at first, so I was learning as I went along. This freaked me out a bit, since Duwayne didn't seem to make many mistakes, and he expected the same from me.

All minds were focused on the upcoming screening. Kersh had taken up residence in the apartment's living room. He'd pace back and forth, finally settling in front of the fireplace, whether the fire was lit or not. He was within earshot of Paul, ready to pounce whenever Paul had something, anything, to show him. Kersh reminded me of Yoda in many ways. It wasn't his physical demeanor; he was tall and slight. No, the resemblance was in his eyes, which displayed an intelligence and seemed to twinkle at the same time, and in his rounded and cherubic face, which often had an appealing smile. *Empire* was a departure from his usual directing fare, so I am sure he was anxious to see the picture put together.

As Paul finished a reel, we were handed the film to check and clean. I mounted the picture and track on my rewind, one in front of the other, locked them into the synchronizer, and lined them up on their start marks, eight feet ahead of the first frame of the picture. Shot by shot the splices were checked. They needed to hold when running through the film projector. For the more forgiving KEM editing machines, splicing tape was applied to only one side of the film, covering two sprockets on each film frame. For the added strength needed for projection, the splices would be replaced with a single splice on both sides of the film.

As I watched the film wind through the synchronizer, messy grease-pencil marks were cleaned up without altering the specific animation markings that indicated temporary visual effects. These marks helped the screening audience understand the film in its present state and also provided a blueprint to those doing the visual-effects work. For example, a series of grease marks over several frames might animate a shot fired from a laser pistol. The viewer could see where and when a shot was fired and follow the tracer to its final impact. The 1,000-foot-long editing reels were then combined into 2,000-foot reels. I attached the first reel to the second, the third to the fourth, and so on. Finally, although exhausted by the day-and-night preparations, we were ready to go.

This was my first rough-cut screening, and it went well. No film breaks, and everything was in sync. When it finished, though, I almost wished I hadn't gone. I didn't know what to make of the movie I had just seen. It seemed like a big mess. I couldn't make heads or tails of the sequences. The imagery was so rough I couldn't connect to it emotionally. It seemed like there was so much work to be done. But everyone in attendance—Paul, George, Marcia Lucas, Ben Burtt, writer Larry Kasdan, and producer Gary Kurtz—was experienced enough to see beyond the crude imagery. We left the Park Way screening room and returned to the editing room to review what we had just seen. I walked back with Ben. He knew what I was thinking: that the film was a disaster. Ben tried to reassure me by telling me it had been the same rough jumble on *Star Wars*, and in the end it all turned out great.

Airing out my fears with Ben helped release the tension of the screening preparation, and I felt much better. Everyone huddled around Paul's KEM as he ran the film reel by reel. Paul would let the film go until someone, anyone, including me, had a note to give. Everyone was allowed the time to voice an opinion. Of course, I was too timid to speak up. The discussions went back and forth, and careful notes were taken. Following a consensus on what notes to address, the recut was divided up between George and Paul. We also had a guest editor.

George asked Marcia to put on her editing hat and take a fresh look at the romantic scene between Han and Leia, and I was told to assist her. I think Marcia missed editing. It had been so much a part of her life. She cut on the KEM in my room. Being assigned as a dedicated assistant to an editor was a first for me. Although I did not look over her shoulder at every cut she made, as assistants often do, she kindly showed me her work in progress. First, she scoured the dailies of the scene, every size and angle, pulling out every bit of film that might have been overlooked. Armed with these new gems, she replaced some of the shots in the cut. She weighed whether it was more powerful to be looking at a character's reaction or at the person delivering a line. She might add a reaction leading into the next line of dialogue, which often added emotional depth to what the character was about to say. All these small changes had a profound impact. Strangely, as we worked together, she never brought up her warning about the demands of editing work and the toll it would take on my relationship with Liv. I suppose she accepted that I had considered what she said and decided to go for it anyway.

Within a short amount of time, the picture was considered locked, which meant that, at least structurally, any forthcoming changes would be minimal, and visual effects and sound could move ahead full steam. Black-and-white dupes, or copies of the film, were made for sound, music, ILM, and the LA-based visual-effects vendors to use as a bible. If changes were made, I would write up a change sheet, specifying exactly which frames were added or deleted from a shot or scene. The picture would undergo changes until the last shot was finished, the negative was cut, and the film went to the lab for printing. Despite the daily changes, everyone needed to get started.

ILM had not waited for the picture to be locked to start working around the clock. They had been working six-day weeks since the summer. Element after element was being shot on their stages with models that had been built months in advance and others that were still under construction. The optical department was running 24 hours a day with both day and night shifts, trying to keep up. As visual-effects shots came into the editing room, they were scrutinized by George, Duwayne, and Paul, and detailed notes were sent back to ILM. George was a harsh critic. For a guy who had all his own money on the line, when it came to getting a shot right, he was relentless, no matter the cost.

I USUALLY came in on Saturday when it was quiet, in order to catch up. One day I heard someone cutting in the front editing room. George was there all alone at the KEM. "What's up?" I asked. "I'm selecting cloud backgrounds for the approach to Cloud City." Cloud City was where the heroes in the film flew to take refuge. During the approach, all the shots looking out the windows in the cockpit of the Millennium Falcon had been shot against a blue screen. The blue would be replaced by the clouds and the city. To start this process, thousands of feet of puffy, white clouds were photographed from a plane soaring through the formations. The clouds were shot in VistaVision, a large-format film, in order to maintain the highest possible quality. The footage was screened at ILM, and selections were made for editing. The VistaVision selections had to be reduced to a 35mm black-and-white copy so it could be viewed on the KEM. With this roll of selects in hand, George came to the editing room and carefully chose the cloud backgrounds for each shot in the sequence. Before editing, I would normally use a coding machine to stamp a code on the edge of the film every 16 frames, so I could identify where the footage came from in the roll since the numbers on the VistaVision original print were not visible in the black-and-white reduction. Since the rolls George cut from were not coded, it was nearly impossible to tell where the cuts of film had come from. The rolls were all cut up, with the unidentified pieces removed. The short trims were now hanging on pins in the trim bin.

"The sequence looks good, George, but I'm not sure how I am supposed to know where all the pieces in your cut came from." "I know you'll figure it out." Getting up from the Kem, he shrugged and with a bit of guilt said, "Have fun," and left for the day. I spent the remainder of that Saturday reassembling the rolls as they were before George cut them up. Using a light box, I had to stare at the film and match the subtle movements of the passing clouds in order to put the pieces back together again. This took hours. I had marked the pieces George had selected so they wouldn't get mixed up as I reconstituted the rolls. Then I put them back in the cut and gave ILM the information they needed to start putting the shots together. When Duwayne dropped in, I told him what had happened. He smiled knowingly. He had faced similar situations while assisting George.

Paul would cut the new shots in his edited reels as they arrived, making sure there were no errors or sync problems. He was also cutting in the ADR, the rerecorded dialogue that replaced inaudible lines of dialogue that had technical or noise issues. Sometimes performances could be improved by rerecording a line reading. When Darth Vader revealed to Luke that he is his father, the real line was recorded for the first time on the ADR stage. During shooting, where the actor was behind a mask, he was given an alternate line to read so that the secret of who Luke's father was would not be leaked. Only the small group of us in the editing room knew the truth.

One day, we gathered around the KEM with George and Paul to consider the auditions for the voice of Yoda. On set Frank Oz, who puppeteered Yoda, had done the performance and lent his own voice to the character. No one ever thought that Frank would be the final voice. But after listening to tape after tape of voice performers, George asked, "What's wrong with Frank's voice?" We all shrugged our shoulders. No one had a problem with Frank's voice. I guess we had to fully explore all the possibilities to fall in love with the original voice. It was settled. After reviewing countless alternatives, Frank Oz became the voice of Yoda.

WE ALL NEEDED a break from the relentless work in the editing rooms around the Bay Area, and Walter Murch came up with the perfect antidote. Walter, a film editor and sound designer, decided to host the first ever Droid Olympics at his farm in the tiny hamlet of Bolinas. Editorial assistants were affectionately called droids by their superiors in a nod to *Star Wars*. At Walter's invitation, all the crews of the feature films working in the Bay Area crawled out of their dark holes, rubbed their eyes, and along with their families took the winding roads to West Marin. The competitions were fierce for the biggest laugh. Here was a chance to show off the arcane skills never witnessed by those outside of the editing room. Who could wind a 50-foot length of film that was stretched out on the grass back onto a film core, using only the hand you felt the least comfortable with? Worst Hand Anyway, as the event was called, caused spasms in the wrist of many competitors.

All assistants in the editing room are required to wind the picture and track through a synchronizer, down to a chosen frame as quickly as possible as the editor stands by impatiently. During the Demolition Rewind event, much film was shredded in an attempt to break the speed record. Then came the Bobbing for Smidgee competition. Have you ever lost something and torn through the garbage as a last resort? Well, a trim bin was filled full of film and deep within was a buried smidgee—a single frame of film. With a stopwatch ticking, droids had to dig for the smidgee without disturbing the film pinned to the hooks on the trim bin. This seemingly impossible feat was accomplished in a matter of seconds, when my pal Duwayne grabbed hold of the film, flung the ends out of the bin, and grabbed the smidgee in midair!

For a group relay event, film boxes were stacked in the arms of the competitors, high enough to block their vision, and they had to race back and forth without dropping a box or running into their opponents. Finally, Francis Ford Coppola demanded everyone's attention. His competition was simple: Come up with an idea for a film, get it financed, shot, and released. "Now go!" he hollered, then announced that his homemade pasta was ready to eat. For the editorial folks whose work made them necessarily antisocial, the friendly competition and picnic were a chance for all of them to see one another and share war stories. In addition to the Droid Olympics, we started a softball league, another way to socialize with those in the sound department and ILM and take a break from the long hours of work.

Steve Starkey

AT THIS STAGE of the production, the effects shots were pouring in. Managing the LA-based vendors long distance was becoming too unwieldy. Duwayne decided I needed to go down south to personally coordinate the work there. I was put up in the Oakwood Apartments on Barham Boulevard, across the street from the back gate of Universal Studios, where I had sneaked onto the lot and found my first job as an electrician. Small world. This was my first time working out of town, so I took what they gave me. It was convenient, but that's about it. I think someone broke into the apartment next door the night I moved in. I was a bit embarrassed showing Liv my location digs. She wasn't inclined to visit very often.

I set up an office at the Egg Company, a building George had recently purchased on Lankershim Boulevard, across from Universal's front gate. The offices were designed for Lucasfilm company employees and those working on film projects. I brought in an editing bench that doubled as a desk with a phone. I moved in a KEM Junior editing machine to view dailies as they came in. *Raiders of the Lost Ark* was in prep, so the place had good energy. The producers, Frank Marshall and Robert Watts, maintained production offices in the building for when they were in town. Norman Reynolds, the production designer, had taken over the conference room. I loved looking at his set designs and models. The office proved to be a good base of operation for me, and an easy drive to all the places I went to on a daily basis. All of a sudden, though, I found I was alone. I had gotten used to the company of experts in the editing room. Now I had no immediate supervisors to answer to and no one's advice or guidance to fall back on. It was both freeing and daunting.

I set up a routine. The day started at Deluxe Lab, picking up dailies for each of the effects shops. Often the dailies were late coming out of the soup, or developer, usually because the color of the film was off, so I would sit in with the expeditor, Dash Morrison, as he color-corrected the film and pushed it through for a quick turnaround. We were a big client at the lab, with film from the LA optical shops and ILM pouring through each day and the promise of a big-release print order in a short time. The president of Deluxe, Fred Austin, occasionally invited me to sit in his overly large office. Leaning back in his leather desk chair, Fred amiably joked with me through his bushy mustache. Fred had worked his way up at the lab and knew everything about the inner workings of the place. I thought that in order to do my job well, I needed to learn how everything worked. I made my way around the lab, following the entire path taken by an exposed piece of film to the delivery of the final print, ready to be projected. I even knew everyone's name, which gave me the privilege of avoiding normal security protocols and giving me access to the whole lab.

Armed with the latest dailies in hand, I stopped by every vendor on the show each day. We would review their latest attempt at a shot. Sometimes, the first attempt was good enough to be the final version for the film but generally not. If not, I would review the print of their latest version and discuss whether or not they had addressed the change notes from George, Duwayne, and Paul. I also brought with me newly assigned shots that had just been sent from the editing room up north, and we would review the instructions to be sure they were clear. This was all much easier to do in person than on the phone. I learned as I went, disguising my lack of knowledge. All the vendors had much more experience than I did doing what they did. But I knew the movie, and I had a shorthand with the editing room. For that reason, I was welcome.

Ray Mercer's effects company operated out of a small storefront.

As he had done on *Star Wars*, Ray was doing the many wipes in the film, visual transitions from one scene to another. George had lots of fun designing the wipes. Sometimes a bar would wipe across the screen, revealing a new scene as it traveled left to right. Another wipe might iris out, starting as a pinpoint in the center of a film frame and expanding until a new scene appeared. In one case, Chewbacca was behind bars, so the wipe was a series of equally spaced vertical lines, each of which moved across the frame to free up the next shot. Often Ray would scratch his head as he attempted to understand the design, so we would review it together. When the shot came back, sometimes the start of the incoming shot—the shot the wipe was transitioning to—appeared to start on the wrong frame. We corrected it together. Since the color often shifted dramatically from one scene to the next, it could be startling when a new shot began, so we would also need to correct the color or density in order to soften the blow.

Nina Saxon had big eyes and energy to burn. She needed both, when her company took on the mind-boggling number of laser pistol shots on the show. In many cases, with multiple guns going off at the same time, it was hard to tell where the gunshots were coming from based on the grease-pencil markings on the film. We would pore over these shots, making sure we had the source for each shot in the right spot, that the trajectory of the tracer was correct, and that the location and the timing of the laser's impact worked. Nina was an astute animator, and once again, even though I was a good second set of eyes and studied what she did carefully, Nina knew more about what she was doing than I did.

Winding up Laurel Canyon and pulling up to Lookout Mountain Studios, I felt like I had opened the door to a rock 'n' roll artist of the sixties. Pat O'Neill, who ran the shop, was first and foremost

The Empire Strikes Back

an artist. Really, all these vendors in LA were artists, but Pat seemed to be working on the show to fund his other artistic pursuits. He not only made short experimental films but also had drawings and sculptures around the studio. Mounted strips of 35mm film in picture frames, presented as art pieces, lined the walls of the office. Pat had long hair and a good beard to go along with it. Our conversations about his art often took us away from the subject at hand, which were the laser sword shots in the movie. These shots were tricky. There was more to them than simply animating the wooden sticks that the actors used during the filming of the sword fights. The shots and the swords themselves were dramatic. The timing and speed with which they turned on was critical. As the light from the swords pulsed, they carried with them the emotions of the characters. Moving through space, the swords had difficult forced perspectives, making them challenging to draw and animate. Also, the color had to be just right. If, say, if the blue aura of the glowing sword was a bit off, in order to correct it, you might inadvertently alter the color of the background. It was important to maintain the color of a scene from shot to shot. Pat might have to redo a shot so that both the color of the laser sword and the background color were correct and in balance with each other. Leaving Pat, descending Lookout Mountain into Hollywood, I usually had to make a mental adjustment. I went from feeling like I had spent time in another era—the time of my high school days, when I hardly had a care in the world—back to my current reality, full of responsibility, finishing a big movie.

In addition, Van Der Veer Photo Effects, Westheimer, and Modern Film Effects were enlisted to do various shots for the film and were all part of my daily journey. Often, a second set of dailies would be finished at Deluxe, so I would head back to review the new shots before sending them north to the editing room. As the number of weeks to finish started to close in on us, they opened the lab on Saturday exclusively for our film. Although it was costly, we couldn't afford to lose any more time. ILM often needed immediate feedback from their latest work in order to know how to finish a shot. Since we "owned" the lab on Saturday, I had the run of the place. And run, I did, with Dash Morrison. He was slick and fast and kept the lab buzzing. I freely roamed the hallway, while the film slowly made its way from one station to the next. I'd peek into the darkroom where the film went through the developer, giant chemical baths large enough to be a backyard swimming pool. I often found the attendant asleep on a wooden folding chair in the corner. The color timer, the person who adjusted how much color and density to apply to each piece of film, sat all by himself in a darkened, miniature viewing room, with a postage-stamp-size screen. He operated a small projector with a foot pedal, much like an old-fashioned sewing machine, quickly advancing to the area he was working on. As the film was projected at high speeds, all you saw were bands of color waving across the screen. The timer knew exactly where he was in the film by those shifting colors. He could identify subtle alterations and knew how to balance the whole. When I described the artistry of the color timer to George, he claimed that if you only watched the bands of color as they played on the screen at high speed, you could tell the pace of the film, revealing where there might be a section of the film that was moving too slow or too fast.

AS THE VISUAL-EFFECTS shots were getting updated and cut into the film, the lab was churning out film morning, noon, and night, and the sound mix was going forward at a frantic pace.

The Empire Strikes Back

Everything was converging toward a major screening in the large screening room at 20th Century-Fox. This would be the first time the Fox executives had seen the film. It would not be finished but close enough. On the day of the screening, sitting in my small editing room at the Egg Company, I threaded up the latest visual-effects shots for George and Duwayne to review. They had to decide if the new shots should replace the works in progress we had in the film. Duwayne stood back and let me take control. I took notes carefully and cut in the shots, making sure I replaced what came out to the exact frame. One frame off and we were out of sync. Before they arrived, I had carefully measured the length of each reel, from the start mark at the head of the reel to the last frame of the picture. I scratched my measurements down on a piece of paper and had taped it to my rack on the editing bench. I was moving quickly. Using my numbers as a guide, I built the small 1,000-foot working reels into 2,000-foot screening reels, attaching Reel 1 to Reel 2, Reel 3 to Reel 4, and so on, just as I had done for our screenings in Marin. I ran the film on the KEM to be sure I hadn't made any mistakes. I was ready to pack up and go. We were hours away from the screening, ready to head across town to Fox, when Ben came into the room and dropped some rolls of full-coat sound film on the floor and said, "Here's the new mix."

There was silence as we all looked at one another. "Are you kidding?" I finally said. "In the 11th hour you want me to use this new version?" There was no answer to the question. I just had to do it based on the lengths of the reels I had scribbled on the piece of paper attached to my rack in front of me. I found the audible sync pop at the head of Reel 1, then rolled back and carefully marked the start frame with a big X with my grease pencil. Lining up the X on zero in my synchronizer, I rolled down the new track to the footage I had noted on the piece of paper. I scribed a mark on the last perforation of the final frame and cut it with my splicer. I then rolled down Reel 2 to the first frame of picture. I cut off the leader and hung it in my trim bin. When someone asked a question, I said to stop talking. This had to be right. I attached the tail of Reel 1 to the head of Reel 2. I had no time to double-check my work. Reel after reel I repeated this procedure until the show was again on the 2,000-foot screening reels. Usually I would code the picture and track, so if the film broke, I could quickly resync the film and carry on with the screening. Not this time. After carefully preparing for the screening all morning, I now had to go in blind. I was terrified.

In the theater, I sat at the edge of a row in an aisle seat. That way I could run up to the screening booth if there was a problem or simply run out of the theater. As the lights went down, the Fox logo came up with the usual fanfare, and everyone whistled and screamed in anticipation. I slunk down in my seat, began to sweat, and became deaf to my surroundings. There were six reels and five changeovers to new reels. Each changeover was a potential problem. In addition, if I had attached the reels to one another incorrectly, any given reel could be out of sync. Each new reel gave me a heart attack. I knew the last shot of each reel and sat tensely, hoping, praying the movie stayed in sync. I would listen and watch the first bit of dialogue or anything to give me an indicator we were OK. By the end of the screening, I was exhausted. Everyone was ecstatic with the outcome. I was the only one in the theater who couldn't wait for the show to be over.

By then, I had seen the film so many times I almost had it memorized, cut by cut. I sat by the editors as they ran scenes forward and backward. I cut in hundreds of visual-effects shots and checked them. I stood by on the mixing stage as George and Ben supervised the sound mix. When the final prints came out of the lab, I viewed the movie in both 35mm and 70mm, part of a team checking prints for distribution. It would take weeks for me to let the images go, so I could think other thoughts without the film winding through my mind. But it gave me a thrill to think of what I had just accomplished. I knew very little coming into this job, yet by playing a small but important role in finishing the film, I felt completely satisfied. While I looked forward to a break, I couldn't wait to do it again.

CHAPTER 6

Behind the Scenes

I WAS TAKING a nap when I was suddenly awakened by the rumble of pounding feet and the rising din of indecipherable voices. Images from *The Empire Strikes Back* were becoming a distant dream. The streets had been abandoned when I laid down to rest. I looked out the window to discover that shops up and down the small street had reopened and were teeming with people walking with purpose, speaking and gesturing excitedly. Our *pensione* was on Via Della Vite, at the base of the Spanish Steps, a fashionable shopping district in Rome. For years I had harbored a desire to return to Italy, the country whose films had stirred my initial passion for making movies. Liv and I were finally there, with no work responsibilities and the time to explore. We dressed quickly and stepped out for an early supper at Nino, our favorite restaurant, just blocks away from our modest room. For dessert that night we were treated to *fragole di Nemi*, the first baby strawberries of the season. Liv and I decided we would venture up to Nemi the following day and find the source of this delicate fruit. Lucasfilm suddenly seemed far, far away.

We took a bus to the outskirts of Rome to a transfer station that dropped us off in front of Cinecittà, the famed movie studio built in the Mussolini era. It was a thrill just to see the imposing walls, as impenetrable as Universal had seemed to me not long ago, knowing that Visconti, Rossellini, and Fellini had worked there. Another bus took us into the Castelli Romani to the town of Castel Gandolfo, the summer residence of the Pope. We went on foot the rest of the way to Nemi, a small village with a view overlooking Rome. Most of the cafés were closed, but one proprietor invited us in, displaying a rabbit he was cooking on his indoor grill. When he asked where I had picked up my rudimentary Italian, I described how I came to study the language when I had fallen in love with the Italian films made during and after the Allied liberation of Rome during World War II. He said he was in Nemi at that time, watching the smoke rising and the tanks rolling into the city. Suddenly, those images that I knew so well on film became real as he told his war stories.

A few days later we left Rome for Sicily. As I gazed out the window of the train at the vine-covered hillsides of Calabria, my thoughts drifted back to my recent film work. It was clear to me that my career journey had changed dramatically through my experience on *The Empire Strikes Back*. I had found a group of filmmakers who were thinking of film on a whole new level from what I had known through my experiences in LA. I was challenged in my work and invited to contribute to the art of film as never before. My passion had increased. The seed that had been planted in college was now starting to burst open. With an excitement for my future, I could now enjoy experiencing the settings of my favorite Italian films and the source of my inspiration for my thesis in college.

Heading to the beaches and fishing villages along the southern coast of Sicily, we traveled through small towns in the interior of the island. Scenes from *The Godfather* ran through my mind as we passed outdoor cafés in places like Piazza Armerina. The town square was occupied solely by men, all dressed in black, drinking coffee and smoking cigarettes and either reading the newspaper or huddled in small groups in heated discussion.

We arrived in the fishing village of Selinunte in a single train car. It was the end of the line. As the train reversed direction and left town, the gatekeeper raised the hand-cranked railroad-crossing arm that was blocking passage on the only road into town. There were no cars to be seen. A young boy was unself-consciously relieving himself on the wall of the train station, which looked as if it had been closed for some time. I asked the gatekeeper for directions into town. He pointed toward the sea. With no help in sight, we picked up our bags and started walking. We arrived at a seaside restaurant and were greeted by the hosts of both the restaurant and the apartment we had taken on the outskirts of town. We returned for dinner to a nearly empty restaurant. This was mid-May. The crowds would start arriving in the summer.

We shared a family-style table with a lone fisherman. At the end of the meal, he asked us to share some Averna, a popular liqueur that tasted of the earth. The more we drank, the more fishing stories he told. He had lived a hard life, heading out to sea late at night, fishing at first light, returning to the harbor to make his sale. He could have been one of the locals who portrayed the fishermen in *La Terra Trema*, the Visconti film I had written about in college. As he got up to leave for his boat, he invited me along. Since the sea was rough and the bottle of Averna was almost gone, I declined the invitation. In hindsight, I am sure he took his boat out each night under the same conditions, so I would have survived.

As Liv and I walked back to our apartment, the full moon led us to the ancient Greek temple that overlooked the village and the sea. We crawled under a gap in the chain-link fence and climbed up to the site. As we hugged one of the columns, we could not touch each other's hands. We were enraptured by the reflections of light on the calming sea, hoping our fisherman would be safe under the guidance of Selene, the goddess of the moon.

When our trip ended and Liv and I returned home, we felt that we had been on our honeymoon, so we decided to get married. Our wedding was presided over by the Presbyterian minister from the seminary across the street from our cottage. Attended by only a few friends and a neighbor perched in a tree, we kept the ceremony brief. We threw a party a few weeks later, surrounded by close friends from our old Berkeley days as well as the new friends we had made since moving back to Bay Area. All my Lucasfilm friends came, along with their wives or husbands—George and Marcia, Jane, Chrissie, and Lucy, along with Ben, and Duwayne. Liv invited all her friends from the Nancy Van Wyck Catering Company. They were all great chefs and filled the tables with wonderful food. It had been a rich summer, and I was now ready to return to work.

MY NEXT-DOOR neighbor, Hal Barwood, was producing a film called *Dragonslayer*, directed by his writing partner, Matt Robbins. They had been in production while I was in Europe on holiday. I hoped to get a position on their show. Duwayne was hired as an assistant editor, but the editor, Tony Lawson, had brought along someone from London to work with him. I was out of luck. At the same time, George Lucas and Steven Spielberg had gone overseas to film *Raiders of the Lost Ark*, which Steven was now editing in Los Angeles. Executive producer Howard Kazanjian had hired filmmaker Phillip Schuman to shoot a behind-the-scenes documentary on the making of *Raiders*, and he was brought back to San Anselmo to edit. Howard wanted me to be Phil's assistant editor and act as the post-production coordinator of the show for Lucasfilm. Although I had taken on some of those supervisory responsibilities on *Empire*, in this case I would have no immediate supervisors. I would be on my own. Even though this was a documentary, not a feature film, I would have the added pleasure of being a voyeur on *Raiders*, watching and listening to others in the trenches during the shoot, with at least the feeling of being part of the production. After meeting Phil, I decided to take the job. As writer, director, and editor, he was happy to have my help. I don't think he had been able to afford to have a person like me on his previous shows, though I imagine he was probably a bit suspicious of having a company guy snooping around.

Phil and I could not have been more different. He was a mess. I liked to keep things in order. I started work rather early. He stumbled in sometime before lunch. I would arrive to find his editing room in disarray. Film was hanging everywhere, even taped to his KEM screen or the console of the machine. Empty coffee cups sat next to full ashtrays. I felt like a maid, attempting to restore order before Phil got to work. I often wondered what took place during the early hours of the morning while I was home asleep.

I appreciated the footage that Phil shot on location. I think he had a point of view and knew how he intended to use it. The interviews were good, whether they were done on set, in makeup chairs, or during car rides into work. They all had an in-the-moment feel, capturing both the working process and the off-camera personalities of the subjects. The film focused on the problems faced by the production and were covered in detail. Whether it was removing TV antennas from the rooftops of a Middle Eastern city to maintain the period look of the film or moving the crew into a remote area of a Third World country, the problems they faced were dramatized to capture your attention and imagination.

In the middle of assembling his cut, Phil's little world was turned upside down. Lucasfilm asked Phil to put together a 10-minute show reel for a gathering of NATO, the National Association of Theater Owners, which would take place in Las Vegas. The short documentary would be used as a marketing tool to raise awareness and enthusiasm for *Raiders of the Lost Ark*. The producers and the studio marketing department wanted to showcase the teaming of George Lucas and Steven Spielberg by showing them working together. Studios generally relied on traditional trailers to hype films for the theater owners at the convention. Movie stars were paraded out and expected to wave and say a few words. A lavish lunch was served, with each studio trying to outdo the other. But for *Raiders*, the producers and the marketing department decided to try something new: a longer piece and one that took the theater owners to a place they were never invited to go—behind the scenes on a movie set. Phil understood what they were asking him to do, but it put him into a tailspin. He was a filmmaker, not someone to be exploited to make promotional films. He really had no choice, however, so he reluctantly took on the job. The 10-minute reel was a huge success. I'm sure most of the marketing heads at other studios were asking, "Why didn't I think of that?"

Finishing the promotional documentary for NATO introduced me to the world of independent and documentary filmmaking in San Francisco. My previous experience had been working with ILM and Deluxe Lab. The Big Boys. By checking in at Monaco Film Labs, a boutique lab in San Francisco, and Cinematte, which did titles and small effects work, I became aware of a different group of filmmakers trying to get their voices heard. Every trick they employed or print they made put pressure on their minuscule funds. Rather than rely on NATO to showcase their work, they pinned up fliers about screenings in the windows of Cinematte or Monaco

Labs or on lampposts nearby. Their enthusiasm grew on me, leading me to films that probably never saw a movie screen again. Whether it was out of guilt or simply because I was impressed by such diligence, these filmmakers created a desire in me to watch every penny I spent on our documentary. I was wearing a different hat now. I had joined another club in the filmmaking world.

All the film clips from *Raiders of the Lost Ark* that were used in the documentary needed to be reduced to fit the smaller documentary format. *Raiders* was shot and released in wide-screen anamorphic, which means that the projected image had an aspect ratio of 2.39:1; the picture's width was 2.39 times its height. The documentary was 1.33:1. Shot by shot, the feature-film frame had to be panned and scanned to create a much more limited image. I was chosen to do the work, even though I had never done this before. I suppose there was no one else to do the job. I spent a few days on a Moviola at Modern Film Effects in Hollywood, slowly going through the film shot by shot, giving instructions on what part of the image to use. I used a very crude sliding window device, framed to the size of the 1.33:1 format, which I placed over the view screen of the Moviola. Stopping at every new shot as I ran the film, I selected which part of the wide screen would be or could be shown. It is a very subjective process.

Generally, you start by framing the middle of the image, where most of the action takes place. Often, if two characters are in the frame at the same time, unless you wanted to cut both of their heads in half, you had to choose which character would be in the frame. This was clearly not what the director or the cinematographer intended, so you ended up feeling kind of rotten about the whole process. But since the footage needed to be changed into the documentary format, it had to be done. This can be avoided on TV; if you put black bars at the top and bottom of the frame you can keep the entire original format intact. I ended up panning and scanning the whole film, despite the fact that Phil only used small sections of the film in his final cut. I'm not sure if someone else redid my work for airing on television, but if so, I never heard about it.

UPON COMPLETION of the documentary, I moved back to an office next to Ben Burtt in San Anselmo. Phil had taken off, and Frank Marshall asked me to put together some short *Raiders* featurettes using the documentary footage. They were mash-ups, cut-down versions of sections of the documentary and the NATO featurette, but they still had to make sense on their own, with a beginning, middle, and end. I had never actually cut anything before, so this was a fresh challenge. I did a number of these. One was about stunts, while another focused on shooting in North Africa. I was on my own. Just me and no assistant. It was like writing with film.

While I was cutting the shorts, Ben set up an 8mm camera on the ceiling of my room, framing me editing at the KEM. He rigged it to shoot a frame once a minute. He called this time-lapse footage of me working *The Making of the Making of....* He figured that since the film was shot in 35mm and my documentary was shot in 16mm, his footage should be in 8mm. I don't think this film was ever seen by anyone other than Ben and me. I should have cut it into the documentary.

Ben often rapped on my door and asked me to listen to his latest sound creation. The bullwhip crack from the beginning of *Raiders* nearly took my head off. It definitely took me by surprise. The sound was so layered and complex it filled your entire body and then exploded. As it ricocheted and tailed off, you could hear the sound of a jet fighter soaring past your head.

Behind the Scenes

"What do you think? Too much?" "No, Ben, I love it."

Frank Marshall seemed determined to keep me on payroll. He had another behind-the-scenes doc up his sleeve. He had a few young USC graduates shoot some footage on the set of another Amblin film, *Poltergeist*, and wanted to put together a featurette, just like the NATO show reel we did on *Raiders*, about 8 to 10 minutes long. Although Frank directed the guys shooting B-roll when he was around, generally they simply covered shooting days that had the most production value. They photographed the giant gimbal, which looked like a Ferris wheel with a built-in bedroom set, that gave the appearance on film of the actress tumbling around the walls and furniture of the room. They shot the little girl as she faced the ghostly light emanating from her bedroom closet for the first time, scaring her to death. And they captured the giant tree coming to life outside the boy's bedroom window during a lightning storm. All good behind-the-scenes moviemaking material. There were also a limited number of interviews conducted on the set. It was a challenge to make some kind of sense of it all, since none of the filmed events were tied into one another. But I was determined to make it work with the material I had.

There is nothing in the world, no experience, no destination, no festival that can prepare you for Comic-Con, the madcap convention for film and comic book fans. That would be like going to a jazz club or an art museum and thinking you knew what it was like to attend Mardi Gras or Burning Man. The Comic-Con revelers live in a world unlike any other. They're the largest gathering of fanatical Halloween-costumed devotees of fantasy in the world. This was where Frank and I took the short *Poltergeist* documentary to be screened. No sooner had I cleared the entrance and was feeling lost in the lobby before one of the attendees approached me and offered to buy the Sprocket Systems jacket off my back. Sprocket Systems was the post-production company that George had just started at Lucasfilm. All the employees were given a jacket, a blue baseball warm-up jacket with a large S embroidered on the back. Who even knew that the company had been formed or that these jackets existed? These fans did. That was the world we entered. They knew everything about their idols. Parading around as Dr. Spock with prosthetic ears, or a Jawa from *Star Wars* mumbling gibberish, hardly anyone had their face uncovered. Except us. We were looked upon with either scorn or pity.

Since the audience clamored for a chance to attend the different presentations, when the featurette was shown, they were already pumped up and excited. We were almost guaranteed a positive response. They loved the documentary featurette and talked it up, quickly spreading the buzz to fellow geeks who wanted to be first in line to see what pleasures they had to look forward to in the movie theaters. I came away with a few life lessons: It was time to get away from there as fast as possible and get back to moviemaking, and never wear your Sprocket Systems jacket to Comic-Con.

I also learned that watching a movie on the making of a film only increases your desire to be there. You want to be part of that filmmaking team. You want to mingle with the actors. You want to face the problems the production is facing. Go to war for the sake of Art. Live that extraordinary life. Working on films in the editing room, I felt one step removed from the production. I only heard the war stories of those who were there during the shooting of the film. But I was still looking forward to my next feature-film experience, even if I wasn't on the production battlefield but nestled in the confines of the editing room.

CHAPTER 7

Return of the Jedi

IN THE SPRING of 1979, a film crew descended deep into the desert near Yuma, Arizona, to film a sequence for *Return of the Jedi, Episode VI* of the *Star Wars* trilogy. This U.S. location would be the next-to-final stop in the shoot that had been going on for months in London and various locations around the world. In our new San Rafael, California-based editorial suites, I awaited the arrival of the first set of dailies from Deluxe Lab. The shooting crew was suffering from intense heat and swirling, dusty winds. In the comfort of my editing room, I only had to deal with scratched negatives and prints that displayed streaks of green or red, depending on where the negative had been damaged. Keeping up with the damaged film added a layer of difficulty to the usual synching of dailies. Most importantly, I needed to notify the set if any film was unusable. Generally, it was fine. A bit more leniency was called for, given the adverse conditions of the shoot. When I spoke to the lab processing the film, I first asked that they run the negative film through a wash and make a new print. Scratches in the emulsion were more difficult to deal with. Often the problem could be solved or, at least, mitigated.

I had been hired as the first assistant editor on *Jedi*. Duwayne was going to be cutting on this film. I stepped into the role that Duwayne had filled on our previous stint on *The Empire Strikes*

Back. Although Duwayne was clearly in charge, now I would take over as much as I could to free him up to edit. We hired Conrad Buff as an additional assistant editor to work with me. We were lucky to have him.

Conrad was a very experienced effects editor from ILM. Whether it was a spaceship, a matte, a piece of animation, or a wisp of smoke, it all came through the editorial department at ILM. Then the editors lined up all the elements of a shot to be combined properly in the optical printer. Tough job. And Conrad was good at it. He was interested in getting involved in film editing and taking a break from visual effects. From the moment he came into the room and we started syncing up dailies from the desert shoot, we got along famously. We both had casual dispositions, usually joking as we plowed through the mountains of film. After syncing, I usually logged the film in. Conrad was also assisting the editor, Sean Barton, so he had his hands full.

Sean was the editor that the director, Richard Marquand, had brought in from England. Sean was a hang-loose Brit. He would almost wrap himself up in his own arms as he laughed his way through a story or two, standing in the doorway of our room. We also hired an apprentice editor, Debra Seligman, to assist both of us and take care of coding the film for identification purposes. Debra had come from the independent film world in San Francisco and carried that spirit with her into our editing room. It was very refreshing. It was a great, hardworking group.

The editorial department, the sound department, the administrative branch of Sprocket Systems, and the computer division had taken over an entire industrial warehouse complex in San Rafael. The editing rooms were all squeezed into one wing of a building on the ground floor. We had four rooms for the editors and two rooms for the assistants, a closet for the coding machine, a private bathroom, and a kitchenette. That was it, but it was all we needed. On the entry end of our hallway, the door led to the lobby/reception area. Across the reception area from our suites was a door that led to the film's sound department. At the other end of the hallway, next to the exit, a heavy soundproof door led directly onto the sound-mixing stage. Out the back door was our lunch area. ILM sat across a parking lot. The lot never had any cars in it, just scaffolds, miniature sets, film equipment, and film crews shooting one thing or another. Everything was incredibly centralized. I had never worked on a film where all the departments in post production were in such close proximity to one another. For the most part, it was great. Only when you wanted to hide from the endless questions was it a pain in the ass.

There were endless questions because the editing room was the hub for all information. ILM demanded information all the time. They needed to know which blue-screen shots or background plates we used in the cut of the film, along with very precise frame counts for each shot, so they could begin their work. When they delivered shots, they needed immediate feedback. Preliminary feedback was given during dailies at ILM, which George often attended. Once the shots arrived in the editing room and were cut into the picture, they were reviewed in their context. If we didn't like a shot, ILM needed to know what changes were required. The shot as designed might not be working. Or the action might not match the shot that preceded or followed it. All this information needed to be passed along quickly, since departments often stood by, waiting for a response.

The sound department was also full of questions and demands. They knocked on our doors daily, even hourly, begging for our cut footage to begin their work. Dialogue editors needed to know which takes we were using. The sooner they knew, the sooner they could check the dialogue tracks that were recorded during shooting. Often, if the wind was blowing or if machines were running, or if an actor mumbled, the dialogue would have to be rerecorded. A list of problematic lines was made and reviewed in the editing room. If the tracks could not be switched with a clean alternative reading by the actor, the cast members would be contacted and called in to rerecord the dialogue. Everyone disliked rerecording dialogue. The director hated it. The actors hated it. It took hours. The original dialogue recorded on the set was always best. But if it was unintelligible, you had to rerecord it.

The sound-effects editors had endless questions about the unfinished images in the movie. They often did not know what was going on. Where did the tie fighter fly into the frame, for example? What frame did it enter on? How fast was it going? When did it open fire? Often these very specific actions were not clear at all. We also had questions from the composer, John Williams, who was writing the music for the film. In order to get the composer and music editor started, we huddled around George's KEM and ran the film from beginning to end. We would stop whenever George or the editor of the scene thought a music cue should begin playing, then continue running the scene or scenes until everyone felt the music should stop. There is an art to figuring out where music is needed and where it should subtly begin and quietly go away. In a movie like this one, there was less subtlety. The music was almost wall-to-wall. The editors had laid in temporary music where they thought it should go and picked music with the correct tone or style that fit the scene. At one point, John said, "That works nicely. Where is that music from?" Ben Burtt told him it was his score for

Superman. John Williams had written so many film scores, he did not recall that he was the composer or which movie the music had come from.

Since George usually could be found in the editing room, most marketing questions came our way. New trailers and TV spots were previewed in the editing room. Once a trailer or TV spot was approved, a breakdown of every shot in it was created. The trailers had unfinished VFX shots, so those would need to be prioritized for completion at ILM to make the deadline for the delivery of the trailer, which was long before the release of the film. Otherwise, ILM finished shots in the order that suited them best. All this came through the editing room. And, more often than not, it came through me. Despite the fact it was a bit overwhelming at times, it was easier for one person to do it. We didn't have a traditional post-production supervisor, so in addition to assistant editing, I took on that role, just as Duwayne had done in the past. We also had to coordinate the VFX venues we were working with in LA that were producing laser swords, laser pistols, wipes, dissolves, titles, and so on. Just like on *Empire Strikes Back*, except more. At least it felt like more.

WHILE I WAS coordinating the work for effects and sound, Richard Marquand was with his editor, focused on getting his director's cut ready for a screening. This would tell us how much recutting work we had. Sean was a fast editor, so it didn't take long to learn we had a lot of work to do. Soon after the director's cut screening, Richard went back to England. Then George took over. George liked some of the bits, but he was ready to roll up his sleeves and add in his own two cents. The editing room was humming.

Duwayne took one of the rooms across the hall and started work on the Ewok battle. He was very self-sufficient, so he didn't need much help, thankfully.

George took the room next door to me and started at the beginning of the film and changed things as he went. Around this time, Conrad was stolen back by ILM. I don't know what the original arrangement was between the two, but his time was up. That was unfortunate for me, to say the least. Looking back, I'm not sure how we handled all the work. Duwayne was reluctant to do the assistant's work. It was tearing him away from what he really wanted to be doing, but he had no choice. There was just too much to do. Then Marcia came in. George asked her to recut the Jabba the Hutt battle, which was incomprehensible. She also cut some of the more intimate scenes. Now there were three editors.

What complicated things more was that Marcia cut on a Moviola. On a Moviola, you run each take individually on small rolls and make your selects for editing. For working on the Kem, or a flatbed editing machine—which both George and Duwayne did—the film was assembled into roughly 900-foot rolls, with one take spliced onto the next. I had to break down the KEM rolls for the scene Marcia was working on into small, individual rolls as she needed them. She started work in the late afternoon and worked late into the night. I would get in around eight in the morning, get myself settled, catch up on ILM and sound, and see what Duwayne or George needed. Late in the afternoon, George would take off, and Marcia would show up. I stayed until 8 or 9 p.m., and if she said she was good for the night, I would take off. I couldn't figure out why their days were split like that. When I asked George, he said she was a night owl.

Each editor was an artist and had a different style and approach to their work. I have no idea if George knew exactly what his plan was when he sat in the chair, or if he let it flow as he went. Probably a bit of both. What I do know is that he did not mind distractions. He often had rock 'n' roll music playing while he was cutting. The music somehow energized him without making him lose focus.

On Saturdays he would tune into a college football game on the radio and listen as he cut. I loved hearing either the music or the football game from my room next door. I overheard the Cal-Stanford game in 1982, which was a thriller. I even came into his room to listen. Toward the end of that game, the Stanford marching band flooded the field, thinking the game was over, but time had not run out. In the melee, a Cal player scored the winning touchdown, dodging the band as he ran. I could not have been more thrilled. George cared less, since he was a USC fan.

George was fun to be around. He just loved to edit. It was like the pressure was off. His writing was done. The shooting was done. Now he could shape the movie with the film he had to work with. No one could assemble *Jedi* as well as George, even with the same footage. He would occasionally show his work as the cut progressed. When it was in disarray or out of sync, he would ask me to get his cut back in order. "Steve!" "Yeah, George." "I need some help." He would throw his hands up in the air as he was leaving the room, as if to say, "Sorry, it's a mess. Please fix it."

Marcia, on the other hand, was wired up. Her thoughts moved at lighting speed. Her eyes would dart around the room. She would think, pause, then think again, then grab a piece of film. She worked standing up, as most Moviola editors do. She held the film up to the light to double-check it was the frame she was looking for. She marked it in the air with a grease pencil and ran it on the Moviola. Then she double-checked her mark and cut the film. No doubt, she had the puzzle pieces in her head. If I went into her room, I was careful to make sure she was at a break in her flow before asking a question. Often I would not bother her at all if I sensed it wasn't a good time. She was a method editor. In the zone. When she was in that head space, there was hardly ever small talk. As soon as she decided to take a break, though, she could not have been more fun. She just turned it off, whatever it was. She would declare we should go out for a sandwich, maybe even stop by a local softball game at a nearby park, just to clear her head. She knew a few players on the team that she was quite friendly with. Arriving back at work, she went straight into her room and back to work.

Duwayne was a tenacious editor. He approached his editing like chasing down a line drive in left field, diving for the ball. He dove into his scenes with the same passion, taking risks if necessary. He worked and worked until he was satisfied. He was hard on himself. He wanted to please George and thereby please himself. He would do anything to get it right. I tried as much as I could to assist him, but he was quite the solitary guy. It was best that I cover the other demands of the editing room to free up his mind.

With George, Marcia, and Duwayne cutting, the change notes were hard to keep up with. If we had the time, which we didn't, we would have waited to copy the film for the sound department and the composer until we were closer to a locked picture. Since we had committed to copying the picture for everyone after the director's cut screening, however, we had picture change notes for just about every scene as it was recut. The notes would go something like this: Roll down to 16 ft. 3 frames, cut 7 frames at the end of the shot. At 15 ft. 8 frames, remove shot. Hold to reinsert later. At 15 ft. 8 frames, add new shot.

When Marcia finished recutting the battle on Jabba's ship, there were more than 30 pages of change notes for just that one scene. These notes could not have a mistake. If they did, both sound and music would be out of sync, or they might end up working on the wrong shot. A disaster. And it was all on you and your notes. When a recut reel was completed, my first priority was to take care of the change notes. Of course, along with the sound and music people, the visual-effects folks also needed to know right away if a shot changed. They were already busy on the director's cut version. They could not afford to waste time on a shot that had been cut from the movie or a different take of a shot than what they were working on. I would usually give them a preview of the changes right away. Then I would go carefully through the cut and give specific counts indicating the exact change. It was nuts. Day in and day out. All of us could not wait until this all settled down, and we could focus on finishing. Unfortunately, that never happened until the film was done.

Every visual-effects shot in the film was put into motion when I sat down at my editing bench and, using a loupe (or magnifier) and a light box, I recorded the first and last frame of the shot. This provided ILM and the outside effects companies with the crucial information they needed to begin their work. On *Jedi*, I went through this exercise nearly 1,000 times.

Since I was the one most familiar with the progress of each shot from the beginning, I followed them as they came in for review. Commonly, George and Duwayne would review the dailies of the effects shots together, and I would be there to take notes. I would communicate the updates to ILM or LA, and we would go from there. Since there were so many shots to keep track of, I mounted two, four-foot-by-eight-foot magnetic boards onto one of the walls in our hallway. It was a magnetic status board. Every shot had a line on the board with a little box next to it. In the box I placed a small magnetic dot to signify the status of the shot. If it was blank, we had not received anything yet. If it was blue, the shot was omitted. If it was yellow, it was a temporary shot. If it was green, it was considered OK, but if time permitted, it could be better. If it was red, it was final, and no more work was required. As a daily ritual, I would update the board. Each day I cried out to George that I was updating the status board. I strapped a box around my neck, as if I was a cigarette girl, with divided sections in the box for red, yellow, green, and blue dots. With the updated daily status of the shots scribbled on paper in my hand, I would either add a dot for new shots or replace the dot on the board if the status had changed. George just loved watching me update the board. He would often step out into the hall, rub his hand on his chin, and just stare at the board. I might stop and ask if everything was all right. "Yes," he would say, "just looking." It didn't make the finals come in any quicker, no matter how hard he stared at the board. It was a beautiful thing when every shot in a reel had a red dot.

COMPUTERS had made their way into the editing room at the outset of *Return of the Jedi*. George had set up a computer division to tackle many filmmaking tasks and artistic endeavors. He saw the future of film, and it was digital. But it was all in its infancy. The transformation was taking much longer than he had the patience for. The whole building was attempting to move into the computer-aided digital age, and departments started to communicate through the computer. A file-sharing program was designed and set up to input and update shot information between the editing room and ILM. I was responsible for initiating the process. One day I freaked out. I stepped into George's room and told him I was fed

Return of the Jedi

up. I couldn't input the status of the shots on the computer any longer. If the shot information needed to be updated on a daily basis, they were going to have to hire another body to do just that. From now on I was going old school. Paper and pencil and a xerox machine. I simply did not have enough time to keep up with my own paperwork and then redo the work in the computer. ILM accepted it and from then on they input my paper-status reports themselves.

I embraced the computer. I just didn't have time for it. I even took a nighttime computer programming class given by Ralph Guggenheim, a video-graphics designer. For an assignment, I designed a hangman game. Very cool. Ralph was also heading up a group designing the EditDroid, a digital editing machine. Periodically, I was called upstairs to play around on the prototype, giving the group feedback on how it was working and what might make it more user friendly. A competitor, AVID, was racing ahead with a similar system and ended up winning the race. Computer graphics for film were also slowly moving forward, but none of the technology was ready for *Jedi*. The computer division was the foundation of what became Pixar.

This was the first film where I was around the sound mix from beginning to end. I loved having the ability to drop in next door to hear the mix as it progressed. Sometimes the temporary image was so crude, the mixers were unclear what was going on in a shot. I remember moving a wooden pointer across the movie screen to show the mixers the speed and trajectory of a ship moving through frame, so they knew how to pan or move the sound across the screen correctly.

In the middle of post production Sid Ganis, the head of marketing for Lucasfilm, and George came into my office and asked me if I would put together a 10-minute behind-the-scenes featurette on the making of *Jedi*. It wasn't really a question. A filmmaker was making a full-length documentary on the movie, and they wanted me to create a short show reel using his footage, similar to the one on *Raiders*. I was flattered that they asked me, since I had very little editing experience. I got another room to work on the short film. I recall that I started the featurette with a shot of a helicopter flying slowly toward the set in Yuma. I had *Star Wars* theme music playing in the background. When George saw the first shot, he said, "Stop! That's a really boring way to start the show. At least tell them how long it took to build the set, how much lumber was used, or something to impress the audience and hook them in." I thought, oh, no, here we go. This is going to be a disaster. As it turned out, that was just about the only change he asked for. Thank God. I really enjoyed working with Sid, along with Nancy Hult, the creative executive from KQED, which was going to air the featurette. The two of them enjoyed supervising the project more than I suspected. Their budding romance while working on the short film turned into a lifelong marriage.

In order to celebrate the delivery of the first completed reel to the negative cutter, Bob Hart, I went to LA and made a personal visit to see him. I conversed with him daily, but I rarely saw him. Knowing all the work that had gone into each shot he was cutting, I found it to be nerve-wracking to watch him cut the negative. He told me I had to make a cut myself. Hold the scissors and cut the film? I couldn't live with myself if I made a mistake. He handed me the scissors. With my hand shaking, I cut the frame. "Not that frame!" Bob joked. That got me. He and his partner just laughed and laughed while I was still shaking. This is what they did all day long.

And then we were finished. The reels were all delivered. The mix was completed. The answer print at the lab was approved. It

Return of the Jedi

is amazing how these things suddenly just end. I sat down for one of my final lunches out on the patio. I brought my peanut butter sandwich, or something simple, in my *Star Wars* lunch pail that I attached to the rack of the bike that I rode to work. George joined me. Duwayne was there as well. George reflected on the film and the toll the *Star Wars* trilogy had taken on his life. He said that for nine straight years, he had spent every day working on *Star Wars*. Every day. It could be writing. Or prepping a film. Shooting. Editing. Mixing. Approving the final print. Marketing. Novelization. Games. Merchandise. Every day. He was tired of it.

I asked, "Why don't you make a small independent film, like the ones you made in film school?" He said he had that idea in mind. And then the movie was done, and lunch was over. We got up from the table for the last time.

LIV AND I decided to let go of our work and take a bike trip in France for a few months. Just before leaving, I got a surprise call from the producer, Howard Kazanjian. He knew of our upcoming trip to Europe and had a proposal. He needed someone to supervise the Italian sound mix in Rome. Since I was going to be in Europe and I was familiar with the picture, he thought of me. He said he would put us up in Rome and fly us both home when we finished. Even though I had no idea what the job entailed, and my Italian was a bit rusty, I thought it would be a great experience. Liv and I started our trip in Paris, where we rented bikes, and traveled by train to the Loire Valley. We cycled there, then went to the Dordogne. We planned to end the cycling trip in a small hill town, Cordes, further south in France. One of the great pastry chefs in France, Yves Thuriès, had a Michelin-starred restaurant there and had agreed to meet Liv and discuss a possible pastry apprenticeship in his kitchen.

Even though Liv had been the pastry chef at L'Ermitage, this would be a great honor for her and provide her with additional training. Monsieur Thuriès greeted us warmly, possibly too warmly in Liv's opinion, and treated us to a nice room overlooking the beautiful Cérou River valley. That evening, after a long day's cycle, I sat on the balcony and read the news in the international edition of *Time* magazine. I had not seen the news for weeks. While flipping through the pages, I suddenly stopped. My heart sank. In the Milestones section, listed under Divorced, were the names George and Marcia Lucas. I had to catch my breath. Tears formed in my eyes. I should have seen it coming during the editing of the film, but I didn't. "Liv, read this," I said. I couldn't tell her myself. Every day from that day on, I thought of the news. I couldn't shake it.

After touring the kitchen and seeing all the French men ogling her as she walked through, Liv decided that an apprenticeship in this French restaurant was not what she wanted after all. Instead, we continued our cycling trip. First, we picked another river, the Lot, and had a wonderful time cycling along the banks. As we cycled, we gave some thought to the future. I wondered what I would do for work. Liv pondered what would be next for her.

After returning to Paris to drop the bikes, we were off to Rome for the sound mix. Howard had put us up in The Hassler, a wonderful hotel at the top of the Spanish Steps. We had stayed at the bottom of the steps in a *pensione* on an earlier trip., so we knew the neighborhood but had experienced nothing as luxurious as this. Upon our arrival, I found a note from Howard, telling me that the mix was delayed, so to enjoy ourselves for a few days. We felt like royalty, except that the concierge and doormen were a bit snooty, probably because we had not tipped them enough. Then came another note from Howard. The Italian actors, who were set to record their dialogue over the past few days, had decided to go on holiday. No mix at this time. Head home. Wow, after a luxurious stay in Rome, without doing any work and without any idea of what might be in store for us when we landed, we flew home.

WITHIN DAYS after returning, I got a call from Duwayne. "I have a job for you if you want it. I am cutting a documentary for Richard Schickel, and I want you to take over for me. I need to get out of here." And just like that, I met Richard and went to work. It was a documentary called *From Star Wars to Jedi: The Making of a Saga*. Richard was producing what I call a "clip" show. Richard had interviewed George and was using clips from the *Star Wars* trilogy to illustrate his story. Editing this show was different from my other documentary work. Someone was looking over my shoulder as I cut, someone who had their own ideas of what they wanted. Maybe that's why Duwayne needed to leave the show. Still, I worked alone without an assistant, going back and forth from my old assistant's room to George's old editing room, using George's KEM to cut on and my old room to do the assistant work. Richard's ideas were clear, so the clips from the films intercut nicely with his interviews with George.

Since George had made clear that he was taking a break from *Star Wars* and film in general, I was about to be on the street looking for a job. I realized how much I cherished my experience at Lucasfilm, working so closely with George all those years. George, Duwayne, Ben, and many others had shared their knowledge with me and allowed me to grow. I developed confidence in my own voice, giving me the courage to be creative and speak my mind. Yet where would the experiences I had during the past six years at Lucasfilm lead me?

Then, one day, while clearing up my work on the *Star Wars to Jedi* doc, a crate the size of a coffin dropped at my feet. I looked at the return label on the huge box on the floor of my editing room: Frank Marshall, Amblin Entertainment. I resisted opening the crate until I finished the show at hand. Now the time was right to pry it open and see what Frank had in store for me. The contents of that crate contained the beginning of a new chapter in my film career—working for Steven Spielberg's Amblin Entertainment, and the end of my days at Lucasfilm, where George gave me a look that said, "May the force be with you!"

CHAPTER 8

Behind the Scenes at Amblin

I PRIED OPEN the crate on my editing room floor and found it full of 16mm film. The film was labeled with sound-roll numbers but with very little other identification. Over the summer Frank Marshall and I had seen one another at a softball game at Skywalker Ranch. I was standing at third base, and Frank came up and mentioned he had some film he was sending my way.

"Don't worry about it. You don't need to get into it until you finish up what you're doing. I am just giving you a heads up that I will be shipping it to you." The more I got to know Frank, the more I learned that this was not an unusual thing for him to do. Although tempted to look in the crate, I had pushed it aside until I finished editing the *Star Wars to Jedi* documentary. Now that I was staring at the contents inside the crate, I called Frank to find out what he was thinking. He said it was documentary footage that had been shot during the production of *Indiana Jones and the Temple of Doom*. He thought we could make a documentary together. Although it was technically a joint project with Lucasfilm, George took very little interest in the documentary. On this project, I would report directly to Frank.

As I was about to go to work, I got a call from the editor on *Amadeus*. They were cutting over at Fantasy Films in Berkeley and were looking for an assistant editor to work with Milos Forman, the director of the film. Working alongside the visionary director of *One Flew Over the Cuckoo's Nest?* That got my blood moving. I was flattered by the call, yet my decision was easy. First of all, I had committed to Frank. That was important in my young career. Also, I wanted to spend more time with him. Hearing his stories from the set got me excited, and I wanted to learn and hear more. Also, I would be the editor, not an assistant. That meant a lot to me as well. I turned down the *Amadeus* job and suggested they hire my apprentice editor, Debra Seligman. They did. Once again, a romance blossomed in the editing room. The next time I saw Debra, she invited Liv and me to join her for dinner with Milos. They were living together.

I set to work on the documentary. I loved working alone. I methodically went through the film and tried to make some sense of it. Some rolls had accompanying sound. Others were MOS, or without sound. Other times, a shot might start with sync sound, then continue without it. The sound man might have been separated from the cameraman, so they would have tried to sync with one another whenever they could, but when that was not possible, the cameraman would shoot on his own, without sound. Basically, the film was all a jumble. One roll at a time I organized, labeled, and logged in the film with detailed descriptions of what I was seeing. Often I did not know the context of what I was looking at, so I would give it my best guess. There were shots of working with elephants in Sri Lanka. Art department prepping. Dance rehearsals. As I organized the film, I became acutely aware of the elaborate logistics involved in shooting on location and the difficulty of getting scenes ready for stage work. Every day and every scene had its difficulties. Watching how the film company overcame the challenges it faced would be the dramatic backbone of the documentary.

Strangely, despite the endless problems, it all seemed like a wonderful challenge and a lot of fun. Everyone on the crew had derived great satisfaction in overcoming the obstacles and completing the work. It was very different from quietly sitting in an editing room figuring out what to cut next. Working on the production started to needle me a bit. Maybe the editing room was too confining, too sheltered from the excitement of the production. These were all thoughts I had as I peeked into the window of the production and watched the footage.

The film production on *Indy*, like *Raiders*, was on a much larger scale and appeared much more exotic than the TV shows I had worked on as an electrician. The movie company had filmed in Sri Lanka, Macao, and various locations around California, even at Hamilton Air Force Base in Marin. My desire to be part of the production increased when Frank would come up to visit me in the editing room and tell me stories of working on the film. Often, Kathy Kennedy would come along with him. They would laugh and reminisce about the work. I told Frank that one day I would like to follow a path that would lead me to what he was doing. For now, I was having fun. But I was developing a new long-range goal, even though I didn't know how to make the transition or even take the first step.

When Frank and Kathy returned to Amblin, Spielberg asked about the progress of the documentary. Frank called to say, "Steven (Spielberg) wants you to come to LA and edit the documentary down here. We have a new building on the Universal lot, and there is a room for you to work in. We also have an apartment in Marina del Rey that you can stay in. We will give you a per diem and a car." Now that sounded like an adventure. My only request was that they give me unlimited tickets to fly back and forth to the Bay Area, so

Liv and I could go home whenever we wished. They were fine with that request. So just like that, we moved back to LA.

What a culture shock! Looking out all the windows of our Amblin apartment in the marina, I could see myriad sailboats tied up to the docks. The trees and greenery that we were used to in Marin were replaced by water and boats. Instead of the chirping birds at home, we would hear the soft clinking of metal on boat masts, as the sails fluttered in the light ocean breeze. At night the seawater lapped against the docks, and the ropes made a straining sound as they attempted to hold the boats in place. While looking around the apartment, we found a film print of *E.T.* in a closet. I guess Steven had rented this apartment for some time. We never would have dreamed of moving to Marina del Rey, but it became a refreshing refuge from the city. Liv had been commissioned to write a pastry cookbook. The kitchen was airy and light and would prove to be a perfect place to develop and test her recipes.

Amblin turned out to be a nice place to work as well. The new southwestern-style company bungalow had just opened, and I quickly became part of the Amblin family. Like Lucasfilm, they valued their employees, and similarly, there were not many of us. Lunchtime gatherings and festive holiday parties bonded the group together. The offices were on two floors surrounding a center courtyard. After passing through the lobby and entering the courtyard, I got to my editing suite in the front corner of the building, quite separate from any of the other offices. Down the hall was a conference room, and in the back corner was the kitchen. The chef prepared lunch every day, so I rarely went out. In the back of the building was the screening room. It was small, well equipped, and had a good sound system. I got to know the projectionist, Rene, quite well over the years.

On the opposite side of the building was another, smaller conference room next to an open office that was used for illustrators prepping on movies. Then came accounting. Bonne Radford was the head accountant. She was attractive and smart and savvy about film production. In the other front office on the ground floor sat Jim Warren. As the building manager, he ran a tight ship. A set of stairs in the courtyard took you up to the offices of Frank, Kathy, and Steven.

When not in my editing room, I spent most of my time in Frank's office. Mary Radford, Frank's assistant, was his gatekeeper, much like Jane Bay had been for George. That is where their similarities ended. Mary was rough around the edges. She liked to smoke and drink. She knew where all the bodies were buried and was rarely caught by surprise about anything. I had great respect for Mary, and she helped me time and time again. In order to see Frank, I went through Mary. She would often encourage him to drop by and see my latest cut of a scene. She also gave me a realistic picture of whether I'd be able to show him any material on a given day. After all, Frank was producing movies for Amblin, and the *Indy* doc was low on the priority list. There were no fires in my room, I just needed feedback to move forward.

Amblin was humming with movies. Lucasfilm was quiet. With George taking a break after the saga of *Star Wars*, I had made the right choice with the move. Frank was producing or executive producing all the shows that came through Amblin, so I became acutely aware of films that were starting up. For the moment, I put the idea of following in Frank's footsteps in the back of my mind and focused on editing. It seemed that the next reasonable step might be to try to get hired as a second editor on one of the Amblin feature films. On *Fandango*, one of the smaller Amblin features, Artie

Schmidt was the editor, and he had Steve Semel as his second editor. Artie was a very pleasant man with a great reputation. He was known to give guys a break.

As the shows geared up, I would ask Frank if there might be a slot I should interview for. *The Goonies*, directed by Dick Donner was the first show to begin crewing up. Michael Kahn, Spielberg's editor, was chosen to cut that film. Michael had a loyal group of assistant editors, so if a second editor was needed, it would surely go to one of them. I would have to wait for the next possibility when I finished the documentary, which, at the rate I was going, would be a while.

I never set up a time for Steven to come down to view the cut. He would stop in unannounced. I might receive a call from his assistant telling me that Steven just left his office and was heading down to see me. That gave me about 30 seconds' notice. I found it strange to screen for Steven, since most of the footage was centered on him. I had no idea how he would react or for what reason. Usually he laughed and said, "Great." Just like George. I heard "great" a lot. So much that I really didn't know what it meant. But, as they say, take yes for an answer.

Steven might also stop into my room in the morning to ask what today's pastry was. Since Liv was testing cakes and other goodies for her cookbook, I would bring whatever was freshly baked to the office in the morning and leave it in the kitchen for the employees to enjoy. Steven got into the habit of checking to see if there might be surprise pastry he could taste along with his coffee. If he was looking forward to a treat, he became disappointed if Liv had not baked anything for him. I appreciated the fact that Steven and the others enjoyed her cooking. She was, after all, a top-notch pastry chef. And these morning visits with Steven, even if they were focused on a craving for pastry, provided me a chance to show him what I was up to. Any excuse to have Steven stop by helped to keep me going.

The more I watched the footage, the more I could see Steven's directing style. Before he shot any scene, he had already shot and edited it in his head. All the camera setups were in his mind. He could frame every shot for the cameraman. The performances were in his mind as well. He could act the parts, which he often did. At first, when I watched him acting a role, I thought he was acting for the behind-the-scenes camera. Some of the time I am sure he was. But most of the time he was roughing in the scene he saw in his mind's eye for the actor or actress. He then gave the actors space and let them show what *they* were thinking. He loved this collaboration. He listened and fed on their creativity. I tried to let the footage speak for itself, only using interviews when absolutely necessary.

True to his word, Frank dropped by to tell me that Artie Schmidt, who was finishing up the editing on *Fandango*, was going to be the editor of *Back to the Future* and was interviewing candidates to be the second editor. I set up a time to meet with Artie. As the interview progressed and I detailed my career to Artie, I could see it was a long shot. I had no experience editing on a feature film. Only on documentaries, which were completely different. I was an experienced *assistant* editor on large-scale feature films, but that was it. I had not cut any scenes on *Jedi*, as Duwayne had. But I felt it was worth a shot. I might be in the right place at the right time. It turned out I wasn't. They decided to go with a much more experienced second editor, Harry Karamidas. I wasn't surprised. I could see that the only way to advance in editing was to line up with an editor and stick with him until he let you cut some scenes. Then once you proved yourself, as Duwayne had done with George, you might be ready to become an additional or second editor. With that experience, you might eventually be given the opportunity to cut a film. This was going to be a tough and long road.

I met with Frank and told him the outcome of my interview with Artie. Frank already knew. He said he had another idea. Amblin was starting a TV series called *Amazing Stories*. Steven had given the mandate to the producer to hire young, up-and-coming talent whenever possible. Frank thought I might just fit in. I met with David Vogel, the producer of the series, who seemed nervous meeting with me. I suppose, since I came from the Amblin camp, it put him on edge. The interview went well, though, and I really thought I had a shot. Until the next day. Frank called me up to his office. "Do you still have an itch to try producing rather than editing?" Even though I was wondering where this was going, I said that I did. "If I asked you what you would like to be doing in five years, what would you say?" I told him it would be great to be an associate producer on a feature film. "In that case, I want you to give this some thought. David Vogel just met with me and wanted me to speak with you about working as an associate producer on the series rather than as one of the editors. This would be a great first step to producing."

I let it sink in. I realized in my heart it was what I really wanted to do. I wanted to follow in Frank's footsteps. As I sat there and thought about it, I could understand David Vogel's perspective. Most often, the associate producer in TV oversees post production and visual effects and quite possibly more. David could see I had done just that on the *Star Wars* films and could easily continue the work in a more elevated capacity on *Amazing Stories*.

Breaking the silence, Frank said, "If you really think this might be something you want to do, you should try it." Clearly, the editing positions were going to other people. Either I accepted this job or started looking for an editor to work with. There was no doubt that this was a unique opportunity. I started thinking of the downsides of taking the job. I wouldn't be working with Frank. But that was ending with the documentary anyway. Instead, I would be working with David Vogel, someone outside the Amblin/Lucasfilm family. Second, I would be cutting my editing career short. All that work, climbing the ladder in the editing room would suddenly be ending. "Let me sleep on it."

I went home and talked it over with Liv. "What's the worst that can happen?" she asked me. "If you decide you don't like it, you can always go back to editing." After giving it some thought, I concluded she was right. We had the world premiere of the *Indiana Jones* documentary in the Amblin screening room for all the employees. Then I said good-bye to Amblin and all the comforts and security that came along with it and took the job on *Amazing Stories*.

CHAPTER 9

Amazing Stories

"I HAVE MADE a terrible mistake, and I don't know what to do." I let out a breath and sat facing my dad in the living room of my childhood home. My dad listened. Only once before had I sought out his ear. That time, years earlier, I sat with him for hours, late into the night, trying to figure out a way to end the conflict in Vietnam. I slowly filled him in on my current dilemma. "Amblin has started up a TV series called *Amazing Stories*. I interviewed for a job as an editor only to be offered a job as an associate producer. Since I had considered working as a producer, I decided to give it a try. We are currently in preparation and scheduled to start shooting soon. There are two associate producers on the show. We alternate working on every other show. He will do the first, third, and fifth show and so on, while I do the even numbered shows. My associate's name is Skip. He is a buttoned-up sort of guy. He wears slacks and a collared shirt and tie to work each day. He talks budgets and schedules with ease. He was the former head of post production at Universal Studios. He never talks about the scripts, the directors, or anything creative, which is all I care about. I immediately felt we had little in common. He set a meeting to introduce me to the production guys at Universal. The room was filled with executives much like Skip. They were all dressed like Skip. They all had very pleasing smiles. All they spoke of were schedules and budgets. And rules. They handed me a big binder filled with rules. I immediately felt uncomfortable. I don't even want to look at the rules. I just want to work on movies and have fun. I really don't think I am suited for the job. Right now, I feel like quitting. But I don't want to let down Steven Spielberg or Frank Marshall."

My dad considered what I said. He had listened to me carefully. "They hired you for a reason. Everyone at Amblin knows you and what you can do. You have a relationship with Spielberg. They don't. They did not hire you to be like someone else. They hired you for who you are. So be yourself. If you do that, you won't disappoint them or yourself."

I TOOK my dad's advice to heart. I have a pattern of bouts of insecurity when faced with new challenges. Once I settle in and my confidence grows, my nervousness seems to diminish, a fire grows within me, and my smile returns.

Liv and I packed our bags and moved to Los Angeles again. This time, we found a place to live in Benedict Canyon, only a few blocks away from Wanda Park Drive, where my parents lived. We rented the house from the same landlords who had rented to us on Beverly Glen. Our cottage was nestled into a hillside, quite small and cute. One of the drawbacks was we lived across the street from Dan Haggerty, aka Grizzly Adams, who enjoyed taking his big chopper out early on Sunday mornings. Otherwise, the place was central and quite cheerful. Following the completion of her book, Liv had developed a food-styling career, where she designed and prepared food for photography. She did most of the prep for her work at the house. When she doubled as a prop stylist, she would run around and gather items before heading over to the photographer's studio. Meanwhile, I went over the hill to the offices of *Amazing Stories* on the Universal lot.

The production announced that Steven Spielberg would be directing the first episode, and Skip would be the associate producer working on that show. Skip was the first one hired so he got the first show. I had looked forward to getting a chance to work with Steven. I was deflated, until I learned who I would be working with first.

MARTIN SCORSESE

After working with George and Steven, I now had the chance to work with another of the great directors of my generation. Marcia Lucas had spoken to me of her wild experiences working on Martin Scorsese's films. Those were in the '70s. Steven and George seemed tame by comparison. Marty was set to arrive only a day or two before the first day of shooting. I think he was doing Steven a favor by fitting the show into his busy schedule. Our first chance to meet was at the production meeting that was held just after he arrived. All the heads of the departments were present.

I had never been around a show at its inception and certainly had never been invited to a production meeting. We went through the script, scene by scene, discussing or confirming the requirements from every department. At the end of the meeting, Marty pointed out that since the location was quite far from the editing rooms and the screening room for dailies, he wanted to set up an editing suite on location. That way he could watch dailies and oversee the editing without taking time at the end of the day to return to the studio. Of course, I said sure. It did not seem like an unreasonable request. Vogel glared at me with look a of disappointment, a look that said, "Why did you say yes to that?" I returned his look. "What, David, would you have said no?" I did not pause to think that this would probably exclude David from interacting with Marty in the way he had hoped. I arranged for the KEM editing machines to be transported and set up on location.

I drove out to the location to make sure everything had been set up right, giving me an excuse to watch Scorsese work. What a change from *Star Wars* and *Indiana Jones*. Marty was directing a psychological thriller about a self-centered horror-story novelist who is terrorized by a phantom of his own making, one who only appears in reflected surfaces, mostly mirrors. Not only was the material completely different from what I was accustomed to, but so was Scorsese. He spoke faster than anyone I had ever met, and his ideas were coming just as fast. Although I was not needed on the second day, I returned to the location to see if I could observe the shooting again and watch the dailies with Marty and the editor.

I asked Deborah Schindler, his assistant, how I might speak with Marty. Deborah was like Jane Bay with George and Mary Radford with Frank; she was the conduit to Marty. She coached me and gave me the courage to approach him. He welcomed me but made clear that he didn't want anyone else around to watch or discuss dailies, just the editor, the assistant editor, and me. Not even David Vogel, the producer. While watching him shoot, we had a few moments where I was able to tell him the work I had done with Lucas and Spielberg. I hoped to give him confidence in my abilities in editorial so he would not feel nervous handing over the show to me to finish. Since he was going to be back in New York for post production, he fed me ideas as we watched the dailies, so I might understand what he expected for the look of the show and the sound mix.

I had no idea if this first show would be the norm, but I was given creative responsibilities and the reins to make decisions on my own. I worked closely with the editor, Joe Ann Fogle. Joe Ann had most recently worked on *Hill Street Blues*, a well-respected TV series created by Steven Bochco. She was very instinctive in her cutting and listened well to Scorsese. I felt confident with Joe Ann cutting. As I watched dailies with her and Marty and listened to her notes for editing, I had a bit of longing to be back in the cutting room. I had really wanted a shot at it to see what I could do. But I had taken the leap into the producing world, and, so far, I was embracing it.

Marty selected Michael Kamen to do the score. Michael wrote a very tense and baroque-sounding piece that delved deep into the psyche of the main character. Up until this time, I had become accustomed to the work of John Williams. I had heard his music for six years on all the *Star Wars* and *Raiders* films. This was a huge departure. But Marty knew what he wanted for the score, and it worked very effectively. The scoring was done in New York under Marty's supervision. Before he left town, we watched the final cut of the show together, and he gave me specific instructions on how to mix the show—when it should play very real, when to play up the dialogue or the sound effects, and when the music should take over. When I sent him the final mix, I fully expected to have notes of changes he wished to make. I was happily surprised to learn he thought the work was fine. This was the first mix that I supervised, and his approval gave me the confidence to do mixes for other directors who did not have the time to do the work themselves.

Marty also shared his ideas with me for the look of the show, so when I went to color-correct the print, I could achieve the cool tone he was looking for. Once the print was completed with Marty's approval, I immediately created an interpositive, a direct copy of the negative, made on negative film stock. I carried this along with me, as well as the final color-corrected answer print to Modern VideoFilm, where I supervised the transfer of the show from film to tape. I usually spent a few days going scene by scene, then shot by shot, trying to make the videotape version look as beautiful as it had looked on film. Usually, the interpositive had the closest look to the original. At times, more contrast or clarity could be achieved with the print. We would bounce back and forth as we fought our way through the process.

I had never supervised a color-transfer session, but I was a quick study alongside Lou Levinson at Modern Video. Lou went on to become a premier colorist in Hollywood. It seemed we always worked late into the night getting the work done. And there were endless technical problems. I often found myself wishing to go home but having to kill time in the second-floor employee lounge, which looked out to the corner of La Brea and Sunset Boulevard. Next to the gas station was a motel, directly across the street from where I stood. Prostitutes roamed the streets and often followed a john into one of the motel rooms. I watched them coming and going as I waited for Lou to call and say he was ready again, snapping me out of my trance. When we finished, the final master was delivered to the network for broadcast on TV. I worked hard to make it great, since Marty's short film would only be seen on television, not on the big screen in a theater.

Every week one of my shows was either in prep or shooting. After the shooting was wrapped on Marty's show and went into post production, my next show would begin prepping. As time went on, I would not only be in prep on a show or following the shooting of a show but would also be involved with overseeing the special effects, doing ADR, music scoring, and final mixing of shows in post production. The work ramped up slowly, then got busy really fast.

Amazing Stories

MY OFFICE on *Amazing Stories* overlooked the Amblin compound. I only had to go out the back gate and take a set of concrete steps down to the main entrance of Amblin, which I still considered home. Across the street from the front gate were the editing rooms, also a short walk away. Our offices were a cluster of bungalows. I shared my office with Skip Lusk, the other associate producer, and our joint assistant. Artwork and set models filled the hallway separating our offices from the art department next door. Whenever I needed a break, I would get up from my desk and wander over to the art department and lose myself in the designs for the upcoming show. I might look for Rick Carter, the production designer, who would happily riff on some idea before we both needed to return to our tasks at hand. This marked the beginning of a long list of film projects that Rick and I would share with one another.

Across the walkway from our office was the production office. Joan Bradshaw and Kevin Donnelly, the two alternating production mangers on the series, worked hand in hand with me on the shows. This was the first time that Joan and I worked together and, as with Rick, we became soul mates on many of the films in my career. Across the parking lot was the producer's bungalow, the main conference room, and casting. The producer's bungalow not only had David Vogel's office but also the office of Joshua Brand and John Falsey, who were the co-writers and developers of the series along with Steven. Josh and John had produced and written the highly acclaimed TV series *St. Elsewhere* and went on to create other memorable series, including *Northern Exposure*. I don't think writing and overseeing an anthology series like *Amazing Stories*—where each story had a life of its own and the tone and storylines changed from week to week—was their strong suit. Maybe they thought that

Steven would become the voice of the series, like a Rod Sterling or Alfred Hitchcock, but somehow it never really jelled. Every show was different. Some were whimsical, some had a horror bent, others were mysteries. Individually they were often good pieces, but, as a whole, the audience didn't know what to expect week to week. One clear example was Paul Bartel's show, which didn't fit into any box that Steven, Josh, or John could have ever imagined.

PAUL BARTEL

All the episodes were like mini movies. No two were alike, and the directors could not have been more different. The tone they set was an extension of themselves. The first time I saw Paul Bartel, he and his boyfriend were getting into his 1985 convertible Chrysler LeBaron. When I introduced myself, he was polite and effervescent as he shook my hand. He seemed so happy to be in Hollywood making a little film. I found his enthusiasm to be contagious and immediately wanted to help him in whatever way I could. He seemed like a fish out of water. Coming from more offbeat independent films, he did not appear to know the correct protocols of the Spielberg world. He was always politely asking, "Do you think this would be all right?" Maybe Vogel had told him he was giving him this chance and not to screw it up and make him look bad.

Paul was doing a remake of a short film he had done called *Secret Cinema*, the story of a young girl whose daily life is secretly filmed, with the help of those closest to her, for the pleasure of theater audiences, until she suspects something is amiss. Along with Griffin Dunne and Penny Peyser, Paul appeared in the show alongside his longtime friend and actress Mary Wornov. They both played multiple roles. I had seen Paul's film *Eating Raoul*, so I knew a bit about him, but working with him opened up his world to me. *Secret Cinema* was campy, the performances were intentionally broad, and it was full of laughs, especially when Paul or Mary were on the screen. In the production meeting, I often found Paul looking my way, seemingly paying more attention to me than the meeting. He was happy with everything that the departments were doing for him and shot the show in a very simple style.

Paul, quite possibly at the suggestion of Spielberg, had Billy Goldenberg do the score. Goldenberg had written countless scores for film and television, including *Duel* and a *Night Gallery* episode for Spielberg. This was the first of many composers, both new and old, I was exposed to on the series. Since the time frame was short, and the number of minutes that were required to be written for each show was limited, many great composers were able to fit the work into their schedules. Often the composers had worked with the director of the show, sometimes exclusively for the director, so they were up for the challenge, big or small. It certainly wasn't for the pay, since they were all getting union scale.

We had a minimal budget for each show on the series. It usually only allowed for 36 musicians to play for one day. The pieces needed to be written for that size of an orchestra and had to be recorded very quickly. Fewer takes were done on every cue in order to finish in one day on time and on budget. Sandy DeCrescent, the music contractor, watched the sessions closely and guided us through the most efficient way to make use of our time on the stage. She also booked all the musicians. She knew every player on every instrument in town and was even familiar with the musicians that each of our composers preferred. Composers had their favorite players—their first-chair violin, flutist, bass player, or pianist. When their favorites were busy, Sandy found a competent alternative. On the scoring day, she checked each player in, called the breaks (which were mandatory), and prepared all the paperwork. It was all done with ease. *Amazing Stories* started my long career working with Sandy, a person I respected so much. I think she knew my love of music and included me in all her decision making. It was a tutorial in scoring.

When the show was complete, I took the print over to Amblin to screen it for Spielberg. He watched all the shows and gave notes to the directors. I usually attended the screenings, with or without the director present. In the case of *Secret Cinema*, Paul was not present. When the lights came up after the screening, there was silence. I broke the silence and asked Steven, "Should we ship it?" He laughingly responded, "I don't know what else to do with it." Nothing he could say or do would affect the little movie Paul had made.

Paul came back and worked on a second show in the series, *Gershwin's Trunk*. I was fortunate to work with him again. In this show, a composer, played by Bob Balaban, is desperately trying to write his next musical. While facing writer's block, he seeks help from a psychic, played by Lainie Kazan. She helps him overcome his dilemma by channeling Gershwin. Paul and John Meyer wrote the songs. John had recently worked with Paul on a small film called *Not for Publication*. His task for *Gershwin's Trunk* was difficult. He would have to write a series of songs, clearly reminiscent of Gershwin, while at the same time staying clear of actually quoting the composer or having any recognizable Gershwin in the music. The signature song was "I Discovered You."

> *Balboa thought it was terrific*
> *When he discovered the Pacific*
> *Columbus sailed the ocean blue*
> *And Marco Polo, found China solo*
> *But I discovered You.*

And it finally concludes:

Consider Hudson and de Gama
They brought the bacon home to Mama
We give them credit where it's due
Take Spain or Thailand, I'll stick with my land
Cause I discovered You.

There were also other whimsical songs in which you could hear Gershwin lurking in the background yet were distinct enough to be original. "I Discovered You" hearkened back to "They All Laughed," "Agitated Ankles" had the spirit of "Fascinating Rhythm." Since my exposure to Gershwin was limited up to that point, I enjoyed immersing myself in his music.

After John Meyer and Paul had completed the songs, Universal business affairs required that I hire a musicologist whose positive evaluation could stand up in court if the Gershwin Estate sued Universal for copyright infringement. This required a long lead time before we could actually begin shooting.

Following the completion of *Gershwin's Trunk*, Paul hosted a gathering at his house, where everyone sat around after dinner and sang songs. They each took turns, singing mostly show tunes. Carrie Fisher got up and sang a few songs. She had a cameo in the show as Balaban's girl. John Meyer accompanied her on piano, as well as everyone else at the party. It seemed like he could play anything. When it came to my turn, I was too embarrassed to sing, in addition to which I hardly knew any songs. All the partygoers encouraged me. John suggested we sing "I Discovered You." It was like having sex for the first time with everyone watching. At least I knew the lyrics. No one else did, except Paul, so I was singing alone with the pianist. Even though I had never performed a song in front of another soul before, with John's lead, I had fun with it. Paul clapped exuberantly at my performance.

I WAS CONSUMED with my work. I was using all the skills I had learned while assisting on the *Star Wars* films, only my responsibilities were growing. I was still involved in the editing of the shows, though only giving my opinion when asked. I attended the ADR sessions, often supervising on my own, which I had never done before. I always attended the scoring sessions and took part in the management and creative decisions. I negotiated songs for use in the shows. I obtained and licensed stock footage when needed. I supervised the film-to-tape transfer and delivery of the show. I also attended the final sound mix of the shows, sometimes supervising on my own. During the shooting of the shows, if any special effects were required, I would oversee their production, not just watch the shots as they came into the editing room. I worked closely with the vendor and the production manager and defined what the effects crew requirements would be on the set. I budgeted the effects with the vendor to keep it in line with the money we had to spend. In fact, I oversaw the entire post-production budget on every show. I really did not have the time to think about the fact that I was not pursuing my editing career. The show and the directors kept me too busy.

BURT REYNOLDS

In walked Burt Reynolds, dressed like a Hollywood cowboy. Tight jeans, cowboy shirt with a few buttons open, and cowboy boots. He could not have been more polite in a Hollywood sort of way. He directed a rather sappy script called *Guilt Trip*, laced with ridiculous one-liners, that the cast did their best to make into something. Dom DeLuise was cast as the personification of Guilt, who, when taking a much-needed holiday, falls for Love, played by Loni Anderson. An unlikely couple, for sure, but not in the world of Burt Reynolds. At our production meeting, Burt asked who would be in charge of music clearances. He was hoping to get clearance to use "As Time Goes By," made famous in *Casablanca*. All eyes were on me. As we were leaving, Burt came up to me and said this song was really important to him. I got it. This became a daily focus for me.

I contacted music business affairs to get the ball rolling. I learned that the publishing rights for the song were with Warner Bros. Music, one of the largest music publishers. An agreement among the studios for the use of songs in TV shows had set rates that were much lower than for feature films. By saving a small bit of money during the scoring session, the cost for the song was not going to be the issue. What became the issue were the terms of the agreement. Universal required that the rights to any song that they licensed be cleared for use in all media, in all territories, in perpetuity. Warner Bros. did not grant the rights to use their songs in perpetuity. I asked the name of the person in business affairs to hear it straight from the horse's mouth. Warner Bros. would not back down. Not even for Burt Reynolds? "Not even for Burt Reynolds." I was amazed that they wouldn't grant favors to anyone. Not even to a star as big as Burt Reynolds.

Burt was going to play the song during shooting in the coming days, so I had to get it cleared. I didn't know what to do. I called back Warner Bros. I told them that Burt intended to use the song, and I didn't know how to get around the problem. My contact said, "Tell Universal I will give them the use of the song for 999 years, but

I can't give it in perpetuity." Universal said that wasn't good enough. I couldn't believe it. It was ridiculous. They were entrenched. Neither would budge. Since the shooting day was approaching, I decided to bring Burt up to speed. He said he wasn't surprised. I guess you choose your battles, because he quickly moved on. I think he wanted to see how far I would get with his request. Or you could say he was testing me. He decided to use "I'll Never Smile Again" by Ruth Lowe. I told him I would quickly check on it. The song was with the Universal Publishing Group, so we were fine to use it. Although the song spoke to the film, it wasn't the same. Damn business affairs.

I did not usually get introduced to the actors while the shows were shooting. I would stop by, just to say hello to the director, watch the filming a bit, then get back to my job. When it came time to do the ADR for the show in post production, I had not met Loni Anderson or Dom DeLuise. When they did their recording session, I introduced myself and joined them on the stage, rather than in the soundproof booth. I wasn't shy about it, and the actors never seemed to mind. I liked communicating with them about their performance while sitting on the stage. The directors, when they were present, generally sat in the soundproof recording booth with the ADR recordist and the ADR engineer. We generally started by playing back the line or series of lines with the actor, until they were warmed up enough to try to record. After a take or two, we might play back the recording to see how they were doing. Usually the actors knew if they liked what they heard, so I would wait for their reaction. If they were unsure of the line reading and looked to me for a reaction, I would point out what I thought might improve what they had done. Often the sync with the original line wasn't perfect, so we would redo the line for that reason. Or the pitch could be off. Or the line reading was rushed. Or a word or even a breath changed the intent of the line. Even if the line appeared to be okay, I might do another take for the director so he would have a variety of readings to choose from. When the new line was fine, I would give the actor the confidence they needed and encourage them to move on. This became my method for many years to come.

You can never tell which actor might excel at ADR and which ones can never redo a line anything close to the performance they did while shooting. Matching their performance in production is usually the goal. I always told the actors, "Do what you did on set." Loni Anderson was great at ADR. I was in the middle of overseeing Loni Anderson's recording when we broke for lunch. She suggested we go up to the Universal commissary. I never went to the commissary. That's where the suits went for lunch. That's where the writers or actors went to lunch, but not me. I felt self-conscious eating with Loni Anderson. She was as cute as could be and knew countless people, who all stopped by to say hello. Poor girl, she had to introduce me to everyone. Then she looked up with a big smile. Burt walked up and asked if he could join us. As if it was a question. To my surprise, Burt chose not to attend the ADR session. For a moment, I had that uncomfortable feeling that I was with his girl. It turned out he was simply stopping by to see how the ADR was going. I am sure he was fully confident that she could handle the session by herself. I was still surprised he did not want to supervise the session. When I think of any detail that might alter the outcome of even the smallest of scenes, even in an *Amazing Story* episode, I consider it a life-or-death issue. I learned, as time went on, that painting with a slightly bigger brush could be fine. I certainly found this out working with Clint Eastwood.

CLINT EASTWOOD

Clint definitely painted with a bigger brush. He shot fast. There was never any fuss. Not his style. David Vogel stopped me in the parking lot and asked if I wanted to come along with him to visit the set where Clint was shooting. I rarely visited the set since I was so tied up in post production. I jumped at the chance. On the way, David told me that he was afraid that Clint was going over the allotted number of shooting days. More than anything, David feared going over budget on an episode. I had seen the production reports. Clint was shooting an incredible number of camera setups each day. More than anyone had done on the show. David decided to confront him anyway. I'm not sure what solution he planned to offer. They were shooting a scene with Sondra Locke in a rose garden. In between camera setups, David approached Clint, and after a bit of small talk, he said that he feared the show was going to go over schedule. Clint looked at David, didn't say a word, then walked over to his director's chair. He retrieved the script from the chair's side pouch and brought it over and handed it to David. He said, "Here's the script. Tear out any pages you don't want me to shoot." And walked away. I was happy I wasn't holding the script in my hand. I don't recall if we said good-bye or not. Clint never seemed to hold it against me. He recognized that this was Vogel's issue.

When post production began, I often came to Clint's office on the Warner Bros. lot if we needed to meet about anything. I met his longtime editor, Joel Cox, and even his music arranger/collaborator of many years, Lennie Niehaus, who composed the music for the show. Whenever possible, I arranged for Clint to do his post-production work on the Warner's lot, which was the case when the time came to do ADR. I took my usual seat in the recording studio alongside each actor when they did their work. Clint was not present when we started, so I decided to make use of the time and get started with Harvey Keitel. Keitel was not a very exacting ADR performer. His lines were very loosely in sync at best. Also his energy level seemed to drop when redoing his lines. I had him try his first line over a few times to see if we might improve the performance and the sync. After a few takes Clint's voice came on over the intercom speaker in the room. "That's good enough, let's move on." A bit defensively I explained we were attempting to improve the sync a bit. He said, "That's good enough, let's move on."

Clint painted with a bigger brush than I did. But I didn't learn. He got out the same size brush again later. We were doing the final mix of the show on the big stage at Universal, usually reserved for their big features. The room was a large theater with a mixing console two thirds of the way back from the screen. Once again Clint was not there at the outset; I started without him. I was never one to waste time or money on the stage, so I wasn't shy about taking a stab at what I thought the director might want. During the course of mixing, if I noticed a problem, I would raise my hand and motion for the mixers to stop. I would point out what I thought the problem was, and we would roll backward, find a spot to jump back into the mix, and try to improve it. It is a painstaking process. Inching forward, stopping, tweaking one thing or another, then taking another pass at it. Every time you stop, the mixers need to know the balance of all the elements, so they could find their way back into the mix and match the levels of everything rolling forward, so you could restart without hearing a jump in the sound. Often the mixers would stop when they heard something that wasn't to their liking, and I would watch and listen as they did a fix. They were much more experienced than I was, so if I made an inane request, they would politely let me know if I had my head up my ass.

The next time I waved my hand at the mixers and they stopped the film, a voice caused us to turn our heads. Clint, who had quietly walked onto the stage said, "I hope this is going to put another ass in a seat." Which meant, I hope you're making a change that is going to really make a difference to the outcome of the mix, not something so subtle only you would be able to hear it. I gave it a bit of thought, and in that context, I decided I couldn't justify my reason for stopping. I told the guys to move on. Clint painted with broader strokes. I was a bit of a perfectionist. Some filmmakers are perfectionists, even more so than I. But not Clint. The mix was done rather quickly and sounded just fine.

At the end of shooting, I sent a bouquet of yellow roses to Sondra Locke. I thought she had done a wonderful job. After we finished the show, I saw Clint in the parking lot outside my office. I came out to say good-bye, and for some reason I said that if he was ever in need of any additional help on any of his shows, I would love to have the chance to work with him. With the door to his pickup truck still open he said, "I had that idea in the back of my mind, so I will push it a little further forward." I thanked him for that. He then said, "That was really nice of you to send those flowers to Sondra." He then got in the truck and drove away.

THOMAS CARTER

Thomas was a Black man with a quick-witted intellect. He was an actor's director, which was a good thing, since the piece he was offered to direct was an ensemble film, led by Joe Pantoliano, James Cromwell, Al Ruscio, and Geoffrey Lewis. *One For the Road,* a dark comedy cleverly written by Jim Bissell (who was also a great art director), took place mostly in a tavern, where a group of barflies hatch a plan to kill a drunk for his life insurance money. But the guy won't die. Once the plan was hatched, the music of Johnny Mandel playfully heightened the dark comedy.

I stopped by the set on my way to lunch, just to get a few laughs and watch Thomas at work. Before breaking for lunch, the cast was rehearsing the scene they planned to shoot right after they returned. I watched as the main character, Mike Malloy, played by Douglas Seale, stumbles out of the bathroom in the bar singing a song. What is he singing, I wondered? No one gave me a heads up he would be drunkenly attempting to sing. When the crew left for lunch, I approached Thomas and asked where the song came from. He said he had added the song and thought it would be a great way to start the scene and would show Malloy's increasing drunkenness as he heads back to the bar. I agreed. That all worked. But I needed to clear the song before it could be sung on camera. Otherwise, we could be held hostage by the publisher and forced to pay their price for the licensing fee. That's assuming we could get the rights to use the song at all. The publisher might not like their song sung by a drunk in a bar. In any case, it could take days or weeks to clear the use of the song, not an hour.

"OK," Carter said. "Find me a song that suits the scene ready for the actor to sing after lunch." My lunch plans suddenly changed. I ran out the door and turned to the only one I thought could help me: Julian Bratolyubov. By this time I was good friends with Julian, a Russian immigrant who was the supervisor of music prep and copying in the music department. I had first ventured over to the department to chase down some rewritten parts needed for some players in the orchestra. After that visit, I would occasionally stop by and say hi to Julian and shoot the breeze a bit. He was now the only one I thought I could turn to. Thankfully, he was there on his lunch break.

"Julian, I need help. The director of our latest episode has put in a song for an actor to sing in a scene coming up right after lunch. I told him he couldn't use it because it wasn't cleared. I need to replace it with an original song, *really fast.*" Julian just kept listening. "The scene is in an Irish bar, and the character is Irish. What if we write some words to an Irish standard, and I will run back and teach it to him when they get back from lunch." I started to sing out loud the melody of a song everyone knows, *da dum de dum de dum de diddly, dum de dum de dum.* He went to the piano and played and said, "Do you mean this?" "Yeah, that's it." "It's the Irish Washerwoman song." "Is it in the public domain?" Which meant anyone could sing the song at no cost. He said he thought it was. OK, slow it down to the tempo of a slurring drunk, and I'll make up some words to go with it. And that's what happened. With a piece of paper in hand, I ran back to the set and found Douglas Seale and explained that he needed to learn a new song. He said no problem. I handed the piece of paper to him, and I sang it through a few times. It ended something like this:

….or lament for that which is.

Will only bring despair and hate,

For death is where justice is.

He said, "I got it." Thomas Carter walked up and said, "Let me hear what you got." Douglas sang it for him. Thomas said, "That'll work." And that was it, I had written a song.

Some weeks later, the music department was preparing the cue sheet for the episode, which identifies the writer for each piece of music in the show. Julian called me and said to stop by his office. He said, "Remember that song you wrote in a panic that day here in the office?" "Yeah." "Well, I need to name it and add it to the cue sheet with you as the writer." "Really? OK." "What shall I call It?" I named the song "Malloy's Lament." Julian then said I needed to join ASCAP or BMI to register the song and track the residuals. He suggested joining BMI, which I did. I still collect residuals on that song.

WILLIAM DEAR

By far, the show with the biggest laughs was *Mummy, Daddy*. Bill Dear was a delight to work with. He lived in Carmel. We shared a bit of a Northern California sensibility that connected us instantly. He tried to find the humor in every scene. The show had a great idea for a short film. While shooting a horror movie in a southern swamp, an actor dressed in a mummy costume hears that his wife is about to give birth. He leaves the movie set and hurries to the local hospital, and while running through the swamp, he is mistaken by the local rednecks for the legendary mummy believed to still live in the area.

Bronson Pinchot played the director of the film within the film, clearly trying to mimic none other than Spielberg. Brion James knew exactly how to play the stereotypical redneck trying to chase down the mummy. And Tom Harrison chewed up the screen while wrapped in a mummy costume as the father-to-be. Since Tom's mouth was covered by his mummy costume, most of the recorded lines were unintelligible. When we rerecorded his dialogue in ADR, it was an open-ended chance to have fun with his lines. Lip sync was not an issue. Tom could act against what both he and the other actors had done, often saying lines that could not be heard by the other actors but were clear to the audience. He put a kerchief over his mouth, giving a slightly muffled effect to the recordings so they were not too clean. Just for laughs, we recorded many risqué lines that, sadly, did not end up in the show, since they were not suitable for Sunday-night viewing on NBC.

We chased down Danny Elfman to compose the music for the show. His score gave an upbeat tempo and light tone to the chase through the swamp. Danny followed the Nino Rota style of the music in *Pee-wee's Big Adventure,* which he had written a year earlier. When Bill and I took the film down to Amblin to screen for Spielberg, Steven laughed throughout the screening. That was a first. Most of the shows didn't have many laughs. Steven complemented Bill and then said, "Do you have any movie scripts lying around that you want to make?" As it turned out, he did. He briefly told Steven the story of *Harry and the Hendersons.* Steven said to send it to him right away. The story was right up Steven's alley. *Harry and the Hendersons* went into immediate production. How lucky was Bill Dear? To his credit, he had the screenplay ready to go and directed a delightful episode of *Amazing Stories.*

TRUE TO the concept of bringing in young talent to the show, quite a few directors with little experience got a shot at working on the series and a chance to prove themselves to Steven. This opportunity cut both ways. Steven was always looking for young and, therefore, cheap talent to direct shows for Amblin. The young filmmakers were desperately trying to get a movie to direct. It happened for Bill Dear, maybe it would happen for them. I worked with many of these first-time directors. The two youngest were just 24.

Amazing Stories

PHIL JOANOU was born nervous. He was skinny. He was wired. He had just come out of the USC film school with a short, *Last Chance Dance*. Steven was his idol. Phil tried to emulate his style. He arrived on the set with an ambitious shot list and plans for complicated camera moves. As the hours ticked by, he complained when he was not able to finish the day's work. He thought that the crew was just not good enough. They weren't fast enough. They couldn't get the work done. The crew felt his frustrations as he moped around the set. His daily game plan wasn't possible within the time constraints of *Amazing Stories*. He learned his first lesson, the need to compromise. This was incredibly disheartening to Phil. He would speak with me endlessly about the difficulties he was having.

I was honest with him and suggested simplifications to his game plan. I encouraged him. I told him he should compliment the crew not berate them. They'll work harder for you if you show kindness and respect. He came to dinner and talked more about his difficulties. Despite his angst, he shot good shows. We worked together on *The Doll*. The show starred John Lithgow as a shy, loveless man who purchases a magical doll that changes his life. The show displayed a very sensitive side to Phil's directing. Georges Delerue was chosen to do the score. I was a huge fan of Delerue, having listened to his scores on numerous François Truffaut films, including *Jules and Jim*, *Day for Night*, and *The Last Metro*. I was fortunate to get invited to visit Mr. Delerue in his home at the top of Laurel Canyon, where he played a sketch of the music on his piano. The music tied together a nice, gentle story for Phil. Phil was the first to jump right into a feature film following *Amazing Stories* called *Three O'Clock High*. David Vogel was his producer. That was a mistake since the two did not mix well. If I had had more experience at that time, I might have been a better fit as a producer for Phil.

Steve Starkey

TODD HOLLAND fell in love with Kyra Sedgwick, the actress who was costarring in his show, *Thanksgiving*. This was not uncommon in the world that I worked in. Steven had fallen in love with Kate Capshaw on *Indiana Jones*. Clint Eastwood became involved with Sondra Locke on *The Outlaw Josey Wales*. Burt Reynolds married actress Loni Anderson. Danny DeVito had been married to Rhea Perlman for many years. Phil Joanou was dating Molly Ringwald at that time. Todd was in good company. In *Thanksgiving*, Kyra played the stepdaughter of a greedy farmer, David Carradine. Living on a drought-stricken ranch, she discovers gold at the bottom of a well while desperately looking for water. I could see why Todd fell for Kyra. Beautiful eyes, a softness to her presence, and a huge smile. She even sang a bit of Patsy Cline. She created a sweet and sympathetic character in Todd's little film.

Todd was so full of energy it was hard to get him to stop bubbling, even for a second. He listened, but his mind was moving so fast you might have to repeat yourself. It all came from a very childlike enthusiasm for the craft. He simply had too many ideas. He had a real sensibility for edgy comedy, even though this episode only showed hints of that. It revealed itself in a short he had done, *Chicken Thing*, which he had made earlier. He did such a fine job on his first episode of *Amazing Stories* that he was invited back. His second show was *Welcome to My Nightmare*, which he also wrote. It was the story of a complete movie geek, much like Todd, who finds his life turned upside down when he steps into his worst nightmare—a scene from the movie *Psycho*. The script was very complicated to shoot, but Todd was unfazed by its complexity. These shows really jump-started Todd's career. Soon after *Amazing Stories*, he directed a few episodes of *Twin Peaks*, which was all the rage at the time.

Amazing Stories

LESLI LINKA GLATTER was a completely different filmmaker. Unlike Phil and Todd, she had a more independent and artistic side. I would not say she was avant-garde, but she certainly had an idiosyncratic sensibility. She was always looking for a different way to tell a story. Also she invited ideas and collaboration much more than Phil or Todd. She decided to shoot her show, *No Day at the Beach*, in black and white. I was really excited about this, as was the cameraman. They collaborated well on the choreography of the players and the camera on the opening half of the show, which took place inside the close living quarters in the belly of a ship. Here we are introduced to the meek soldier of a wartime naval unit who unexpectedly and miraculously saves the lives of his comrades.

The show looked beautiful. We used stock footage for establishing shots of large-scale scenes that had more production value than we could afford, like ships approaching the shore and landing on the beach. Then we had to try to match the photography of her film to the found material. Lesli took a risk, but it really worked. The cast, led by Charlie Sheen, just loved working with her. I remember sitting on the mixing stage, listening to the provocative score by Leonard Rosenman, as Lesli pondered the most effective way to end the show. "What music should we play?" she kept asking. We tried all sorts of things, including having the troops sounding off as they walked away, letting the audience ponder the miracle. But in the end, we couldn't top Rosenman's score. What were we thinking? This was the guy who wrote the music for *Rebel Without a Cause* and *East of Eden* and countless other scores. But Lesli never said she was done until she had tried any and all ideas. I loved that about her.

Steve Starkey

TWO SEASONS and more than 20 shows with different directors, actors, and composers were enough to make your head spin. In the middle of it all, Skip Lusk, my co-associate producer left the show. I don't think he quite fit in. It is ironic how when I started the series, I thought I wouldn't fit in. It shows what insecurity can do to you. His replacement could not have been a nicer, more competent guy, Steve Semel. We had similar backgrounds. Steve had also been an assistant editor on numerous features, including *Apocalypse Now*. We had the San Francisco Bay Area and the Bay Area filmmakers in common. It was so easy to work together and commiserate about our shows and their problems. We were both blessed with a wonderful assistant, Cheryl Bloch, who, with a small push, could have done our jobs. She had also done quite a bit of assistant editing before coming to help us out on the series. When she left the show, she worked with the executive producers, Brand and Falsey, for quite a few years.

As luck would have it, unlike the first time around, I was able to work with Spielberg on his second show in the series. All in all, it would be the most challenging work I did in my two years on *Amazing Stories*.

CHAPTER 10

My Amazing Story with Steven Spielberg

IN ONE OF his interviews during the making of *Raiders of the Lost Ark*, Steven Spielberg said that when he was faced with a seemingly insurmountable problem on a film set, he enjoyed the challenge of painting himself out of a corner. On his episode of *Amazing Stories* called *The Mission*, a gunner holed up in the belly of a B-17 bomber uses his imagination and artistic skill to paint *his* way out of a corner. He draws cartoon landing wheels that come to life on his crippled plane, bringing the aircraft in for a safe landing.

As in this case with Spielberg on *The Mission*, I have often found that directors seem to be consciously or subconsciously attracted to material that has a resonance in their personal life. The material or story may not be autobiographical, but it's still very personal. Even when Steven's films were shrouded in special effects or predicated on extraordinary events, they still seemed to resonate deeply.

ARRIVING ON THE SET of *The Mission*, I found the damaged aircraft engulfed in smoke and surrounded by a white cyclorama. Almost the entire story took place inside the body of the airplane. Whenever the camera looked past the actors and out the windows of the aircraft, it would appear that the plane was airborne. It was a tight set with little room to move. A handheld camera was used to shoot most of the show. Steven was at home here. With all the angles and shots already blocked out in his mind, there was an amazing economy in his filmmaking style, particularly in the small space.

Piece by piece, the movie was assembled by Steve Kemper, his editor. Steve had assisted Michael Kahn, Spielberg's usual editor, on quite a few shows before getting his first opportunity to edit on *Amazing Stories*. Michael had probably given him scenes to cut when they were working together. When I learned of Steve's background, it came as no surprise that he had been chosen as one of the editors of the series instead of me. I did not regret or resent the decision that had been made more than a year before. At this point, I was not looking back. I had been challenged in many unexpected ways while working with a diverse group of directors, helping to put their shows together.

Kemper quickly put together the cut of the show and screened it with Steven. When they completed the director's cut, we had a group meeting to review the movie for ADR and sound. The meeting included John Stacy, who supervised the sound on all the shows, along with Lettie Odney and Denise Whiting, the ADR editors. Steven announced that he would not be present for ADR or the final mix of the show and asked that I oversee its completion. He was going off to shoot *The Color Purple*. Despite the fact I had accomplished the same tasks with numerous directors, I suddenly felt a heavy weight on my shoulders. We knew each other well, but he was handing over a little movie almost an hour in length, twice as long as most of the other episodes. I knew that I could do it, but I could not help feeling insecure. As we plowed through the cut, Steven gave all of us directions for completing the show. When it came to ADR, Steven made it clear that he hated loops, the dialogue that was rerecorded on the ADR stage. On this particular show, that was a problem. Most of the dialogue had been clobbered by the sounds of the wind machines, smoke machines, the rocking of the plane, and all the other mechanical devices on the set. You could hardly hear a word that was said. Steven made an exception for one scene that was particularly noisy. But that was his order. Somehow we had to make the dialogue recorded on the set work in the final mix.

Since this was a busy show and the action was confined to the aircraft, the sound design would be particularly crucial to the emotion of the drama as it progressed. When the mission was going along smoothly, the engines and ambience in the plane would have a different personality than when the plane was in jeopardy. The sound on the show required special attention, so I called Richard Anderson. Richard was the same sound editor I had assisted on *More American Graffiti,* when he came up to Lucasfilm to help out Ben Burtt. He agreed to come and supervise the sound. It was fun to work with Richard again, albeit in a different capacity, and he was a great asset to the crew.

As we played through the show with Steven, reviewing the dialogue and sound, we came across "shot-missing" banners in the work print. Steven pointed out that these banners represented shots that he failed to get while shooting. He asked that I pull together a second unit and shoot these for him. Up until that moment, the only experience I had shooting inserts was on the stage at Universal, and usually the director was there to supervise. This time I would be gathering the crew from the show on the large sound stage with all the bells and whistles that were there on the filming day: the set, the lighting, the props, the special effects, in other words, everything. Then directing the shots. There were even shots that included the actor who played the belly gunner, Casey Siemaszko, which would require makeup, hair, and wardrobe. This was a big deal. To say I was intimidated was a gross understatement.

Steven gave his direction for the shots—there were quite a few—as if he were speaking to a seasoned second-unit director. I simply nodded in agreement and hung on every word that might guide me through the day. Of course, as with any crash course, I would remember little after he left the room. Steven said to do the shots, cut them in, and he would review them when he had a chance. Of course, if they were not to his liking, I would have to mount the crew all over again and reshoot. The first series of shots were from the final sequence of the film, when Casey draws a picture of the landing wheels. The camera would be looking down over the shoulder of the belly gunner, as he furiously colored his drawing. The camera was meant to move in tighter on the drawing as the shot went on, matching the slow pace of the camera on the shots before and after in the scene. A different series of insert shots followed the cartoon drawings as they were blown across the tarmac, with one final drawing landing on a kerosene runway light and catching on fire. The final insert shot of the show was an over-the-shoulder shot of Casey, surrounded by his mates, holding the drawing that saved their lives.

When we finished running the picture, Steven stood up to leave and said, "Call me if you have any questions." I had my marching orders, as did the sound crew. Shoot the second-unit shots. Complete the visual effects. Supervise the ADR. Attend the scoring session. Do the final mix. I hoped that I would get approvals from Steven along the way so I could redo whatever might be necessary. We had to do the second-unit shots right away, before they struck the set and the film crew was needed to shoot their next show.

My Amazing Story with Steven Spielberg

HEADING OVER to the sound stage, I was upbeat yet nervous. I had reviewed the shots over and over again in the editing room, so I knew what was needed. I had a shot list. I even had a picture of the shots in my mind. All I had to do was shoot them. I walked on the stage and saw the crew huddled by the plane set. John McPherson, the cinematographer, was lighting the set to match what he had done during the first-unit shoot. John was about 10 years older than I was and had shot quite a few TV shows and had even directed some. I really didn't know him very well. I had only watched him work from a distance and seen him a few times in dailies on some of the shows. As the associate producer, I was delegated the role of second-unit director, so I would be in charge, although clearly, I was going to need all the help I could get.

When I approached the group, John waved to me and asked that I follow him toward the stage door. When we stepped outside, he assumed a rather ominous tone and said, "Look, I don't want you to get the wrong idea. I am in charge of this set. Don't go trying to make it anything different." I stood there agape, not knowing what to think. I assured him I had no problem with that. It felt like he had picked me up by the lapel of my shirt with one hand, threatened me with a finger pointed in my face, then set me down. Where the hell had that come from? I was pretty unassuming, certainly not out to prove anything. I just wanted to get through the day. While quite shaken when we walked back onto the stage, I tried to act like nothing unsettling had happened. In any case, John's mood improved after he set things straight with me. Now we had shots to do. He set up the camera and selected the appropriate lens, then I took a quick look through the viewfinder, and we were ready to go.

The first series of shots had Casey sitting in his gunner's seat, furiously filling in the yellow wheel on his drawing of the plane. Saying "Action" was always a bit strange for me and has really remained so to this day. But Casey was good. He knew exactly what he had done when the scene was shot. He did it over and over again as we changed lenses and got closer and closer to the action, pushing in tighter and tighter on the drawing. Finishing this part of the shoot was a big relief, since I didn't have the actors to deal with anymore.

As it turned out, the most difficult shots of the day were up next. These were the penultimate shots in the show, where the camera follows different drawings skipping along the tarmac, as if blown by the wind. The first lands on a blue runway light; a second one lands on a burning kerosene runway lamp and catches on fire. All we had for the set was a piece of tarmac with some dried-up weeds growing up through the cracks, a blue landing light, and a lit kerosene lamp. For the first shot, we dropped in a drawing on the tarmac, and with the help of a small electric fan, watched it blow along the ground and finally stick to the blue light. We could not, for the life of us, get the drawing to land properly on the light, so you could actually see the drawing. It was always crumpled or facing away from the camera. The prop man tried over and over again. Finally I asked to have a piece of monofilament tied to the drawing and on cue, with the camera dollying alongside the moving paper, I pulled it to where it was supposed to go and land correctly. It worked. You could clearly see the drawing.

Having done that, we moved to the shot where a different drawing skips along and lands on the burning lamp and catches on fire. Now we had the method, but it took numerous tries to get it to land correctly. When it finally did, it didn't catch fire. Damn. I said to pour some kerosene onto the paper. Hopefully it would be moving so quickly and catch fire so fast, no one would notice that the drawing was dampened. That way when we got the shot right, at least it would start burning. Another perfect shot and still no burning drawing. Then I really doused the paper. I was not going to leave the set until we had that shot. I was obsessed. Finally, with the paper almost soaking wet, and after many more takes, the drawing landed perfectly and caught fire. We got the shot. I was elated. I have no idea how many takes it took, but this was my introduction to second-unit directing. I sent the shots to the editor, who said they all cut in fine. Now we waited for the effects shots to come in.

Dream Quest Images was the company that did all the visual effects shots in the series. They were a smart group of guys who worked very economically. The creative team was led by Hoyt Yeatman and Scott Squires. Quirky guys and very resourceful. This was not ILM, but we always got shots that worked for the show. ILM would have been too big for the series. We could not have afforded them, and they probably would not have been able to do the work on our tight schedule. Each show had its set of challenges. Whether we were looking for animated playing cards flying through the audience or a simple animated spark that displayed the magic of a ring, the guys always provided what was needed for the show. *The Mission* presented one of their greatest challenges. Dream Quest had to somehow create the oversize animated yellow landing wheels and bring them to life on the real plane. The wheels first appear when you see the crew emerge from the belly of the plane. The cartoon wheels continue to hold up the plane as the crew walks around them after a safe landing. Dream Quest added clever shadows on the animation to make the wheels appear to be part of the live action.

Steve Starkey

AS THESE SHOTS came dribbling in, I turned my mind to ADR. Steven had said to leave the dialogue alone, but when I listened to the soundtracks again with the sound supervisor and the dialogue editors, we decided to record the lines for the whole show as a backup. There was only one scene where we thought that the original recording would probably be OK. I ended up spending a few weeks on the ADR stage directing the actors through the rerecording of their lines. Kevin Costner, who played the pilot of the bomber had, by far, the greatest number of lines. In addition, Kevin proved to be the most exacting of all the actors. He found the original production dialogue to be just right, and he wanted to do everything in his power to recreate what he had done on set. Every breath, every subtle shift in volume, every nuance of performance. He was never satisfied with a reading until the line was done perfectly. Of course, I was of the same mind. If I was going to use a rerecorded line, I wanted it to be the same as what we were replacing. I knew that Steven would know the difference.

Kiefer Sutherland had some very difficult performances to redo. I asked him if he found it difficult to get his head back to that time and place when he did the original on the set. He said, "It's all acting. It's my job as an actor to perform the lines as I did on the day." I never forgot that, but I remained in awe of the actors who could reenter their original mind-set. Casey Siemaszko was lighthearted about the whole process, despite the fact he had done little ADR before. In between takes, he told me that he was in the circus as a kid and had been shot from a cannon. I guess after that, he was fearless and could do anything. All the other actors really stepped up and did remarkable work as well.

Getting the lines right enabled the sound effects to shine. Using the ADR and clearing out the on-set sounds, we had clean dialogue to work with and were able to get very creative with the sound effects and do a well-orchestrated mix. John Williams had written a sweeping score that enveloped the whole story. The music was particularly moving when the crew was saying their final good-byes to the belly gunner. Then it shifted to a tense cadence as the plane headed in for what should have been a fatal landing. John Williams proved again the unique creative relationship he shared with Steven.

The sound crew, with their collective experience, ended up creating a great track. Bill Varney, the head mixer at Universal, ran the mix. I was in good hands. All eyes looked to me for approvals, scene by scene, reel by reel, but the editors and mixers did all the heavy lifting. We were ready for Steven. We scheduled the screening for him in the Hitchcock theater, which was the largest theater on the Universal lot, usually reserved for mixing feature films. In addition to listening to the mix, he would be watching all the second-unit shots on the big screen and quite a few visual-effects shots he had not had a chance to approve. My hands were sweaty as the movie ran. When the lights came up, there was silence for a brief moment. Everyone held their breath. Steve Kemper, Bill Varney, the sound editors, and ADR editors were silent and waiting.

All Steven said was, "Great. I have only one note. Why didn't you loop that one scene? All the other loops were great." In that moment I quickly learned that it was not appropriate to remind Steven he had said not to do any ADR at all, except possibly for one particularly loud scene, and to leave the rest of the entire show alone. All I could say was, "I thought that scene was OK." He then said, "You are going to have to go in and loop that scene. Otherwise, everything else is great!" I couldn't believe it. No mention of the second-unit shots. They were fine. The effects shots were fine. The mix was approved. I said I would get it done right away and fix the mix. I had to call almost all the actors back in and go to work. This time, I did the ADR with more confidence. Steven had blessed our work, and I knew what to do.

I shared the news with Liv. She was excited for me. I told her I hoped I could do more of what I had done on *The Mission*. I loved the creative and logistical responsibility. Also, the show felt more like a movie than an episode of a TV show. I wanted to work on movies. Do the same work on a larger scale. With timing and a bit of luck, I was ready to make the leap.

JUST THEN I heard rumblings about a Robert Zemeckis show called *Who Framed Roger Rabbit* starting to gear up over at Amblin. I was surprised that Frank had not mentioned it to me. The more I heard about the movie, the more enticing it became. I started to build the show up in my mind, even though I really knew very little about it. I wondered if they needed or had hired someone to help oversee the post production and visual effects. I couldn't stop thinking about it. I had to put my mind to rest. I decided to meet with Art Repola, the in-house post-production supervisor at Amblin. He had his finger on the pulse of their upcoming films. He said everything I heard was true. The show was huge. The director, Bob Zemeckis, was a great guy to work with. Frank had always said the same thing about Bob—great guy, great filmmaker, fun to work with. This was the director of *Romancing the Stone* and *Back to the Future*. Big movies. *Roger Rabbit* was a show I wanted to work on. What should I do? I sheepishly asked Art if he was going to try to get a position on the show. Art had been the post-production supervisor on *Back to the Future*. I knew if he wanted the job, he would get it. He said he was thinking about it. I couldn't push him any further than that. Around the same time, Warren Franklin, the head of ILM, called me up and said if I had a chance, on my next trip up north, he would like to meet with me about an upcoming show called *Roger Rabbit*. What a coincidence...

Liv and I always loved an excuse to get out of LA and escape to Northern California. Taking walks in the woods and visiting with our close friends provided us with welcome relief. I couldn't wait to hear what Warren had in mind. ILM was still located among the warehouses of the canal district in San Rafael, with The Kerner Co. name on the door. Warren had been in the optical department when I worked on the *Star Wars* films, so we had gotten to know one another in those days.

For our meeting, Warren ushered me into a small conference room and had Ken Ralston join us. Ken was going to be the visual-effects supervisor on the show. He was one of the premier effects supervisors working in the business at the time. Ken was awkward at the meeting. I later learned that he was always awkward in these situations. When I asked if he could tell me anything about the show, he said, "It's a live-action movie with a bunch of cartoon characters running around. It's huge and really complicated." Then Ken took off, and I stayed behind with Warren. First, he said that he and Ken would love to have me work on the show as the effects coordinator. I was happy to hear that they would like to work with me, but the offer to work as a coordinator rankled me. Following what I had just done on *Amazing Stories*, the job seemed like a bit of a demotion. Then again, what did I expect? This was ILM and this was how they ran their shows. They had effects supervisors, who were in charge, and coordinators, or glorified assistants, keeping track of things. I am not sure why I expected something different.

STEVE STARKEY

Also, the pay scale was lower than what I had been getting paid. The dream was fading quickly. I thought I could handle the job, but I wanted more. I wanted to oversee all the post production on the show *and* the visual effects. I told Warren, at the very least, if I were to take the position, I wanted to be an effects producer, not simply a coordinator. In order to effectively work with Ken, overseeing a large budget and schedule, I needed to be on a more equal footing with him. It would be a collaboration. I would do everything in my power to give him the creative freedom he needed, and to organize the show the way he was used to, but at the same time, he needed to respect my need to maintain a schedule and budget.

Elevating my role to effects producer would be a first for ILM, but Warren understood my position. In fact, I think he welcomed the idea. The less oversight required by him the better. I told him that I had not thought about working at ILM, but I would give it some consideration. We parted ways optimistic that something would work out. The more I thought about it, taking the job Warren had offered wasn't enough. I really wanted a bigger role with more oversight. More like the associate producer position I had on *Amazing Stories*.

With all my misgivings in mind about the offer at ILM, I decided to meet once again with Art Repola at Amblin. I was on pins and needles. My role on the show hinged on his decision. He told me he did not want to take the job as post supervisor on *Roger*. It was a tough decision for him, but he had decided that going away to London for six months would be too long to be away from his family. He said if I was interested in the position, I should contact Robert Watts, the producer on the film. I quickly contacted Robert, whom I had met on the *Star Wars* films. He moaned and said he really didn't have any money for the position, although he knew it was needed. He was having huge budget problems as it was, and he couldn't afford to put in any money for a post-production supervisor. He did say he would be in the Bay Area, visiting ILM and Jimmy Bloom soon, and he would give it some thought. Jim Bloom. Great. My old pal from Lucasfilm. Maybe *he* could help me. I called Jim and told him what I was trying to do. I wanted to be both the post-production supervisor and visual-effects producer on the show. He said he would bring it up with Robert and try to convince him it was the right thing to do.

I received a call from Warren who said he had spoken to Robert Watts, who now wanted me on the show as his post-production supervisor. Clearly Jim Bloom had recommended me. Robert and Warren thought I could handle both jobs, but Robert pleaded poverty to Warren. He said there was no money in the production budget for a post supervisor. What was he thinking when he prepared the budget, I wondered? Warren told Robert that the ILM budget could bear the cost of my entire salary, then called me and said my deal was done. I was set to work on *Roger Rabbit*. I would be making the leap from TV to feature films. I was taking the next step in the career path that I described to my mentor, Frank Marshall. Even though I was not hired as an associate producer, I would be taking on all of the same responsibilities, and hopefully more, and on a much larger scale. I had somehow cobbled together this position. Now I had to make a leap of faith and hope that everything would work out.

Lunchtime with my posse at Emerson Jr. High, Los Angeles, 1965.

Sitting on a banister outside my seventh-grade math class, 1965.

With my sister Michele in 1974.

With an Indian friend, Sukumar Nambiar, and my college roommate, Kevin Caldwell, in 1975.

On our wedding day, August 16, 1980.

George and Marcia Lucas at the wedding party.

The Empire Strikes Back softball team, 1980
(standing left to right):
Paul Hirsch (editor), Ben Burtt (sound designer), Steve Starkey,
Brian Johnson (effects supervisor), Duwayne Dunham (first assistant editor);
(seated left to right):
Jane Hirsch, Peggy Burtt, Olivia Erschen, Brian's wife, and Chrissie England.

Looking for that special piece of film in the editing room on *The Empire Strikes Back*, 1980.

Updating the visual-effects status board with magnetic dots on *Return of the Jedi*, 1983.

Shooting *Roger Rabbit* with Bob Hoskins riding Benny the Car on the streets of Los Angeles, 1986.

Bob Hoskins hanging on wires in front of the blue screen at ILM, during the Toontown shot on *Roger Rabbit*, 1988.

Judge Doom puppet in front of the blue screen at ILM.

Roger Rabbit, jumping out of Valiant's coat,
has something to say to director Robert Zemeckis.

Roger Rabbit comes to life in Maroon's office.

My wife, Liv, as an extra, with Bob Hoskins while shooting a scene for *Roger Rabbit* in Oakland, California, 1988.

Charlie Fleischer on set in his Rabbit costume with director Zemeckis, 1987.

Richard Williams, Steven Spielberg, Robert Zemeckis, Robert Watts, Simon Wells, Steve Starkey, Ken Ralston, and Don Hahn at the animation facility in London on *Roger Rabbit*, 1988.

One of many turnover sessions in London on *Roger Rabbit* with Artie Schmidt (editor) seated at the KEM, Bob Zemeckis (in red, standing), with Ken Ralston seated behind him. Richard Williams and I are seated taking notes, 1988.

Roger's crew photo in London (left to right):
Robert Watts, Don Hahn, Robert Zemeckis, Steve Starkey,
Richard Williams, Ken Ralston, and Artie Schmidt, 1988.

Frank Marshall, Kathy Kennedy, myself, Liv,
and Robert Zemeckis at the *Roger Rabbit* premiere
in June 1988 in New York, wearing our Roger bow ties.

Rick Carter (production designer), Robert Zemeckis, Simon Wells, Joan Bradshaw (production manager), Neil Canton (producer), and myself on the *Back to the Future II* set, 1989.

Myself with Steve Irwin, Larina Adamson, and Ian Kelly, the *BTF II* video playback group.

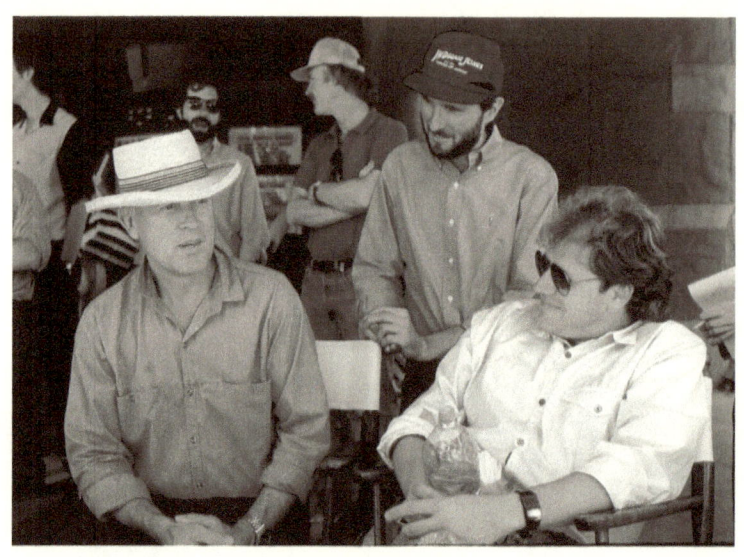

Max Kleven (second-unit director, *BTF II*) and me, reviewing our day's work with Robert Zemeckis.

Shooting second-unit photography in Monument Valley on *Back to the Future III* with Max Kleven, Bob Zemeckis, and Michael J. Fox, 1989.

Robert Zemeckis, Neil Canton, Joan Bradshaw, and myself on a bluff in Monument Valley, with the wranglers and the Native American extras in the background on *BTF III*, 1989.

Striking a ZZ Top pose with Christopher Lloyd, Robert Zemeckis, Neil Canton, and Michael J. Fox in Monument Valley on *BTF III*.

Liv and I with Paul Pav (location manager), Joan Bradshaw (production manager), and Neil Canton (producer) in the Monument Valley drive-in movie theater during the shooting of *BTF III*.

Bob Gale (writer/producer) and his daughter, Samantha, George Lucas, and Inge, Liv's daughter, holding George's baby, Amanda, in the *Back to the Future III* Western town, 1989.

Liv, Michael J. Fox, and Inge in front of the old saloon set on *BTF III*.

The ILM crew about to drive a miniature train over a cliff.
I am wearing the gray/green parka.

Sharing a beer with some of the *Back to the Future III* editing crew.
Peter Lonsdale (assistant editor), me, Neil Canton (producer),
Michael J. Fox, Robert Zemeckis, Bob Gale (producer),
Artie Schmidt (editor), and Harry Keramidas (editor), 1990.

With the director, Peter Bogdanovich, on the *Noises Off* set, 1991.

With Carol Burnett on the set.

Chatting baseball with Michael Caine.

Frank Marshall listens while I arrange
to play tennis with Christopher Reeve.

With a smiling Julie Hagerty on *Noises Off* set.

The cast of *Noises Off:*
(STANDING LEFT TO RIGHT)
Marilu Henner, Christopher Reeve, Julie Hagerty, Denholm Elliot,
Michael Caine, Nicollette Sheridan, John Ritter.
(SEATED LEFT TO RIGHT)
Mark Linn-Baker, Carol Burnett

With producer and personal mentor, Frank Marshall.

CHAPTER 11

Shooting the Rabbit

WHEN I STEPPED onto the set of *Roger Rabbit* in the late fall of 1986, I might just as well have been one of the cartoon characters that were invisible during the shooting of the film. I was unknown to everyone around me. Over time, many of the faces on the crew would become familiar, but on my first day only a couple of people, Robert Watts, the producer who hired me, and Ken Ralston, my cohort at ILM, knew who I was or what I was hired to do. As I looked around, they were nowhere to be seen. I was on my own.

The streets felt more like real life than a movie location. I saw old Los Angeles buildings I had not seen in their original glory, all carefully rejuvenated with loving care by the production designer, Elliot Scott. The streets were humming with electric streetcars filled with people dressed from a bygone era. I had stepped back in time to 1947, the time period of the film. That was when my father, recently returned from the war, was enrolled in law school at Loyola. While in his late 20s, close to my age, he would ride up Western Boulevard to see plays and go to clubs. He would soon meet a beautiful Frenchwoman who was working in the French consulate. She had placed an ad in the *Wall Street Journal* offering to exchange French lessons for driving lessons. She found her prize in my dad. He never learned to speak French very well, and my mother was a terrible driver. But they married and started a life together. Upon graduation from Loyola Law School, he started practicing law in downtown LA. In previous years, when my dad had taken me on a tour of his old stomping grounds, I could only imagine the city he nostalgically recalled from his younger days. Now I could see it.

My reverie of times past soon turned to the present when I met Robert Zemeckis for the first time. I introduced myself as the post-production supervisor and visual-effects producer. After a brief pause, all he said was, "Good luck." His response was memorable and, at the same time, unsettling. He may have been surprised that I was hired without having met him. I am not sure. I *am* sure that he was surprised that anyone was foolish enough to think that they could manage the jobs I described to him. Either that or he figured I had no idea what I was getting into.

As I drifted away from Zemeckis, I watched him direct a scene where a down-on-his-luck private eye, Eddie Valiant, played by Bob Hoskins, runs across the street, dodging pedestrians and a red car, and heads into the Terminal Bar to satisfy his drinking problem. Eddie is hired by a cartoon producer, R.K. Maroon, to investigate an adultery scandal involving Jessica Rabbit, the wife of Maroon Studios' biggest star, Roger Rabbit. They are among the toons who inhabit the world with the live-action characters. When Marvin Acme, the owner of Toontown, is found murdered, Roger becomes a suspect and is pursued by the nefarious Judge Doom and his henchmen, the Weasels. Eddie and Jessica try to get to Roger first and prove his innocence.

I always take pleasure in the first time I see the images and characters jump off the page of a script and come to life during the shooting of a film. In this case, only the humans would be jumping

Shooting the Rabbit

off the page during shooting. The invisible toons would spring to life much later.

EARLIER THAT MORNING, when I arrived in the crew parking lot, I saw a large group of guys huddled around an elaborate go-cart—a bare-bones roadster with a raised driver's seat and a seat for an imaginary passenger. The steering wheel was not functional, only something to hold onto. Then I noticed the drivetrain leading to a seat in back, where the real driver would sit to navigate the car. This is how they planned to simulate Valiant taking a wild ride with the animated character called Benny the Car. Everything I saw on that first day took my breath away. The designs and ingenuity were beyond anything I had ever seen created on a film set. The collaboration between the departments was stunning just for this one car. I couldn't fathom the amount of time and departmental collaboration it took for the designers in the transportation department, the stunt coordinator, and the mechanical effects group to put together a vehicle that could be driven like a cartoon car with the actor safely on board. How many months had this show been prepping? I was full of questions, but with everyone up to speed on the show, I hesitated to appear uninformed. I had some catching up to do, so I watched and listened a lot.

I found Ken Ralston and followed him around as he observed the shooting and answered questions. The visual-effects supervisors I knew were very careful when asked the about the restrictions or rules of a shot or what they thought they could pull off. If they were too scared of what they did not know or what they had not done before, they did not hesitate to impose limitations on a shot. Not Ken. He was a risk taker, and Bob Zemeckis loved that about him.

They had collaborated on *Back to the Future* and formed a tight relationship. Ken was now being asked to up his game. This show was filled with visual effects. There were cartoon characters appearing in half the show. This was not a show where you said no, we can't do that. On this show, it became clear right away, we were going into uncharted territory, and it was going to take the knowledge, ingenuity, and sheer gumption of everyone involved to pull it off. I hoped I could hold up my end of the bargain.

For each visual-effects shot, I noticed a large creature mounted on the dolly where the camera usually was. Actually, this was the camera—the VistaVision camera—encased in a huge, padded blimp in order to minimize the sound of the film roaring past the lens. VistaVision was a film format twice the size of 35mm, used to mitigate the loss of quality, particularly the grain, added during the optical process. I watched as the camera crew placed the camera inside the blimp, snapped the foam cover shut, and hefted it into place. Every time a magazine needed to be reloaded, which was twice as often with VistaVision than with 35mm, I painfully watched this procedure take time away from shooting. I had to look away. The volume of work on the show could not bear this repeated delay day in and day out. Something had to be done.

As it turned out, something was getting done. It just wasn't ready yet. Up north at ILM, a crew of technicians was building the Vistaflex camera. Modeled on the Panaflex, this camera would be sleek, lightweight, and more production friendly. Magazines could be changed quickly. The camera could be mounted on the dolly quickly. And, most importantly, it was soundproof. "Why wasn't it ready?" I asked Ken. "Don't ask." I guess this was a sore subject. It was supposed to have been ready for the start of principal photography in Los Angeles.

Shooting the Rabbit

Following a break for the Christmas holidays, the film would resume shooting in England. The cameras had to be ready by then or in Ken's words, "Heads are gonna roll."

FOLLOWING THE LA SHOOT, I returned to Northern California. Standing outside the front door of ILM, I asked myself, "What have I done?" In a pattern that seemed to repeat itself, I had that moment of dread, like on *Amazing Stories*, when I wanted to quit because I thought I wasn't up to the task. Only this time I didn't want to quit, I was simply having doubts about what I had gotten myself into. Disguising my sudden insecurity, I greeted Warren Franklin in the main hallway. Everyone knew one another. They were quickly going about their business. A wave of fear crawled over me. What was my business here? How should I get started? What made me think I could tackle this position? Up until now, I had managed effects from outside a facility. As an assistant editor, I evaluated the work of ILM and other effects groups when the work showed up in the editing room. We made critiques or suggestions, but I never did the actual work. I collaborated with Dream Quest on *Amazing Stories*, both conceiving shots and determining how we were going to execute them. Then they went back to their offices, and I went to mine. The shots became their problem. In both cases, I was a step removed from the facility itself. Now I was a volunteer in the nuthouse. There was no escaping it. I was stuck with the problems and had to be part of the solution. I took a deep breath and continued up the hallway.

I first wanted to check on the status of the VistaVision cameras, which were being built in the engineering department at the back of the building. "Good morning, boys. I'm Steve Starkey, working with Ken Ralston on *Roger Rabbit*. I was wondering how the cameras are coming along?" Greg Beaumont and Mike MacKenzie were busily working, millimeter by millimeter, to accomplish what had never been accomplished before. Soundproof VistaVision production cameras, ready to withstand day-in, day-out use. They had to run as smoothly as a well-tuned aircraft engine. "We're getting there." "Does that mean you will be done next week?" "We hope so. They seem pretty good but not quite ready. We have more tests to do."

I could not tell if these guys were taking the impending deadline seriously or not. Their attitude was much different from those who work on a film set. Everyone in every department on a film crew runs when it is their turn to run. These guys were simply working at their own pace, never seeming to be concerned by the imminent deadline, which was actually only a few weeks away. "Let me remind you, the cameras are leaving with me on New Year's Eve." They looked up for a moment, then went back to work. With that, I left them to their own devices. I am not sure what they thought when I left the room, but I was serious, these cameras were leaving with me on a plane for London.

I went up to my office to get set up. I had left for the LA shoot so quickly that I only had time to put a pad of paper and a pencil next to the phone on my desk before walking out the door. I hired Suella Kennedy as my production coordinator. She was a delightful person and very meticulous. She had assisted me in the editing room on the *Star Wars* documentary and had gone on to be an associate producer with John Korty. I knew her work and felt lucky to have her help me out. I knew I would be gone quite a bit of the time, first in London, then back and forth to LA, so I needed someone well qualified to be in the office at ILM at all times to run the

Shooting the Rabbit

show in my absence.

I finally got a chance to look at the proof-of-concept test that had been done for the show and that had convinced everyone involved that a movie with live actors interacting with cartoon characters could work. Everyone who had seen the test, from Bob Zemeckis and Steven Spielberg to the brass at Disney, saw the magic on the big screen. In the test Joe Pantoliano played Eddie Valiant in a brief scene interacting with Roger. It worked beautifully. How was it done so convincingly, I wondered? What did it take to do the shot? That's what I wanted to know. Poor Ken Ralston. I had questions about everything, which he patiently tried to answer. The more Ken told me, the more I realized how little I actually knew about what he was describing. I also realized how little I knew about how the departments of ILM worked and interacted with one another. Most of the people at the facility had been doing this work for years, if not their entire working lives. They lived and breathed effects work. I was an outsider. It was daunting, to say the least. Ken tried to calm my fears, though it should have been the other way around, with the producer consoling the artist. One thing we both knew was that nothing could really happen until we got into the shoot a bit and saw a cut sequence ready to be put into post production. Then the real movie magic would be put to the test. That would be a priority once I got to London. Figure out a shot or sequence that we could use to "test" the process and do it in a timely fashion, in order to establish a methodology for the whole show.

ILM was now a facility that catered to more than one show at a time. In the *Star Wars* days, the facility did not entertain any other movies. George had the run of the facility. Now the company had to take on multiple shows concurrently in order to keep the place busy and profitable. While we were getting started on *Roger Rabbit*, a Lucasfilm show called *Willow* was setting up shop. I could not tell how much of a conflict this would be. The management had a plan that allowed both shows to coexist and not jeopardize the work on either one. All I knew was we had similar release dates.

I was scheduled to depart on December 30 and arrive in the UK on New Year's Eve. The camera technicians were working through the Christmas holiday to be sure the cameras were ready to go. I checked in every few days to be sure they were on track for my departure. Meanwhile I prepared the necessary customs paperwork so the cameras could clear customs quickly upon my arrival. They would come in on a Carnet, a temporary import and export permit, which allowed the equipment to come into and out of the UK duty-free and tax free. It felt like a big responsibility to transport the cameras myself, but by trying to give the engineers as much time as possible to finish their work, it seemed to be the safest and only way to get the cameras to the UK. On the day before my departure, I went down to ILM, hoping to get all the camera cases lined up and ready for my pickup the following day. The cases were all laid out and numbered, all 20 of them, but the guys hesitated. They said they weren't done. I said that's impossible. They are going with me. I was adamant. They said they had to do a few more tests. Mostly they were concerned about a final scratch test to be sure no film running through the camera gate would be damaged.

I put my foot down. I told Greg to get a plane ticket. If he had to run another test, it would be done in the UK. The cameras were coming with me. I called Robert Watts and told him the news. In order to leave the following day, I needed to bring a technician with me. Robert was trying to pinch any penny he could. He and his production manager, Pat Carr, were reluctant to have even me fly to London. Now I was adding another traveler. The show was growing in size by the minute, and they hadn't even started the UK shoot. Robert had been around the block enough to know that the show was drastically underbudgeted. I said it was the only way that I could leave the country with the cameras. He reluctantly approved it, and that's what we did. Liv, Greg, and I flew to London together with the many cases filled with brand new VistaVision cameras, lenses, and accessories.

COMING FROM rural Marin County to old world London was a culture shock. Even though I had been to London a few times in the past, I still looked up in awe as we passed through the center of town. The architecture is so grand and rich, it takes your breath away. In addition, what made this particular trip different for me is that I arrived with a job. I had only been in London as a tourist before. Now I had a purpose. I discovered, even at customs, when you said you were there to work on a film, ears perked up. People listened. Things happened. Maybe that's why I cleared customs so quickly. We drove directly to Elstree Studios in the north of London. We were taken directly to the visual-effects room, our dreary little office on one of the sound stages, and dropped off the cameras. Greg planned to stay behind and shoot his test. I had arranged to have the test film sent into the lab. We would be going into the first day of shooting blind, not knowing the results of the test until the labs opened back up after the holiday weekend. I had to put my worries behind me, at least for a night or two. It was New Year's Eve.

Mary Radford, Frank's assistant, had asked Liv and me to celebrate with her. We stopped by our service flat in Swiss Cottage on the way. This small community on the fringe of Hampstead was within walking distance of Hampstead Heath and Mary's flat. Liv and I loved to take walks, so that would prove to be a wonderful outlet for us during our stay. Our little studio was quite drab. It was part of a row of walk-ups, all identical in their postwar efficiency. They were called efficiency flats for a good reason. The studio, no larger than a modest hotel room, consisted of a combined living room and bedroom, with a separate bath and a kitchenette. That was it. But Liv always had a way of making even the smallest, dreary places seem nice. She added little things, like flowers and personal effects, that lit up the flat. We were excited. Here we were in London with a place to stay, a per diem, and I was working on a film.

A few of the other Americans were staying on the same block as we were: Clyde Bryan, the key camera assistant; Ray Stella, the camera operator; and Scott Farrar, the additional visual-effects supervisor under Ken. Scott and I would take the same car to and from work each day, as did Ray and Clyde. Other than the four of us, there were only a few other Americans there for the shoot. Dean Cundey, the cameraman, brought his family and put his kids in the American School. Artie Schmidt, the film editor, also made the trip. On the animation side of things, there were production personnel and a handful of animators from the States. Other than Bob Zemeckis and his assistant, my old buddy Frank Marshall, and Mary Radford and a few cast members, that was about it. Visiting with Mary over New Year's felt like we were with family. Liv and I had grown to be good friends of Mary's during the Amblin days and just loved her daughters, Kyle and Brooke. Liv would end up spending many of her free days touring London with the girls, seeing the city through their young eyes. Liv did have some food-styling obligations back home, but at least she was there to see where I was living and share some cultural activities together. In fact, one of the first weekends we were in town, Frank and his wife, Kathy Kennedy, arranged a trip for Liv and me into the English countryside. They got us a car and driver who drove us to the small village of Woodstock, near Blenheim Palace. We stayed at a rustic 17th-century inn called The Feathers, within walking distance of the palace gates. In the inn's ancient bar I tried an old scotch and toasted to Frank and Kathy. Despite the fact that he had not brought the show to my attention, and I had to seek it out on my own, he treated me graciously and with respect. What more could I ask for from a mentor and old friend? I loved that he was there to temper my insecurities.

THE EFFECTS CREW gathered in our grungy little room at Elstree the first morning of shooting. We were all a bit jet-lagged and filled with concern about the cameras. The technicians had a way of letting their fears seep into your spirit. Ken was a bit nonplussed about it all. I think he knew that their fears were generally unjustified. I didn't. Clyde, the assistant cameraman, was in the room with us. He prepped the cameras for the day's shoot, and off he went with the other technicians. Later we learned that the test was fine, which was good, since we were already shooting. Thank God for that.

My first day at work was unsettling. What was I to do? Production had set up the show, so I felt like an observer, not a doer, with little to contribute. I tagged along with Ken on the set and listened and tried to follow what was going on. The first scene was blocked, and Roger Rabbit played a significant part in it. We were in Maroon's office, where Roger learned that his wife may have been cheating on him. He blows his top. This was a rousing way to start shooting. Eddie Valiant and R.K. Maroon, played by Alan Tilvern, both tried to reason with Roger. They gestured and pleaded with him, both locking their focus in space, in a place that would eventually have a cartoon rabbit filling the void. Hoskins said he had no problem imagining and following the cartoon character in front of him. He said he did this all the time with his kids. To help the actors and the camera department understand exactly what and where Roger's action would be in each shot, either Bob Zemeckis or Dean Cundey would hold a large puppet of the rabbit (or whichever character was in the scene) by the ears and race around the set during the final blocking. This reference would be filmed and would prove helpful in so many ways. First it acted as a way for all department heads to see clearly what the cartoon character's actions would be. It also provided a lighting reference when it came to lighting the animated characters. Then it was up to the actors and the cameraman to follow his every move.

Charlie Fleischer, the voice performer for Roger, stood off camera, dressed in a rabbit costume prepared especially for him, and delivered Roger's lines. It was all a bit surreal. It took a leap of faith for everyone involved. The camera operator had to follow an invisible Roger, taking his lead from the actors, who spoke with and reacted to the cartoon character. The prop men had to move props on the set, anticipating Roger's every move as he leaped around the set. The effects technicians were blowing papers and destroying objects that followed Roger's path of destruction. The coordination had to be perfect for the illusion to work. Then everything had to be reset for take two. This is how it was going to go. Slowly. Everyone involved seemed up to the task. There were excellent technicians in every department.

Charlie wore his rabbit suit from the moment he arrived at work until he left. He even wore it to lunch. All of us, cast included, went to lunch in the commissary. I ate with some of the guys in the

Shooting the Rabbit

cafeteria upstairs, but there was a pub downstairs where most of the technicians had a beer with their brat and mingled with technicians on other shows. Hoskins was often found eating with the guys. One day a technician from another movie spotted Charlie walking by in his rabbit costume. He was overheard saying, "Did you see the rabbit from that *Roger Rabbit* show? It looks really stupid. I bet the show is going to be a flop."

PAMELA MANN, our script supervisor, amassed extensive notes from all the departments on the set in order to provide a blueprint for post production. The editing room would have been completely at a loss without her notes. Pamela had done the continuity on both *The Empire Strikes Back* and *Return of the Jedi*, so I was familiar with her continuity scripts, which I had used extensively as an assistant in the editing room. She was well respected, and as far as I was concerned, her work was impeccable. Strangely, even though I had worked with her scripts, I had never met her. Without too much flattery, I told her how wonderful it was to finally meet her and how helpful her scripts had been to us on the *Star Wars* films. We became inseparable. Even though she had worked on some of the biggest effects films of that era, *Roger Rabbit* was a different beast. She had to chart the moves of all the invisible animated characters in every scene.

Script supervision or continuity was a difficult job without toons running around. First and foremost, Pamela had to keep track of the camera: which camera was used in a shot or setup, which lens was on the camera, and a brief description of what the action was. She would "line" the script, detailing exactly where the action of a given shot would start and end. She devised, along with others, a system of how to number each scene and the shots within the scene, and she numbered every setup and take. If a shot had a Panavision camera, it might start with one prefix, whereas if the VistaVision camera was used, it might get another. A specific identifier was used if a cartoon character appeared in the shot. Or if the shot incorporated a blue screen. All of the labels made it easier on everyone, from the editing room down through the effects process, as the film traveled on its path to completion.

Pamela also had to keep track of each camera roll, so if the film needed to be referred to or retrieved, it could easily be done. She did the same with sound. All the sound rolls had a record in her lined script. All this note keeping was just part of the job, which she seemed to do with ease. Normally on an effects film, a production person from the visual-effects department would keep separate notes for every visual-effects shot. Since the cartoon characters were in a good percentage of the film, this fell into Pamela's world. I relied heavily on her work and helped her gather any info I could. Taking on the task of keeping track of the toons added a big layer to her job. Generally, her quick notes taken during shooting were so extensive that she had to stay behind when the crew wrapped in order to clean up what she had written. She could not afford to get behind.

As the work piled up, a full-time second unit was put into place, and Pamela hired an additional continuity person dedicated to that unit. At first, Frank Marshall took the reins as the director of the second unit. Frank had done extensive second-unit directing for Spielberg, like what I had done on *The Mission* on *Amazing Stories*, only on a bigger scale. He had a great relationship with Bob Zemeckis, so it was easy for him to step in and easy for Bob to trust him to do the work. It is very difficult to guess what the director wants in a scene and to shoot it without his supervision. All the scenes that Frank directed had storyboards, which gave a good indication of the shots needed for a scene, but many decisions still had to be made on the day of shooting. Whenever possible, a video feed directly from the second-unit camera was fed to the first unit, so Bob could keep tabs on the setup. Ian Kelly was the video engineer who set up the link between the first and second units. He was extraordinary. Ian's primary responsibility was taking a feed from a video tap on the first-unit camera and sending the image to a playback monitor. Generally, Bob would watch the scene as it unfolded on his own private monitor. In the old days, directors simply paid attention to the performances of the actors and would rely on the camera operator, focus puller, or first assistant cameraman to tell him if he got the shot in the way he had intended. Now the director could watch the video of the actors and the movement of the camera at the same time on his monitor. Since so much relied on getting the correct timing and placement of the cartoon characters in the frame, Bob relied heavily on Ian.

The first, and possibly the most complicated second-unit scene was the piano duet featuring Donald Duck and Daffy Duck playing the *Hungarian Rhapsody* at breakneck speed. The cameras started out rather conventionally, but as the tune continued, the cameras moved wildly in order to keep up with the ducks. The music for the entire duet had been choreographed and prerecorded in advance. One initial difficulty on the set was getting the computer to drive the piano keys in sync with the music to make it appear like the ducks were playing. Like a player-piano roll, the computer controlled the keys on the piano, only this was much more sophisticated, changing speeds as the song went along.

This was the first time I met Alan Silvestri, the composer of the music on the show. Alan would end up being a lifelong friend and collaborator, but these ducks, or at least the pianos they were playing on, had him stumped. The computer just wouldn't tell the keys what to do properly, but Alan was not going to give up. Once he solved the problem, it was a surreal experience to watch the cameras following the invisible ducks as they fought and played with one another. I don't know how everyone kept it all straight.

Putting together a scene like the ducks playing the *Hungarian Rhapsody* proved to be a puzzle for the editor, Artie Schmidt. He would start by using the lined script, storyboards, and music as a guide, but it was still a daunting task. Fortunately, he also had the filmed rehearsal with the puppets to show him the cartoon characters' actions. I had met Artie when I applied for the job as second editor on *Back to the Future*. He did not select me, and he joked that because he didn't hire me, he was responsible for my getting my job as a producer. In a sense, he was right. Becoming a second editor would have certainly changed my job path. I often stopped by the editing room to keep the staff up to speed with what was going on during the shooting. I could also shed light on the action of the toons in a scene that Artie was cutting, since I had often heard or seen what otherwise might not be clear. I also wanted to keep track of the effects scenes that Artie had assembled for the director to look at, so we could put our first shot or scene into the works. It turned out that the first shot that was ready to go was very similar to the test shot that had been done more than a year earlier.

This time, Valiant exits Maroon's office and walks down some exterior stairs that overlooked a courtyard on the back lot of Maroon Studios. He pauses on the landing and looks down on a hubbub of cartoon activity. Valiant heads down the stairs, avoiding a little leaping frog and squeezing past a large elephant who says,

Shooting the Rabbit

"Excuse me!" Bob Zemeckis called me over on the set and said he was happy with the scene to be turned over to animation and post production. Before we did that, though, we needed to find a voice for the cartoon elephant. I have no idea why, but I thought of Mary Radford, Frank Marshall's assistant. She was happy to do it, and Bob said to give it a try. I booked the old recording stage on the lot. I don't think the room had been used in years. After we dusted off the equipment, Mary recorded the line during her lunch break. We did it multiple times and then I brought it to Artie, who cut in his favorite take of Mary's voice recording, and with Bob's approval, the scene was ready to be turned over to all departments.

I called an all-hands-on-deck meeting during our lunch hour with all persons supervising the work on the shot. We intended to review the shot in detail and discuss the process for all shots moving forward. In addition to Artie and Bob, Don Hahn, who headed up the animation division, was there along with the animators chosen for the elephant and the frog. Ken Ralston was also there. I took detailed notes. This was the first page of notes I ended up preparing for every live action/animation shot in the movie. They provided a blueprint for the shot. First I gave the shot a number. This number would follow the shot from the editing room to completion. Then, listening carefully to Bob's description, I summarized the action of the animated characters in the scene (where the characters were throughout the shot, where and when they moved from one place to another) and how they interacted with the set or props (bumped into an object causing it to fall), detailing the emotion of the characters (sadness or happiness). I also noted their expression (smile, frown) and motivation for a look (a bike crashing into a wall causing a head to turn). The animators would carefully use these notes to guide them while animating. In addition to the action, the notes included all the matte enhancements that were required to put the shot together back at ILM. Roto mattes were needed when characters passed behind a live action person or object; shadow mattes were needed to apply shadows to the cartoon characters; special highlight mattes were created for particular lighting requirements. I took the notes quickly and concisely. Nothing could be left to chance.

When the meeting ended, everyone went their separate ways, except for Don Hahn and me. We were both responsible for our end of finishing the show; Don in animation and me in post production and visual effects. Don said we needed a book or guide, something that described the process step-by-step. Everyone needed to know how a shot went from beginning to end, even though we were making it up as we went along.

We knew it started with the live-action shot, or as we called it, the background plate. Shot in VistaVision (an eight-perforation format), the film was sent to the lab, and a four-perf reduction (like normal 35mm film) was made for editing. The editing machines could not handle VistaVision. When the live action was shot, off-screen voice actors performed the parts of the animated characters in real time. If a character's voice actor was not present during shooting, someone, often the script supervisor, would read the line. If the voice or performance of an animated character needed to be changed or replaced, that would be recorded on the ADR stage. Once picture and track were locked and approved, we would call a meeting to describe the shot in detail with everyone present. A photocopy of each frame of the shot was printed out, along with a corresponding audio track. The photocopy or photostat, as we called it, would be delivered to the chosen animator's workstation. The photostat backgrounds were pinned down sequentially, one frame

Shooting the Rabbit

at a time, with the animator's corresponding drawings overlaying each frame of the film exactly. I thought since the frame counts would be coming from the editing room to ILM, this photostat process should be done at ILM. Thousands of individual frames would be printed at ILM on photographic paper and shipped to the animation studio in England. Since the process was beginning, and I had the first shot in hand, I decided it was the right time for me to fly back to Marin and get everyone started.

WHEN I ARRIVED at ILM, *Willow*, the Lucasfilm show, was in full production. We were definitely playing second fiddle. But I had to get everything up and running. With the supervisors gone, I met with the various heads of departments to give them an idea of the train that was roaring down the track toward them. I devised a tracking system with Suella Kennedy, my in-house coordinator, and set up a giant status board so we could visually track each shot at a glance. The number of shots in any given scene would only be finalized when the scene was edited. But the framework could be put in place.

Despite all the unknowns, I had to prepare a new, updated budget. The budget I was handed at the start was not nearly enough. I had explained this to Robert Watts at the outset of the show. Now we needed to get real. I broke the script down as best I could. As I read and reread the scenes, I was now able to make guesstimates of the number of shots and the difficulty of each particular scene. I thought there could be as many as 1,000 shots. As many as *Return of the Jedi*. Huge show. I also now had an idea of what Ken Ralston was going to need in-house to pull off his magic. I met with the animation division supervisor, Wes Takahashi, and laid out the work ahead, estimating the manpower he would need to keep up with a thousand shots in our limited time frame. I also met with the editorial department. They had to organize and keep track of all the elements for every shot from live action and animation, both in the UK and from within ILM. If it bottlenecked on their editing bench, we would get way behind. Most importantly, every shot and all the elements would converge in the optical department, where Ed Jones was in charge.

When he sat down to run through my projection for the show, I finally understood its scale. Only so much film could make it through the printers in the time we had, in order to make the delivery date. The time was finite. We would have a year to finish once we wrapped principal photography. I wondered what the greatest number of shots was that they had ever finalized in a week with all printers dedicated to a single show. I did some digging. Fifty. Fifty shots. What were the average number of takes it took to finalize those shots? I kept breaking it down further and further. The news was not good. We didn't have nearly enough money and barely enough time, even if we controlled ILM. If anything went wrong, I did not know if we could finish on time. After some deep breathing, I left Ed and methodically continued on the budget, throwing in all the information I had gathered in order to be as accurate as possible. So much was unknown, but a more accurate budget was necessary. I figured I would only be able to go to the well one last time, so I had better offer up a budget I could stand behind. I knew that getting the approval for my new budget would mean a major negotiation with the studio. I was finally starting to understand the process and what was needed. The facility had their overhead costs and profit margins to consider. Even though I was attempting to be as thorough and as accurate as possible, this was my first time doing this. I was insecure about standing up to the big boys at the studio and confidently defending what I was asking for.

The production budget allocated $4.4 million to do the visual effects on the show. When other production departments needed more cash, either during the budgeting process or as shooting ramped up, I am sure the effects budget was cut, and the money was moved to those that needed it. The guys up last in the process always get the short end of the stick. I came up with $7.7 million as my new budget. I met with Warren, the head of ILM at the time and laid it out for him. He panicked. Of course, he had blessed the original budget. He was close to Robert Watts and wanted to call him up and deliver the bad news. He couldn't go into a show that far underbudgeted. I said to wait. Let production finish shooting. I had been with the shooting company in London, and I knew they would be in no mood to hear this news. And, by the way, what could Robert do? Disney was not about to write a check to ILM when they were bleeding money during the shooting of the movie. I consoled Warren by telling him that we really would not be spending much of ILM's money until we wrapped principal photography, and we got scenes cut and locked and into the pipeline. Let's wait until after they wrap. Then we can drop the bomb. He understood and decided to wait. I had discovered that getting what you wish for is always a matter of timing.

With a new budget and better understanding from inside the facility for what was needed to finish the show, I headed back to London. I now knew where all the money would be spent, what the work flow would be, and the time needed to finish. We had put our first shot into the works, the departments were prepped, and we were under way.

SINCE I HAD no idea when I would return to London, I had given up my service flat in Swiss Cottage. As luck would have it, Mary Radford had arranged for me to rent the upstairs flat in her place. The house was owned by the actor Jeremy Irons. He was not working in town at the time and said he would be willing to rent to us. The flat was beautifully located on Well Walk in Hampstead, just a few steps down from The Wells Tavern. After entering the front door from the street, we climbed a rather steep set of stairs to the first floor. The entry led to a large sitting room. The back window looked out on a series of gardens hidden from the road. Old stone walls surrounded each garden, and we could see into all of them from our upstairs perch. Trees were beginning to leaf out, and early spring flowers were starting to appear. The place had multiple bedrooms, more than we needed. In fact, there was more space in the flat than in any home we had ever lived in.

Each day I left the tranquility of our new flat and immersed myself in the intensity of the production. Shooting was now going around the clock with two full crews trying to complete the work in the Acme Factory. Everyone was exhausted. Both Ken Ralston and Scott Farrar were up to their ears, one working days, the other at night, and had little time to give to the work in California. Despite the fact the shooting was overwhelming everyone, I knew I had to start the ball rolling in post production. We had less time than anyone could imagine, and the workload was increasing by the day. The hair-raising estimate that underpinned my new budget was not inflated.

While meeting with Ed Jones during my recent visit to ILM, we determined that an early color timed print would be required for every scene that contained an animated character. This would have to be done before any optical compositing work could begin. Normally, the color timing is done when the negative is cut, and the film goes into the lab to prepare for release printing. In this case, since the cartoon characters would be added into hundreds of shots, their color would be altered as the color of the backgrounds were subtly changed to match one another. If a bit of blue was needed to make a shot look the same as the shot before it or after it, the color of the white rabbit would change along with the background. We would wind up with perfectly matching backgrounds and a white rabbit shifting from red to blue from one shot to another. I cornered Dean Cundey and asked if he would accompany me to the lab and try to make a sample timed print for each scene containing a cartoon character. I could start the process with the timer at the lab, then he could make his adjustments, and I could use that approved print as a starting point. He understood the logic and agreed.

I went to the editing room and sat down and picked a take that the editor was not using for each of the designated scenes and took down the scene and take number and sent it to the lab for printing. This was another time that my stint in the editing room came in handy. The editing room did not need another task at this time, but I had done the color timing for *Star Wars* and *Amazing Stories*, so it came easily to me. In fact, Dean had little to say about the look of the scenes, most likely because he was so busy. I ended up providing the timed clips, called wedges, to Ed Jones for all the scenes we needed.

Another set of scenes was ready to be turned over to animation. I pulled together a turnover meeting, and Don Hahn brought along the animators that Richard Williams, the animation director, had chosen to do the work. Richard was brilliant in choosing the appropriate artist for each character. The more you got to know the animators, the more you realized how a specific artist was suited to draw one character or another. Simon Wells became the Roger animator. Roger could be wild and crazy or sensitive, often in the same scene, but drawing Roger appeared easy in Simon's hands. Some of the best artists from Disney were brought over to London for the show. Among them were Andreas Deja and Phil Nibbelink. At the first large gathering, artists were assigned characters for the scene. Often multiple artists worked on different characters in the same shot or scene.

In the middle of reviewing one such shot Phil stopped us and blurted out, "Why did you shoot it that way? This was plainly pointed at Bob, who was so surprised by the comment he simply asked, "What do you mean?" The question was audacious, and we were all stunned into silence. Phil was criticizing Bob Zemeckis's direction. Phil went on to ask why Bob had put the camera where he had put it and why it was moving the way it did, following the character. Phil complained that the camera did not give him the room he needed to do his animation. Phil was used to doing his animation with a blank sheet of paper, with no boundaries limiting his freedom. Here he had to have his characters follow the path that the camera told him to follow, to move his character to a specific place at a specific time, finally speaking the dialogue where the camera told him the character was standing. Phil basically had a meltdown. He said he couldn't do it. He did not know how to back in his work to what was dictated to him by the shot.

Bob looked at him equally confused. Bob said he thought the beauty of animating cartoon characters was that they could squash and stretch and flow wherever the artist wanted them to go, so in that way he had unlimited freedom. Phil could not see it, at least, not that day, not that time. His mood put a pall on the meeting.

The other animators embraced the challenge. Soon enough Phil stepped up to the challenge as well, and he became one of the most prolific animators on the show. But it was our first indication that these animators were like actors. We would have to hold their hands. They also needed help with the motivation and guidance for the character's emotions. We had a lot of work to do in these turnover sessions beyond simple descriptions. I was going to be busy with my note taking.

MARY RADFORD cornered me and said that Jeremy Irons had called and said that he was going to be in a play in London soon and needed to stay in his flat. I freaked out. The show was going over schedule, and I would have to move. Mary mentioned that to Jeremy. He said he did not mind sharing the flat with us if we were OK with it. Liv and I were fine. Either that or move for a month. There was plenty of room. Jeremy primarily worked at night, and I worked in the day, so we rarely crossed paths. Liv, on the other hand, was often around when he emerged from his bedroom for his morning cup of coffee. He was a pleasant guy, so it was fine, except that he smoked. One particular day a fan showed up at the door to the flat. Liv answered it for Jeremy. This fan was a bit of a stalker, so Liv had to deal with her at the door and agree to pass along a note to Jeremy while Jeremy was hiding in the background.

We took advantage of the fact that Jeremy was performing in town and went to see him in *Richard II*. He was great! We tried to attend the theater as often as possible. Frank and Kathy took us to see a Jeffrey Archer play one night. Frank had had a friendship with Jeffrey over the years. He and Kathy had many friends in and around London since they had been working there quite often on the *Raiders* movies. During the intermission, Frank saw Sir John Mills, the esteemed acter, and said we should say hello to him. He was standing in one of the archways leading from the theater to the lobby. Frank said hello to Sir John and turned to me and said, "I would like to introduce you to the associate producer on my show, Steve Starkey." I shook the actor's hand graciously, not blushing at the job title Frank had bestowed upon me. I was not hired as the associate producer, but Frank had just anointed me. I felt proud and extremely grateful that Frank had recognized the work I was doing. I was going to be an associate producer on a major motion picture. It felt good.

With principal photography nearly completed, our first finished shot for the show arrived: Eddie Valiant walking down the steps outside Maroon's office. Ken gave me permission to show the shot at dailies. The dailies room seemed more crowded than usual. Ken thought it could be better, but Ken always thought that. Let it roll. The gang at dailies clapped. They loved it. They wanted to see it again and again. We now could glimpse what we had on our hands. The shot was pure magic. If the show could look like this, it would be a beautiful film to behold. Word got around to those who were not in dailies, and I ended up showing the shot over and over again. To this tired bunch of hard-working souls on the film, it was a great morale booster. All their efforts were going to pay off. Now we had to go back home and finish the film. Suddenly the year we had left to finish the movie seemed like no time at all.

CHAPTER 12

Bringing the Rabbit to Life

WHEN PRINCIPAL photograpy finally wrapped and I flew back from England, I had not thought about where I would be spending my time over the next year. In the Bay Area, hunkered down at ILM? Or in LA, where the editing room was based? The work would control my destiny. It always did. I knew that the editing room at Amblin in Burbank was where everything started. It was the center of the nervous system that controlled the show. I had been there in the *Star Wars* days. I also knew I had to be careful not to let ILM's pressing needs govern the flow of work. It was my job to figure out how to blend the needs of both the editing room and ILM to the best advantage of the movie. Since I oversaw both, I was in a unique position to do that.

In a perfect world, a show like *Roger Rabbit* would be edited before any animation or visual-effects work began. That way, you would know exactly what your workload was, and you could schedule things in an efficient way that satisfied everyone's needs. In the real world, the work needs to start on shots and scenes while the picture is still getting edited and the scenes are works in progress. They could end up longer or shorter or cut out of the movie entirely. You wouldn't know until the whole movie was cut. If you waited for the final cut to begin work, however, you would never make the deadline. So there we were.

Between a rock and a hard place.

My flight took me back to the Bay Area, so my first stop would be at ILM. If I only had known how many journeys I would be taking on the show. . . I met with Ken Ralston to try to determine which sequence he preferred to sink his teeth into to get the work flow started. I figured that if I could create some order to the delivery of sequences that suited the pipeline at ILM, I might be able to push that same schedule on the editing room. I knew that the cutting room would be editing in continuity from the beginning. I would start with that.

Of course, I also needed to factor in the schedule of the animation. The few shots we already had under way contained unique characters that only appeared in one or two scenes: for example, Donald and Daffy Duck and the toons that Valiant saw looking down to the courtyard of Maroon Studios. These bit parts would only last so long. The pipeline needed more work in a hurry. The main characters had to come into play. I spoke to Don Hahn. Some of these—notably Jessica and the Weasels—were not ready for animation yet. Their designs had not been finalized. But Don agreed to send a list of the scenes he could get started on. Roger was ready to go. We needed to stack up scenes that featured Roger. That shouldn't be a problem since he was in almost every scene. The opening cartoon featured Roger and Baby Herman, and that would keep the facility going temporarily. But the animation facility was growing by the day and needed work to keep the animators busy. I really needed to get into the editing room, see how the cut was going, and figure out a schedule that worked for everyone. I needed to start lighting some fires.

Bringing the Rabbit to Life

BEFORE HEADING DOWN to LA, I had to figure out where to live. I called Frank and asked if the Marina del Rey apartment, the one I used on the documentary, might be available for my visits. Since I didn't know how often I'd be there, and the place was familiar, I thought it would suit me perfectly. He checked with Spielberg, and I was given the OK. At least I would not have to worry about booking a hotel for each LA visit, and I would be saving money. I had budgeted an allowance for my plane flights, a hotel, car rentals, and per diem, but I didn't want to abuse the expense account. Flying from Oakland to Burbank was easy. It was a 12-minute ride from the airport to Amblin. Once again, I had my Burbank-to-Oakland routine. I started to know the flight attendants and the women at the Avis counter. In Oakland I always parked my car at the same place in long-term parking, so I never had to remember where I left it. After my return flights, I often ate at the Chez Panisse Café in Berkeley, particularly if Liv was with me. We frequented the café so often that the maître d', Steve, put us in his little red book of preferred clients. I could call from the Burbank airport as I was about to take off on my evening flight north, and he would have a table ready for us when we arrived. In LA, since I was often alone in the evening, I would eat at various restaurants that had counter service. I became a regular at the counter at Chianti Cucina in Hollywood and the West Beach Café in Venice. I considered writing a food article called "Counter-Culture: The Best Restaurant Counters in LA."

The editing rooms were across the street from the main Amblin building where I had cut the documentary on *Indiana Jones*. It was just down the hill from my office on *Amazing Stories*. It was astonishing to me that ever since I left Lucasfilm, all my work in LA was at Universal Studios, centered around the Amblin complex. As

I started each new job and progressed in my career, I was comforted by familiar surroundings and had a wonderful support group. Frank Marshall was a short walk away, and he was still involved in the project, even though he had other Amblin projects to oversee. Bonnie Radford was still head of the accounting division, so I could go to her for help if I had budget questions. Marty Cohen was the new head of post production at Amblin. He would provide a good buffer between the show and Disney. He had also spent time in the editing room, so we hit it off immediately.

When I opened the doors to the *Roger Rabbit* editing rooms, I felt at ease. There was an empty room next to Artie Schmidt's editing suite, so after a quick hello to Bob Zemeckis and Artie, I sat down in there, closed the door, and started to make my phone calls. I never did get a real office. The editing room was where my work was and where the answers to all my questions were. There was no better place to be. I used an editing bench for a desk. I took away the splicer and synchronizer, set a phone and a legal pad in front of me, and went to work. There was even a KEM Junior, the flatbed editing machine I was familiar with from the old *Star Wars* days. I could review dailies or watch footage by myself without bothering anyone. In a word, it was perfect. Since I had Suella and a production assistant at ILM, I had not considered who would answer the phones or follow through on my work while in LA. I got used to doing that myself. I felt bad that the assistant editors often took down phone messages for me when I was out, but they did not seem to mind.

Artie and Bob were still in the middle of the director's cut, but we needed to get more scenes into the pipeline for the animators and ILM. In preparation for our first animation turnover, we evaluated the dialogue in each scene in case any lines needed to be improved upon or replaced. That had to be finalized before the animation work could begin. I would line up time in the ADR room at 20th Century-Fox. Charleen Richards was our ADR engineer. She had worked tirelessly with me on *Amazing Stories*, when she was at Sam Goldwyn Studios, and I knew her working style. I always had more loyalty to the artist or technicians than I had for a facility. When she moved to Fox, I followed. Usually, when we had an ADR session, I called in the writers, Jeff Price and Peter Seaman. They had worked for years getting the script to where it was. They were not about to let any detail go now. The sessions with Bob, Jeff, Peter, and Charlie Fleischer (Roger Rabbit) were like being at a Comedy Club improv. I was laughing so hard it was difficult to keep the recording sessions on track. In between the laughs, though, we always improved the dialogue.

ARMED WITH COPIES of the scenes to be turned over, Bob and I made the first of a dozen trips to London. Ken Ralston flew from San Francisco to meet us. The first trip involved a tour of the animation facility in Camden Town. The place was filling up fast; animators, in-betweeners, the ink-and-paint department, and the animation cameraman were all busy. The director of animation, Richard Williams, was a joy to behold. He was in awe of Bob's directing and could not have been more excited to greet us. He was shy yet bubbly. Socially uncomfortable, he was happier to be working or showing his work than chitchatting.

I had met him a few times during production. The first time was at his studio in Soho Square. Creaky, steep, wooden stairs led up to his drawing studio. A real artist's studio. He was busy at work on his lifelong passion project, an animated film called *The Thief and the Cobbler*. He loved sharing his work in progress with any artists that came around, including Bob and me. The other time I met Richard was at the Britannia Hotel on Grosvenor Square, where his Dixieland band was playing. He had as much passion for music as he had for animation.

We asked Richard how the Jessica designs were going and revisited the inspiration for her character, all from famous actresses of yesteryear: Rita Hayworth, Veronica Lake, Lauren Bacall. He said that his Jessica designer, Russell Hall, was one of the best animators around, but he had gone AWOL. He couldn't crack Jessica's design, so he simply vanished. No one had heard from him. Maybe creating the ultimate femme fatale was too much for him. "What are you going to do?" "We wait. He is the best artist for the job." As it turned out, it was the right decision. Russell's design of Jessica was inspired—not just her looks. Her walk and her gravity-defying breasts added to her mysterious sexuality.

At the Camden animation facility we gathered around a KEM editing machine, and as each scene was threaded up, the animators who were assigned to each character joined us. I got out my notepad, trying to keep up with Bob as he walked through every detail of the action in the frame. Ken outlined what shadows, highlights, and tone mattes would be needed for each shot. At lunch, I often found myself downstairs in the quiet of the conference room. I set up chairs side by side to form a couch and quickly fell asleep for as much time as I could. I preferred sleep over food and conversation. These transatlantic trips were so short that jet lag persisted until I flew home, at which time I returned to California time immediately. When I got on the flight home, I usually spent the first hour or two rewriting my notes so they could be typed up for distribution upon my return. Then I passed out.

Bringing the Rabbit to Life

WHEN THE PLANE landed at LAX, I usually went straight to the editing room. Every trip seemed to create new cutting priorities for Bob and Artie. Even though we were focusing on getting the first cut of the film into shape, we still had to feed the beast. ILM and animation needed more cut scenes even though it was disruptive to the editing. The truth is we needed both: cut scenes to keep moving forward and the full movie cut so we had a sense of what the final workload was going to look like for both animation and ILM. All we could do was edit, record voices, turn over, review animation. Edit, record voices, turn over, review animation; rinse and repeat.

As Bob started to edit the scenes with the Weasels, they were proving to be too unwieldy. Too many Weasels. Originally modeled on *Snow White and the Seven Dwarfs*, there were going to be seven Weasels. But the scenes in both the Acme factory and Valiant's office couldn't handle that many, so Bob cut them down to five. In addition, each Weasel needed defining characteristics and a distinctive look. Richard Williams flew over from London. We showed him a bit of the cut and told him we needed the Weasel designs immediately. He asked for an office he could work in. I took him down the hall to the lunchroom. With sheets of paper and Sharpies, Richard designed the Weasels in one afternoon. He called us to take a look. The drawings were all pinned up on a corkboard. Each character had multiple poses, from the front and the sides, colorfully distinct costumes, and character traits so you could easily tell them apart. I was stunned. In just a matter of hours, left alone with pens, paper, and his own imagination, Richard had come up with five Weasels. That was it. They were done. The next step would be to find voices for each character. Who would be Smart Ass, Stupid, Wheezy, Greasy, and Psycho?

STEVE STARKEY

Thus far in my filmmaking experiences, I had not been involved in the casting process at all. I was stuck in the editing room. On *Amazing Stories*, I first saw or met the actors when I viewed dailies on film. I occasionally said hello to the actors on the set during filming but really met them for the first time during ADR. On *Roger Rabbit*, the live-action actors had been cast before my work even began. Now, in post production, we were casting voice performers for many of the cartoon characters that only had temporary voices up until now. Some of the characters' voice performers had been selected before shooting began, like Charlie Fleischer for the role of Roger Rabbit, Lou Hirsch for Baby Herman, and Lou Rawls for Benny the Car (who was later replaced). Now I got to work with the casting director, Reuben Cannon, to fill the remaining roles, although ideas came from everyone. Bob Zemeckis wanted the toon Bullets to have the iconic voices of his Western heroes. We got Pat Buttram to come into the studio. Bob also wanted an Andy Devine soundalike, so we got Jim Cummings to imitate him. We also hired Jim Gallant, who could imitate Walter Brennan. Richard Williams said he could do the voice of Droopy, the elevator operator in Toontown. He wanted the voice to be monotone and flat. No inflection at all. He was perfect.

Don Hahn gave us the names of the voice performers for the Disney cartoon characters and provided alternates if the original voice actors were deceased or unavailable. The studio was very protective when it came to which performers could do a Disney character's voice in a film. They had a stable of voices that included Wayne Allwine for Mickey Mouse and Tony Anselmo for Donald Duck.

We tracked down Mae Questel to do the voice of Betty Boop. She had voiced the original Betty, and when she walked in the door, I thought Betty had come to life. She was as short and petite as

Betty was and had that same wink in her eye. There is nothing like having the original performer step into the role and add that unique something that brings the character to life.

The greatest thrill was having Mel Blanc come onto the stage to do all his classic Warner Bros. characters: Daffy Duck, Tweety Bird, Bugs Bunny, Sylvester, and, at the end of the film, Porky Pig. Mel was accompanied by his son, Noel, who held his arm and guided him into the room and up to the microphone. Once there, Mel's voices all came back to him. As he went from one voice to the next, you could hear all the characters, just as I remembered them from my childhood. Mel died a year after the film was released.

But what about those Weasels? Who would those characters be? We set up an ADR session and had an audition party. Bob Zemeckis had the idea of having David Lander come in for the voice of Smart Ass. He remembered him as Squiggy in the sitcom *Laverne and Shirley*. David's whining, New York-accented voice made him the perfect leader of the pack. The other roles were up for grabs. I brought in Fred Newman, who had voiced an alien in one of my *Amazing Story* episodes. He ended up doing the voice of Stupid. On the same day we brought in June Foray to do the role of Lena Hyena, a haglike toon who screeches, "a maaan," as she reaches to grab Valiant. We loved what she did in that small part, so we asked her if she would mind giving a shot at Wheezy, the Weasel with the smoker's cough. She ended up doing that part in the film, too. Charlie Fleischer was at the audition and if we had given him the chance, he would have loved to play all the Weasels. He gave most of them a shot. Charlie found a slimy voice for Greasy and a psychotic cackle for Psycho that won us over. He got both parts. The Weasels were cast.

Another character still lacked the energy and attitude that we needed. Benny the Car. After the other actors had gone for the day, Charlie stepped up to the mike. Instead of the cool cat we had planned on, Charlie started playing around with different personas. At one point, Benny became more belligerent, confrontational, and short-tempered, like a New York cabbie. He yelled out at all the other drivers like he owned the road. And he loved those Brooklyn Dodgers. That clinched it. The writers and Bob were convinced. Jeff and Peter had to rewrite the dialogue to suit the new character, but Benny the Car became Benny the Cab.

One last character, a most important character, still needed to be resolved: Jessica Rabbit. We gave consideration to a number of actresses, but Bob knew all along who it should be—Kathleen Turner. He just did not know how to go about getting her to do the job. Bob and Kathleen had not spoken to one another since they parted ways on *Romancing the Stone*. Nevertheless Bob said she was perfect for Jessica. Sultry and able to deliver the lines with the right irony. No one else would be able to match her. A group of us convinced Bob to call Kathleen. He finally did, and she agreed to voice the part. Bob and I flew to Baltimore, where Kathleen was working on *The Accidental Tourist*. During her lunch break, we waited outside her motor home until she was ready. The production sound mixer showed up with a Nagra portable audio recorder, and we stepped inside and quickly got a reading of every line. The drama was over. Jessica was born.

NOW THAT WE HAD the voices for most of the characters in the film, we could shape up the film for a director's screening. As the picture progressed from scene to scene and reel to reel, the images became cruder and cruder. A few finished cartoon characters were filtered in with the live action at the beginning of the film, but as the movie went on, you really had to use your imagination to follow the story and action. The voices were often laid in over sketches from the animation studio, and finally, toward the end of the film, the only visuals were storyboards that moved like the old flip cartoons we made as kids. Unless you were very familiar with the script and the material, the picture was incredibly difficult to judge. But that was how it had to be in order to screen the picture.

As we approached our deadline for the screening, there were an enormous number of sound effects and temp voices to cut in, especially in the Toontown sequence. I offered to lend a hand. I put on my old assistant editor hat and spent the day cutting in sound effects. I enjoyed the work and loved the fact I could help out. When we marched over to the Amblin screening room, we were all pretty exhausted but excited to have the first pass at the film done. There was a lot to chew on, but the film was taking shape. This milestone in the process helped us understand and prioritize the work ahead. Bob would walk in each day and say, "What do you want me to do now?" He was serious. There was so much work to be done, someone had to tell him what to do each morning. That someone was me.

With storyboards for the Toontown sequence edited into the cut of the film, we were ready to prep the blue-screen shoot at ILM, which involved Valiant running around in a cartoon world. He would drive in a car, fall off a building, ride up a terrifying elevator, and much more. Each shot required a unique blue-screen setup. The director's-cut screening had also revealed a few areas of the film that needed clarification. It seemed logical to complete the additional live-action scenes along with the blue-screen shoot since the crew would be in place.

Robert Watts was in LA to do a bit of early work for the next *Indiana Jones* film. He and I flew up to Northern California together to prep both the live-action and blue-screen shoots. I looked forward to spending time with Robert. I truly respected him and wished I could inherit even a small amount of his precious knowledge of film production. Heading to the airport, I could see I was making Robert nervous. I had taken dozens and dozens of flights from Burbank to Oakland and always showed up at the last minute. Robert liked to show up early, as if he were flying overseas. He was also dreading the live-action shoot. He said he was out of money. I said, depending on the cost, I could probably cover it with my allowance for the blue-screen shoot in the ILM budget. I asked how much he needed. He got out a budget template and said he would do the budget on the flight. As I watched him enter some numbers, I told him I had never done a live-action budget. I had budgeted post production and visual effects, but not live action. He handed the template to me and said to give it a go.

Department by department I thought through the prep, shoot, and wrap needed for each of the crew members and entered in the numbers. He corrected me as we went along, but I got it. The thought process was similar to the budget I prepared for the blue-screen shoot. For example, in my blue-screen budget there were no location fees or set dressing, just a stage rental, rudimentary sets, and a blue screen. I would need to make an allowance in the budget for going on location. Background or extras were not needed in my budget, although they would be for the additional live-action scenes. I looked at what was required as logically as I could and caught on quickly. I felt relieved to get through my first budget, small as it was. And the good news was I could cover the costs with the ILM money. I was Robert's hero.

Bringing the Rabbit to Life

When I approached the blue-screen stage at ILM, I saw a big-rig trailer backed up to the stage door. Dolly track had been laid down from inside the stage to the back of the truck bed. Close to 70 feet of track. The shot started close on Valiant, then the dolly grips pushed the camera away from Valiant as quickly as they could until they reached the end of the truck bed. When the shot was reverse printed, it would seem like Valiant was falling toward the camera. In the next shot, Valiant parachuted into a scene with Bugs Bunny and Tweety Bird, done with Hoskins hanging on wires. Then we reset again for Valiant falling to the ground, standing up, and walking away. That is how the blue-screen shoot went. One setup after another. Ken Ralston had all of them laid out on the stage so we could quickly go from one shot to the next.

When we wrapped, Liv and I had Bob Hoskins over for dinner in our Fairfax house. His stand-in, Sammy Pasha, came along as his driver and our guest. During dinner I asked Bob and Sammy to converse a bit in Cockney rhyming slang. I had heard that they both knew how to speak it. "Apples and pears" meant "stairs," for example. I also loved hearing the story of how Bob got into acting by showing up at a buddy's audition. Thinking that acting looked easy, Hoskins asked if he could give it a try. He got the part. After we'd finished a few bottles of red wine, Bob finally took off with a sober Sammy driving.

NOW THAT THE DUST had settled, and Robert Watts had a handle on his overages during shooting, it was time to present my estimated final budget for completion of the the visual-effects work. I gave my $7.7 million number to Robert to add into his budget. Don Hahn submitted new numbers as well, since he now had a bet-

STEVE STARKEY

ter picture of what it would take to finish the animation (although that would prove to be underestimated). Spielberg, as executive producer, would be the one to submit the new number to Disney. The original budget on the film had been just shy of $40 million. When Steven told Jeffrey Katzenberg or Michael Eisner that the new budget was coming in soon, they said that they hoped they wouldn't see a 4 in front of the new number. They wanted it lower. Steven reassured them they would never see a 4. He was right. The next budget soared past $50 million. That's when all hell broke loose. The shock waves could be felt from Burbank to Marin County and London. The magnifying glasses came out; all costs were now going to be scrutinized in the Disney way.

Robert escaped most of the initial scrutiny, since his numbers reflected costs to date. He had spent his money. I hadn't. My costs were projections. I was called to the carpet. Jeffrey Katzenberg, the Walt Disney studio chief, announced that he was coming up to ILM to review how I was planning to spend every cent in my budget. I was ready. I felt my budget was real. All excesses were relatively invisible. Jeffrey brought quite an entourage. Marty Katz, the head of production. Sandra Rabins, the production head of finance. Art Repola, the new head of post production, whom I knew from Amblin. And a few others. I went through the process, step by step, from when we made photostats of the shots in the cut, through editorial, animation, and, finally, the optical process. We also had the final costs for the Toontown blue-screen shoot. After I defended my schedule and budget, Jeffrey left. Good news came out of my dog-and-pony show. He called, which he had never done before, and blessed my approach and budget. He said to expect daily or weekly calls from him asking exactly how we were doing.

Jeffrey was famous for these calls. He expected you to be there

Bringing the Rabbit to Life

24/7. As he famously said in his widely published memo to Disney employees, "If you don't come in on Saturday, don't bother coming in on Sunday." He lived for his work, and he expected you to do the same.

I now had a similar budget review for post production. That was simpler. I met with Art Repola who analyzed the numbers and gave it his blessing. The other bit of good news was that once that I had proven to Jeffrey that my approach and numbers were solid, he was behind me. And you could have no better ally on a film than Jeffrey Katzenberg. I bumped into Spielberg at Amblin, and he told me he heard that Disney had put me under the microscope, both for heading up visual effects and post production. He warned me that I was walking a fine line by wearing two hats. Imagine you are a soldier, he said, walking across the middle of a battlefield waving a flag for truce during the Civil War. You have Confederate flag markings on one side of the flag facing the south and Union flag markings on the other side facing north. The flag feels heavy. You hold your breath as you walk. All the soldiers hold their fire. All seems well. Then suddenly, the wind changes direction. . . Steven's parable put me on alert.

Bob Zemeckis was happy I made it through this milestone on the film. It freed him up from scrutiny. He realized that Disney would target the cut of the film next, knowing that the only true way to cut the budget was to cut down the film. We left for another turnover trip to London. On my first few visits, I had stayed at the St. James's Club, around the corner from the Ritz. Bob loved the place. I could never see why. I moved to the Meridien Club, farther down Piccadilly. Just up from the St. James's Club was a wonderful, small restaurant, Le Caprice, where I was always greeted at the door by the very affable host. I went multiple times on every trip to London. Just inside the door, a jazz pianist played just the right tunes to keep the place warm and lively. I would settle in for some steak tartare and frites or the thinly sliced, grilled chicken with mashed potatoes and spinach. I also loved the mushy peas.

On this particular night, I told Bob we should venture to Soho and try another favorite restaurant of mine. On the way back to our hotels, walking up Piccadilly, a bit of rain started to fall, and we both put up our umbrellas. The breeze intensified and blew each of our umbrellas straight up, inside out. We folded them up and bent our heads into the wind and rain. That night, October 15, 1987, a violent extratropical cyclone blew into London. My room was situated in one of the turrets of the hotel, and throughout the night the shutters kept banging, waking me up repeatedly. I finally gave up sleeping and called room service for breakfast. "Excuse me, Sir, but you may not be aware of the fact that room service will not be available to our guests this morning. We have had a major cyclone, and our kitchen staff has been unable to get to work." Those English, always apologetic and understated. I quickly got dressed and decided to take a walk. There were no cars on Piccadilly. It looked like the day after the apocalypse. I continued a little farther and looked out onto Green Park. Trees had been felled throughout the park. I could not imagine the force of the winds that toppled these seemingly indestructible, old trees. I wandered the streets, waiting to hear if the roads to the animation facility in Camden were even open. It took a few extra days until the animation staff could get to the facility and we could finish our work. It seemed like the freak storm was an omen of what was to come.

Bringing the Rabbit to Life

IT TURNED OUT that the winds of change were not only on the film but also at home. I received a call from Liv that her daughter had just phoned and wanted to meet her. This was a daughter that Liv had given up for adoption at birth, soon after she arrived in San Francisco in the late '60s. Discovering she was pregnant, Liv had fled Dubuque, Iowa, fearing the reaction to her unwanted pregnancy. Liv had told me about the baby, and we had listed our names in a directory for adopted children who might want to track down their birth parents. This directory was not how Inge Rempel, Liv's daughter, found us, however. Inge's best friend worked for a private investigator, and she had access to information that led to Liv's whereabouts. I heard this news with shock, joy, and fear. Nineteen years of silence had been broken. I couldn't wait to hear how the meeting went. I was happy for Liv and for us that she would be coming into our life, despite the unknowns. We already thought we had complicated lives. It was nothing compared to what lay ahead.

Liv told me that Inge's friend would drive her up to Marin, where she had agreed to meet them for lunch. When she saw the two girls for the first time, she had to look at each one closely to figure out which one was her daughter. We were fortunate that Inge turned out be a lovely girl, if perhaps a bit spoiled by her adoptive parents, who were older than we were, both in age and spirit. We seemed young by comparison. Inge liked that. She was ready to move in with us. That was not appropriate, both because we did not know anything about her and out of respect for the parents who had raised her. I do not think that Inge had mentioned to her parents what she was up to when she drove to Marin to meet Liv. I don't know when she did let them know. I am sure she had a teenager's excuse for why she was going out of town so often on the weekends.

Since I usually started and ended my week at ILM in Northern California, and the weekend visits from Inge became more and more frequent, we were able to spend more time together, and I began to feel comfortable having her around.

AT THE SAME time, shots were pouring in at ILM. I enjoyed watching the dailies, no matter how early in their development. It was relaxing and gave me a shot in the arm. On my birthday Ken gave me permission to "final" shots. That day I finaled almost every shot at dailies, partly because I failed to see their problems or room for improvement, but also because I was given that birthday honor. After I left the room, Ken unfinaled many of them. *Roger Rabbit* dailies were becoming quite popular at the facility. Even workers from other shows who never went to dailies on their own show would crowd in for some laughs. What wasn't funny was wondering how we would get the work done.

Suddenly, the winds of change turned into a tornado. Jeffrey Katzenberg called an emergency meeting. He wanted everyone to assemble in New York to discuss the movie going forward. After receiving the budget, he had started having doubts about the show. I was in Northern California at ILM when I got the message. Ken and I were instructed to fly to Burbank, where a car would meet us and take us to the Disney plane. Bob Zemeckis was there to meet us. Frank Marshall was there. The new head of Disney animation, Peter Schneider, was there waiting for Jeffrey on the tarmac in deference to his boss. Jeffrey finally showed up and briefly apologized for arriving late. He explained that his son had fallen off a jungle gym and hit his head. The boy was safely off to the hospital, so we could board the plane and go. Jeffrey set the tone. Nothing would stop him, not even his injured son, from moving ahead with the business at hand. Bob whispered to me, "Sharpen your finger. There's going to be a lot of finger-pointing."

The reason Jeffrey chose New York for the meeting was that Don Hahn, Richard Williams, and Robert Watts were scheduled to fly in from London and meet us there. We all congregated in a conference room at Disney's New York offices. Jeffrey presided. He began the meeting discussing animation. Were they meeting their schedule and were they still on budget? Don Hahn spoke on behalf of the animation studio, saying he thought they were a bit behind. Richard chimed in that the animators were hitting their stride and would make up for lost time. Jeffrey suggested that they work on the weekends. Don said they couldn't afford to pay them for weekend work. Jeffrey responded saying they should work for free. Don looked at Jeffrey and said they were already pouring their guts into the work, and he couldn't ask them to do that. Jeffrey suggested that he promise them another film to go to on the heels of *Roger* to entice them to donate their weekend work. Peter piped up and said, Jeffrey, you know as well as I do that we do not have another animated film ready to dangle in front of the animators. Jeffrey got serious. He focused on Peter and said if you can't have another animated film ready to go when *Roger* is finished, you are not fit for your job! Jeffrey was willing to sacrifice his own.

We all took a break and wandered the halls, catching our breath. I bumped into Richard Williams who said, "If I'm going to have someone slit my throat, I would rather it be with a sharp blade than a blunt stick." When we returned to the meeting, Jeffrey took out the sharp blade. He continued around the table. He asked Robert Watts how the prep was going for some additional shooting we were planning on. Robert mumbled that he was up to his ears in prep on the next *Indiana Jones* movie… Before he could finish what he was saying, Jeffrey said to Robert, "You are now off the picture. Frank, you are now the producer of the film." I squirmed a bit in my seat. The first throat slit. So that is how it was going to go. When it came to me, little was said. Jeffrey and I spoke regularly, so he knew how I was doing. But for show, he asked anyway. I said we were still moving forward on schedule and on budget. Jeffrey made his point clear. Time to tighten up and get the work done. Shook up, the group parted ways.

Bob Zemeckis and I flew straight to London on the Concorde for the next turnover. As I watched the sun quickly set, I wondered what would happen next. Everything seemed so volatile with Jeffrey micromanaging. The next morning, I woke up to a phone call from Peter Schneider. He said animation was not going to make the deadline. He had looked at the numbers. They didn't add up. He evaluated the output of each animator and extended it to the end of the schedule. There was not enough time or manpower to make it. Despite what Richard Williams and Don Hahn had hoped for, there was no reason to believe that the output for each person would increase enough to change the math. Either the minutes of animation on screen had to come down, or we needed help from outside the facility. With that on my mind, I headed to the animation studio for the turnover. The word was out when I got there. The decision was demoralizing, but we had to move forward. Richard and Don were finally convinced of Peter's assessment. We needed outside help.

We put our minds together. What stand-alone sequence could be farmed out to another company and not feel different from the rest of the work? It was decided that the Benny the Cab sequence was a lot of work and might just add up to the number of minutes needed to get us to the finish line. Next Don and Richard needed to find a supervising animator who had his own facility that lived up to Richard's animation standards. This person had to be available and able to get the work done. It took time to sort out, but they settled on Dale Baer. Dale was very well respected, and they thought, with Richard's oversight, he could manage the work flow. After reviewing the work, Bob trusted Richard's decision, and we moved forward. The good news for Bob was that his film was not going to get butchered or shortened due to the sudden inability to finish on time. What this meant for ILM, though, was that more work than we originally thought would be arriving later in the schedule. The animation would be coming from two facilities instead of one and crashing into the optical department during the final weeks of the schedule. It was going to be hairy. I knew the greatest number of shots that could be done on a weekly basis at ILM, something I had researched early on. Now those limits would be tested.

With the film nearly locked, in a shape we all thought would undergo few changes, we were ready to record the music. In order to save money, we went to London and recorded at Group IV Recording Studios. From the outside, it was a drab-looking concrete structure that defied the art that went on inside. The score for the film was a wonderful blend of orchestral music with jazz elements woven throughout. The London Symphony Orchestra was hired along with a selected group of jazz musicians who flew in from the States. The band included Tom Scott on saxophone, Jerry Hey on trumpet, Harvey Mason on drums, Chuck Domanico on stand-up bass, and Randy Waldman on piano. The first scoring session with the London Symphony Orchestra went more slowly than expected. Even some of the best musicians in the world had trouble wrapping their talent around the complexities of the opening cartoon. With all the tempo and key changes, the entire morning went to rehearsing the piece. We finally got it by the end of the day, but we were already way behind. The orchestra made up for lost time with their immense talent. The jazz musicians were isolated in soundproof booths at the front of the scoring stage, generally recording their music once the orchestra had gone home. Once the recording was complete, with everyone flying high from the incredible music, I booked dinner at the King Tsin in Hampstead for the whole band, along with Bob and Frank and me. I had frequented this place often while living in the area. As everyone piled into cars, and we were ready to take off, I asked about the musician's instruments. Had cartage or a pickup been arranged? I looked at the band manager. Apparently not. I was left behind to do what I thought was a job for the manager or someone in the music department. I learned to never assume anything. Always make arrangements and think ahead, or you will end up doing the work yourself.

WITH THE FILM creeping along toward completion, we prepared for our first audience preview of the film. Disney had decided to go to Granada Hills in the San Fernando Valley. For unexpected reasons, the preview would wind up a disaster. This was my first preview. With all the hard work that had gone into the film thus far, I could not help but be nervous. What could we possibly learn from an unfinished film about its playability with an audience? Still, since time was running out, we needed to know if there were any gaping holes in the story before it was too late to fix them. Once again, in a perfect world, we would have waited until the film had all the animation completed to get a true read from an audience. This was not a perfect world, so we had to move forward.

Bringing the Rabbit to Life

The first three quarters of the film was in pretty good shape, the last quarter ranged from relative unintelligibility to crude placeholders. Disney, or I should say, Jeffrey Katzenberg, organized the screening, and everyone was expected to attend. Along with Bob Zemeckis, Peter Seaman and Jeffrey Price were there. Frank Marshall came along for the ride. Alan Silvestri, our composer; Artie Schmidt, the film editor; and, of course, Ken Ralston and I attended. The entire editing staff prepared the film. At this stage the picture and the soundtrack were not tied together. This was the only print of the film and the only track that corresponded to the picture. On each reel was a start mark where the two could be put into sync, and by hitting the start button, the movie would play perfectly. During the course of the afternoon, we had a run-through of the film. Everything was in sync, and the film looked pretty good. We were ready.

The audience was a good mix of all ages, which included young kids with their moms or dads, elderly couples, and teenagers. The film was getting released under the Touchstone banner due to the film's mature content, so a portion of the audience skewed a bit older. Disney hoped all these demographic groups would show up on opening day.

I placed myself in an aisle seat in the middle of the theater, away from the filmmakers. I wanted to feel the audience reaction during the film. Beginning with the opening cartoon, everyone around me was riveted, laughing in all the right places, and they were very tense when our heroes were in jeopardy. I sat behind a young boy and his mom. At one point in the film, when Roger was about to be killed by Judge Doom, the boy started crying. I felt so bad I leaned forward to tell him that everything was going to be OK. The boy had suspended all disbelief. It was all very real to him. I settled back into my seat, enjoying the playability of the film. Suddenly, the dream turned into a nightmare.

Looking at the screen, I saw the picture give way to the white light of the projector. It did not take me even a minute to know what had happened. The film had broken. Other than being out of sync, this is an assistant editor's worst nightmare. I jumped out of my seat and ran for the screening booth. I leaped up the stairs and raced toward the projector. The film was dangling from the top reel, which normally fed into the projector, flapping as the reel spun freely. The take-up reel was doing the same. I asked for a film splicer and immediately spliced the two dangling ends back together. Now came the difficult task of putting the picture portion of the film back into the gate, finding the corresponding frame on the soundtrack, locking them together in sync, and hitting the go button. Thankfully, the assistants had coded the film, so a matching frame could be located on the picture and track. We locked it in, told the projectionist we were ready, and said to hit go. All this time, while I was feverously working with the assistants to fix the problem, I was unaware of what was transpiring in the theater below. When I said to hit go, I looked out the porthole, giving me a bird's-eye view of the theater. A small portion of the audience had remained in their seats; some were standing in the aisles, but clearly half the audience had left the theater. This was a total disaster. Why they chose to leave is anyone's guess, but the darkest explanation was that the audience was looking for any excuse to walk out the door. Word came up to stop the projectors. As quickly as we had done our work, it was not fast enough. I headed back down the stairs and found the group huddled in the lobby. Everyone looked nervously at each other. After the audience had cleared out, Jeffrey gathered everyone together in front of the theater. He said the official word was we had a great preview. He did not want to hear anything to the contrary. From anyone. "Is that clear?" With that, we looked at each other and decided we needed a drink. There wasn't enough liquor to quell our collective anxiety.

RECOVERING FROM the preview took days, even weeks. I actually do not recall a preview after that. There may have been one, but my memory is clouded by the disaster. In fact, finishing the show was a blur. Back and forth to LA, more trips to London. After one trip, as I was returning from London, Steven's assistant called me in a panic. "Where are you?" I had just landed from London, and I was heading over to the Marina Del Rey apartment. "Under no circumstances can you stay there tonight. Steven is going to be there."

In the 11th hour the filmmakers took a final trip to London to film a new ending for the movie. We needed to go out on an upbeat note. Maybe that's what we all needed. For the last scene we gathered all our live-action heroes with the liberated toons from inside and outside Toontown and had them sing "Smile, Darn Ya, Smile." But truthfully, what cartoon can properly end without Porky Pig waving and signing off with a "Ththat's all ffolks."

The premiere of *Roger Rabbit* in New York culminated a year and a half of turmoil, technical challenges, perseverance, passion, dream fulfillment, and good laughs. The film was screened at Radio City Music Hall, a large-scale theater with 5,900 seats, almost too large for a film screening. The place was full. I still had nightmares of our disastrous preview in LA. I hoped this screening would rid me of that nightmare. That would not be the case. I was coaxed by the lab into making a special print for the screening. When I told the lab the venue for the premiere, they asked where the director, cast, and special guests would be seated. The front of the balcony. In that case, the lab suggested making a print of the film that was two frames out of sync. Oh, no, really? Why? Just so I have another thing to be worried about the night of the screening? Why can't I just sit through a screening relaxed and issue a sigh of relief that we were finally done? They explained that since the screen was so far away from the special section of seats in the balcony, the sound would be delayed. The movie would appear to be out of sync. They suggested advancing the sound by two frames—early in relation to the picture, yet arriving at the front row of the balcony at the right time with the picture. It all made sense, but really?

This was clearly not the lab's first rodeo at Radio City. As I started to give into their idea, I felt terrible, thinking that I was making two prints of the film that would not be any good anywhere else. They would have to be junked after the screening. Also, the prints were being made off the original negative. Every time you make a print off the original negative, you run the risk of something happening. The less wear and tear the better. That is an unwritten law. But I trusted my guys at the lab, so I gave them the order. I also ordered two normal prints that were in sync, also made off the original negative, just in case I did not like what I heard and saw.

When I arrived in New York, I said I wanted to do a run-through the day of the premiere and hear and see this out-of-sync print for myself. During that run, I could tell the lab guys were right. Despite the fact the film played out of sync for many of the audience members up close to the screen, for the special guests at the front of the balcony, it was perfect. We went with the special prints. No one was the wiser either during or after the screening, which went off without a hitch. I finally overcame my *Roger Rabbit* anxieties.

Bringing the Rabbit to Life

The after-party was a raucous affair. Joanna Johnston, our costume designer, had made special blue bow ties with yellow dots, just like Roger Rabbit's, for Bob Zemeckis, Jeff Price, Peter Seaman, Frank Marshall, Robert Watts, Don Hahn, Richard Williams, Ken Ralston, and me. When Jeffrey Katzenberg delivered a toast in the lobby of Radio City Music Hall before everyone headed out for the evening's festivities, he specifically called me out for my "tireless energy" on the show. I felt proud at that moment, despite the fact that Jeffrey had been a tough task master. An even greater celebratory toast was given by Bob in the bar of the Peninsula hotel, where Bob and Jeff and Peter and our loved ones had gathered. For Jeff and Peter and Bob, this had been a long road well traveled. For me, the path had been paved. I soon learned that I would travel with Bob on many roads to come. While waiting for his call to come back to work, a small adventure came my way.

CHAPTER 13

A Solo Performance

IN THE FALL of 1988, a few months following the premiere of *Roger Rabbit*, I found myself back in New York for a brief work trip. After checking in at the desk of the Ritz-Carlton hotel, I lugged my Nagra portable audio recorder up to my room, set it down, and looked out the window at Central Park. How had I gotten so lucky? I had a round-trip ticket from San Francisco to New York, a nice hotel room, and a per diem. I was excited. I looked back outside. The beautiful fall colors beckoned me, so I left for a stroll through the park, switching my attention from the colorful leaves to the reason for my trip. The next morning I would record a series of dialogue lines with Sean Connery for the film *Indiana Jones and the Last Crusade*.

I was a little nervous for a couple of reasons. First of all, I had never operated a Nagra. I was given a quick lesson before I left Lucasfilm. The operation was straightforward, but with any device, something could go wrong. I tried to mitigate that possibility the best that I could. I did a trial run before I left Marin. Then I had the technician thread the tape, so it would be ready to go when needed. All I had to do was turn the switch to record, watch the magnetic tape run from one reel to the other, and let the recorder do its magic, all while I listened to the playback on my headphones. I had suggested going to a recording facility, where none of the technical aspects of the recording would be left up to me, but Sean Connery wanted to do the recording in his hotel room. So that is what I was going to do.

Secondly, I was nervous because I would be in the presence of an actor of great stature. Just meeting Mr. Connery would be intimidating enough, despite the fact I had worked around quite a few well-known actors. In addition, I would be the sole person in the room approving the performance of his lines during the recording. In the past, I might voice my opinion on the nature of a line reading, but the final approval would be left up to the director, who in this case was Steven Spielberg. Since Steven was not present, I was on my own.

It seemed that with every new job I had in the film business up to this point, I never knew what I was doing or what I was getting into, or both. It turned out this was true once again on this road trip. It was an adventure, but it still made me nervous. With the Nagra strapped to my shoulder, I took the short walk to the boutique hotel where Sean Connery was staying. I wondered if I might get mugged carrying my equipment, even though the assailant probably wouldn't know what it was he was attempting to steal. I tried to walk as casually and quickly as possible.

The doorman at the hotel was expecting me. Sean let me in the room and gestured to a small table by the door where I could place the Nagra. When I unloaded the device from my shoulder all hell broke loose. Focusing his eyes on me, the actor launched into a tirade unlike any I had ever witnessed. He first asked who I was and what I wanted. He knew perfectly well, but I meekly attempted an answer. I had been sent to record a few lines of dialogue and handed him the sheet of paper with the lines clearly spelled out for him.

"I know why you're here," he yelled, "but why *you*?" "What is

A Solo Performance

your position on the film?" I told him that I was doing a favor to the filmmakers and that I was not, in fact, working on the show. Then he really cut loose. "Are both Spielberg and Lucas too busy to come out here themselves? They needed to send you in their stead? Are they both cowards? You tell them to come out here themselves or I am not recording the lines!" Gulp, now what? I was speechless, of course. Not only did Sean tower over me in stature, but his booming voice caused me to shrink even further. He was fuming and pacing the room. He threw the pages back at me.

Why I did not move to leave, I'm not sure. I sat in that chair by the door, not knowing what to do. All this was happening in less than a minute. Of course, I could not just leave without recording the lines. This was too long of a trip for that. I could not imagine hanging my head in defeat, trudging back to my hotel room, and phoning the filmmakers to tell them that I had failed on my mission. Then I came up with an idea. I looked up to Sean and said, "Why don't you say what you just said to me into the microphone. You can tell the filmmakers exactly what you're thinking and how you feel. I will record everything you say." This gave him pause. I could tell that the idea was percolating. It slowed him down a bit. His eyes were moving back and forth. He was coming around. I could see that he sensed he had an outlet for his anger. He looked at me and a bit of a mischievous smile moved across his face. He formulated his thoughts, then he said, "OK, tell me when you're ready."

I turned on the machine. It appeared to be recording. I put on the headphones and said, "Go." And, boy, did he cut loose. "You fucking cowards! You don't even have the decency to come out here yourselves! It's insulting! You expect me to do these lines without you! Well, fuck you! I'm not going to do it. If you want these lines, get your lazy asses on a plane and get out here!" And he let out a satisfied breath. He had said his piece. I must say, it was a brilliant performance. I took off the headphones and complemented him, "Well done." I assured him that his feelings came across loud and clear. He seemed satisfied. I was satisfied. Well, almost. I still had those lines to record. Did I dare?

I remained in my seat by the door. I looked up at him and thought, why not? I braced myself. There could be another eruption of anger. But I had nothing to lose now. I must have seen the worst. I went ahead and asked, "Do you want to give the lines a go?" He turned and looked at me but not with the scornful expression I expected. It was with a slightly raised eyebrow. He considered the question. He still had not even reviewed the lines he was expected to record. We had never gotten to that. He asked for the paper with the lines clearly typed out. I handed it back to him. I sat and waited while he read them through. Then, to my surprise, he said, "Are you ready?" Just like that, we were back in business.

I put the headphones back on, turned on the recorder, said I was ready, and he read me the first line. Then he did it again. I just listened, looking down at the tape, as it passed across the record head on the machine. He said, that'll do, let's try the second line. I nodded in approval. On we went, through each line. When he was happy, I was happy. I never responded to his performance, and he never asked me what I thought. When we were done, he handed the paper back to me. I packed up the Nagra, thanked him for his time, and let myself out of the room.

When I returned to the editing room in California, I asked Steven and his editor, Michael Kahn, to come and listen to the tape. I wanted them to hear it with me from the beginning. "What the hell was that? they asked when they heard Sean's rant. "He wasn't too happy you guys didn't come to New York." With that, I left them to

A Solo Performance

choose which of the recorded lines they wanted to put in the movie.

Despite my fear and the near calamitous experience, I look back on my Sean Connery encounter with fondness. I had once again dodged a bullet and come back with the goods. Another narrow escape in the face of disaster. The exhilaration of the process became an addiction. I was bitten by the bug. As it turns out, my next fix was around the corner waiting for me.

CHAPTER 14

Back to the Future II

"Where we're going, we don't need roads." *Doc Brown*

WHAT IS AN associate producer, anyway? The director's girlfriend? The actor's manager? A production company gofer? A friend's son granted a favor by the producer? The writer? The first assistant director? Could be anyone, really. In other words, the credit did not mean any one thing; it was a credit that lacked substance. When I got hired as an associate producer on *Back to the Future, Part II*, I did have some experience to offer, but I was still unclear exactly what my role would be. Bob Zemeckis brought me along for the ride. He already had two producers: Bob Gale and Neil Canton. Bob G. was the longtime friend and writing partner he had met at the USC film school, a creative ally. Neil had worked on the original *Back to the Future*, having been recommended by his, and my, friend and colleague, Frank Marshall, as a line producer. I brought with me a certain expertise in post production and visual effects. That got me in the door. What else would my job entail? I knew I would be expected to oversee the work I had experience doing, but I wanted to parlay that into an expanded role on the film. What else might they have me do? Probably everything that the producers did not want to do.

I did not know that I would be invited back to work with Bob on the *Back to the Future* sequel when we were shooting *Roger Rabbit*. I guess I had not been tested yet. I had overheard Bob and Ken Ralston talking about some ideas in the new *BTF* screenplay that would require a long lead time for some new technology to be developed. Ken was locked in on the show. In addition to Ken, the crew on *Back to the Future II* was filled with faces familiar to me from both *Roger Rabbit* and *Amazing Stories*. Artie Schmidt, the film editor; Dean Cundey, the cameraman (along with Ray Stella, the camera operator; Clyde Bryan, his first assistant cameraman; and Mark Walthour, his gaffer); Joanna Johnston, the costume designer; and Alan Silvestri, the music composer, all came from *Roger Rabbit*. Also a few key crew members from *Amazing Stories* joined the show: Joan Bradshaw, the production manager, and Rick Carter, the production designer. Many others from the LA shoot on *Roger* as well as from *Back to the Future* came aboard.

Bob Z. was fiercely loyal to those he thought worked hard for him and did a good job. I was happy to be included in that tight-knit group. I also learned how important it was to be loyal to your special crew, since they are not only wonderful people to work with and at the top of their game, but they will go the extra distance when you need them to. Once Bob assembled his group of crew members, few jobs were up for grabs.

Not only were many crew members brought back for the sequels, but so were many performers in the cast. Of course, the entire show was dependent on Michael J. Fox as Marty McFly, Christopher Lloyd as Emmett "Doc" Brown, Tom Wilson as the antagonist Biff Tannen, and Lea Thompson as Marty's mother. Others were reluctantly replaced. When Crispin Glover's financial demands to return as Marty's dad spiraled out of control, he was essentially written out of the sequels, with his character only making a brief appearance

Back to the Future II

and portrayed by Michael Weissman (with the help of makeup artist extraordinaire Ken Chase). Marty's girlfriend, Jennifer, played by Claudia Wells in the original, had to be recast for personal reasons and was replaced by Elizabeth Shue. Other familiar faces in the cast accompanied the leads into the various time periods.

SOON AFTER the group assembled, we were all given a 150-plus page script. That is one big script: an epic in the making. Beginning in the present day of the first *Back to the Future* film, the story flew to the future, then back to an altered present day, back further to the Old West, and finally ended in the present day where the saga began. Each time period seemed like its own movie. Each had a unique production design, costume design, and set of props. Each visit to Marty's hometown of Hill Valley needed to be familiar and different at the same time. Both Bob Z. and Bob G. figured the audience wanted something recognizable to hang their hat on, while at the same time enjoying a new spin.

Everyone set to work on breaking down the script and putting together a budget. I was asked to gather the numbers for post production and to take a close look at the budget for visual effects. Laying out a schedule and budget for post was easy enough. I kept it almost the same as *Roger Rabbit*. The crew was virtually the same, so the same rates applied. One difference was that they planned on having a second editor, Harry Keramidas, just like on the first *Back to the Future*. I could roughly model the music budget on Alan Silvestri's work on *Roger*, both in terms of rates and scoring time, with the big exception that we would be scoring in Los Angeles instead of London.

Analyzing the visual effects, on the other hand, was very com-

Steve Starkey

plicated. There were new techniques and all kinds of trickery throughout the film. Bob had learned more about visual effects, and he was ready to experiment. The greatest experiment of all was having actors play different characters or different versions of themselves in the same scene. Michael J. Fox played his older self, his son, and daughter having dinner around a dining table in the future. Michael, Christopher Lloyd, and Tom Wilson all interacted with different versions of themselves in the same shot. All these shots would be breaking new ground in visual effects using cutting-edge technologies.

For these scenes, Ken Ralston had decided they would require a motion-control dolly system, a system where the pan and tilt and dolly of the camera could be recorded and played back numerous times identically, each time for a different character in the scene. ILM had been given the funds to create this by Universal while we were working on *Roger*, so the system would be ready in time for shooting *BTF*. Bill Tondreau had developed the new VistaGlide system, which the crew quickly nicknamed the "Tondreau." I suppose, since they were working on a sequel to a popular and successful film, the two Bobs felt they had the license, and, in fact, a need to expand their ideas and be more inventive on a bigger canvas to satisfy themselves and their audience.

The more I analyzed the script and heard their ideas, the bigger the movie got. The budget for visual effects started to escalate. In fact, the budget grew for all the departments. When it was submitted to the studio brass at Universal, they went ballistic. The studio was committed to move forward with the project, and they even knew the time frame for the release of the film. But they had their limits. So the drama began. The studio shot down the budget. But Bob Z. and Bob G. had something up their sleeve. They regrouped

Back to the Future II

and concocted a brilliant plan. Why not cut the script in half, and make two movies for just over the price of one? The studio bought the idea and wanted us to prove it could be done. If we could pull this off, we had a green light. Of course, it all started with the script. The studio said to move forward with the rewrite and new budget. We were also given the go-ahead to keep working while the budgeting and rewriting were going on, so the crew could stay intact, and the schedule would remain close to the original. Stunned by the brilliance of the idea, it put smiles on our faces. As Rick Carter, our production designer, said, it was "an insurmountable opportunity."

All the departments were called together and brought up to speed. Bob Z. and Bob G. were going to rewrite the script to make the first half a stand-alone movie called *Back to the Future, Part II*, with a second script for *Back to the Future, Part III*. We had faith it would all work out. The good news was that most of the elements in the first script they submitted would remain intact. They reviewed the plot points of both movies, so all the departments could move full steam ahead. New scenes would be written to patch or sometimes fill out the story. The changes that came through could be incorporated in all the departmental breakdowns and budgets as we went along. We had no idea that this process would last throughout the entire production of the film. But we were off and running.

Joan Bradshaw, our production manager, pressured the departments to submit their new budgets for the first sequel. I was able to sit in with Joan as she carefully reviewed the budget for each department. Just in the same way I was familiar with every line item in an effects or post-production budget, Joan had a command of production. I watched and followed her carefully, never adding much but learning why each person on the crew was needed and where all the money was getting spent. As the budgets were pared down further, I saw the subtle trimming that took place. What became readily apparent was that if you started up *BTF II*, gave all the departments the prep, shooting time, and wrap they needed, then shut down, took a hiatus, then started all over again for *BTF III*, we were wasting a lot of money. If we could go straight from one show to the other, we could save a lot. We started to lay out the schedule and see if it was possible. For production, *BTF II* and *III* would have to be treated as one big show. Exhausting, but doable.

The art department would have the greatest challenge. Designs and construction for the second film would be finalized while shooting the first film. It would never all get art directed and designed in advance, especially since the script was growing. For post production, doing two shows at once would be tricky, depending on the start of principal photography on the second show. If we were able to finish editing the director's cut of the first film before shooting started on *BTF III*, we might be able to pull it off. Bob would still be required to continue work on the cut, review the film for sound and music, do the necessary ADR, and oversee the visual effects work. All this could be handled in evenings and weekends while we were shooting. A bit more difficult would be attending the ADR and scoring sessions and the final mix. I could lay out this schedule once we got the shooting dates set.

As far as ILM was concerned, Ken Ralston would have to oversee shots that were under way for the first film while he was supervising shooting on the second. He would have to choose where he needed to be each week, supervising at ILM or with the shooting company. ILM would be able to handle the work just like they were working on two movies. It all really boiled down to production. What would their plan be?

First assistant director Dave McGiffert was small and thin, with the energy of a dynamo. He knew Bob and how he worked and was able to put a fairly realistic schedule in place. Each of the two long shooting schedules were close to 90 days. The greatest scheduling difficulty was with Michael J. Fox. He was also on the TV show *Family Ties*. They were in first position, which meant when they needed him, they got him. At times, the TV show was on hiatus, but for the most part, the movie had to dance around the *Family Ties* schedule. When the sitcom was shooting, each week might look like this: On Monday our shooting call would be bright and early—7 a.m., which was when *Family Ties* was doing their table readings. On Tuesday we started at 10 a.m., with Michael joining us at lunchtime. Wednesday we would start in the afternoon. Thursday, even later in the afternoon. This all led up to Friday, when *Family Ties* taped the show, and Michael would not show up until 7 p.m. We would shoot all night Friday night into Saturday, only to turn around and be back at work on Monday at 7 a.m. Grueling.

After the actors' schedules, production design became the next tail that wagged the dog. The most difficult scheduling puzzle for production design and construction was shooting the different time periods on Back to the Future Square, where the script called for a present-day square, a future version, and an altered 1985. Each time period took time to prepare, shoot, strike, and change over to the next. As soon as shooting was complete on the town square in the future, the entire set would have to be torn down or transformed into another time period. The changes and the costs were substantial. God forbid we needed to pick up any missing shots. After we cleared dailies, we would strike the set and get ready for the next look.

Dave McGiffert had to manage these and all the other logistics that went into laying out a big movie schedule. The shooting start date was set—February 20, 1989. This was my first opportunity to sit in on the review of the schedule as it was unfolding. The complexities of the schedule were not limited to actors' conflicts and production design limitations. There were also issues with location permits (when we could secure a location for shooting), prop designs (hoverboards, for example), costume designs, and visual effects (making sure the Tondreau system would be ready), to name a few. I enjoyed the puzzle process of the schedule, juggling everyone's needs, until it all fell into place.

ONE THING WE KNEW for sure was that we were going to the future. We knew from the end of the first movie that was where our heroes were headed. What would the future look like? Everyone had some idea, drawn from other movies or books or at least the Jetsons! Bob Z. always said, "All ideas are welcome. I only use the good ones." The ideas came flooding in, but at some point, we had to get our act together. Set construction had a deadline. Costumes had to be fabricated. Props needed to be built. What would the buildings look like? We knew that our heroes arrived in Doc Brown's flying DeLorean, but what did the other cars look like? What would the people in the town square be wearing? What were the hairstyles like? The one pitfall was to be too serious or think you could predict future trends. In order to avoid this problem, the Bobs always looked for the comedy or irony in all design decisions. If nothing else, at least you would get a laugh.

We signed up some additional brain power from the art world and industry at large. The entire production staff and all the department heads did their own research and hired consultants. Among our many future consultants were the immensely talented Doug Chiang, whom I teamed up with years later when we formed ImageMovers Digital, and John Bell, who ended up as an art director on the film at ILM. Images came pouring in. Rick Carter, the production designer, and Joanna Johnston, our costume designer, were given the task of sorting out the best futuristic ideas with the two Bobs, creating the futuristic world.

We tapped into major companies that were also envisioning what their future products might look like. As it turned out, the marketing departments of many businesses were happy to loan us their futuristic products and even pay large sums of money if we guaranteed that their products would be seen in the film. That was where things got dicey. We had contracts with these companies. If we did not fulfill our end of the bargain, no payment. Who determined, for example, how much screen time was required of a car in the future to satisfy the deal?

As the budget grew, our appetite for product placement grew along with it. These were desperate times. We had to bring the budget down in any way we could. Often agreements were made and accounted for in our budget when we thought it was likely we could satisfy the terms of the deal. We started to accumulate so many agreements with so many companies that it was too much for me to handle. I said we needed a Brad Globe. Brad oversaw consumer products at Amblin, and I knew him from my time working there. Even though he oversaw Amblin movies, he said it was too much for him to handle. He connected us to Mark Snovell. Mark, along with business affairs, coordinated drawing up the contracts with the major companies. During shooting, Mark would tap me on the shoulder and say if Bob puts that car on camera, we will get another 25 thousand. I would have to make a snap judgment as to whether or not I could approach Bob. If I thought it wouldn't piss him off or that I wouldn't appear to be too stupid, I would point out the product to Bob, and he would either look at me in disgust or possibly reframe the shot a bit. That was yet another job of an associate producer. Taking it on the chin for product placement.

Nike was in from the beginning. Frank Marshall had cultivated a relationship with Nike that was passed down to me. No money exchanged hands, but there were multiple perks for both sides in the relationship. For Nike, their shoes were given prominent display on the lead character. Going to the future gave them a unique opportunity. Marty had worn Nikes in the original *Back to the Future*, but what would the Nike shoe look like in the future? They, along with our design team, came up with a shoe that was suited for space travel, but the big innovation was that it was self-lacing. This was actually called for in the screenplay.

With a little movie magic, the shoes that Marty puts on in the future surprise even Marty. They also became the prototype for the shoes that Joanna Johnston came up with for other young adults in town. In exchange for their assured placement in the film, Nike made the custom shoe at their cost. In addition, due to the exposure of the Nike product, Nike provided us with crew jackets and hats. These alone can add quite a bit of money to a budget, and budgets never have these kinds of discretionary funds to play with. I went down to the Nike headquarters in Marina del Rey. Back in their warehouse, I set eyes on all the Nike products that might be suitable for the crew and that could be made in time for a few hundred crew members. My choice was settled when I got the aesthetic approval of the men and women in the office. Another unheralded assignment for the associate producer.

Back to the Future II

BOB Z. always tends to present a new setting in a film in one big shot, with all the bells and whistles on display. This was certainly the case when we follow Marty McFly into Future Square for the first time in *BTF II*. Flying cars are landing and taking off. Giant video displays have replaced billboards and a three-dimensional marquee announced the latest *Jaws* sequel, leaping out from the local movie theater. Everything that surrounded the square was familiar from the first movie yet redesigned with a futuristic spin. The soda fountain/café from the original film was transformed into the Café 80s, with famous celebrities of the era—from Michael Jackson to Ronald Reagan—taking orders on a video screen. The two Bobs were having a field day.

Creating the playback of the famous celebrities on the screens in the Café 80s was the first of many video displays that made my head spin. When we enter the living room of Marty's tract home in the future, we are greeted by a hanging video painting that displays the image of your choice, much like a large screen saver. Of course, the joke was that this one was broken; Bob wanted a continual line moving down through the beautiful landscape, like what happened on old TV sets. I spent hours at my old video company attempting to make the technicians create a display that appeared to be broken, when they only had the technology to do things right!

Continuing into the dining room, a wall-mounted video screen showed a teleconference call taking place between aged Marty and his boss. Marty was getting fired from his job. To shoot the scene, the actor playing the boss—Flea, from the Red Hot Chili Peppers—was standing in the corner of the stage in a makeshift office, performing in front of a camera with a live video feed going to the video screen in the set. It all had to happen in real time, like a Zoom call, for the interaction to work. All the video playback in the film required daily supervision and became a full-time job, so I eventually hired an assistant to follow through on all the projects.

WHAT BECAME another full-time job on the film was overseeing the second unit. This was a real training ground for me. We had a sizeable allowance for the shoot in the budget, but no one had fully imagined the scope of the work at the outset. The largest scene in *BTF II* was a nighttime car chase where Marty is following Biff, who tries to shake him off and kill him. The second unit worked for weeks in and around Griffith Park, spending most of the time approaching and driving through the Griffith Park Tunnel near the observatory. In preparation for the production meeting on the film, I was asked by production if there were any areas of the car chase that I thought could be trimmed. The length of a car chase is instinctive, with all kinds of ideas that could make it fun and exciting. You never really know what will make it into the final cut until the footage is shot and edited.

To save money, production thought I should make some suggestions now. While Bob was reviewing the storyboards of the sequence in the meeting, I blurted out a few suggestions of cuts he might consider. Generally speaking, no one asked Bob to make cuts in his script or storyboards. He always liked to shoot as much as he could, so he could have fun in the editing room. With all the department heads looking on, he asked me why cut it now? He knew that I knew this could all be edited later. It was a good question, so I said that I had been asked to see if anything was expendable and could save us some money. Fortunately, Bob did not blow a gasket. He knew I'd been set up to ask the question since I had some editing skills and a willingness to bring it up in the meeting. This was my first rodeo in a feature film production meeting. He simply said, sure, Steve, there are shots we can do without, but let's just shoot them all and cut it down later. Fair enough. I felt embarrassed that I had brought it up at all. Lesson learned.

As time went on, and the relationship between Bob and me developed, I would carefully choose the suggestions I would make about saving money on a show. If I understood exactly what he was trying to do, I was not shy about sharing a simpler way to accomplish that. I knew that if he did not wish to make a change, he would tell me. But more often than not he would compromise as long as his vision stayed intact. Sometimes he would go away for a day or two after I had spoken to him, then surprise me with an idea that was better than my cost-cutting suggestion. Every movie demanded this balance between the art and the money we had to produce the art. You had to trust each other in the process.

Juggling my responsibilities between first and second unit made my work life very complicated. The second unit usually had a 5 p.m. call. I would show up soon after the call and spend the night with the unit. A few hours before dawn, when they only had a setup or two remaining, I would head home, try to get some sleep, and come into work around midday. I would spend three or four hours on the set catching up, making sure the other aspects of my job were on track. I might meet with Zemeckis and Max Kleven, the second-unit director, to review the upcoming shots, then head off to second unit. I enjoyed second-unit work. The pressure on the first unit was so great that having time away felt like moviemaking fun. But I was often scared, mostly because I did not know the limits of what was safe for the stunt players.

Charlie Croughwell, who was doubling Michael J. Fox, was a

very physical guy who was willing to take huge, calculated risks. These all involved a moving car putting him in danger. I often stood there terrified, watching the video of each shot, as Charlie tried to make the stunt look as real and as scary as possible. Max Kleven, the second-unit director, knew Charlie well and knew what he could do. Max also knew what he needed to get the shot. Max trusted Charlie, and Charlie trusted Max. The key to shooting an exciting sequence was the cameraman. We had Don Burgess—Burgee, as Max lovingly called him. They had a lot of experience together. Don could not only light the scene and light it quickly, but he was also a phenomenal operator. He was also very athletic and was willing to go to great personal risk to get a shot. Max and Don were a great team. I trusted them and their years of experience (even though Don was fairly young), but I still got scared.

Bruce Moriarty, the first assistant director, also felt very comfortable doing second-unit work. I think he felt more at ease around stunts and physical effects than working with the first unit. Here he was with the rough-and-tumble big boys. No bullshit. I would look back fondly on my days working with them. A few years down the road, I suggested to Bob that he hire Burgee as his cameraman on *Forrest Gump* and Bruce as his first assistant director. Bob did hire them. They did a spectacular job and played a crucial role in making that movie what it was.

In order to get the shots of Michael J. Fox in the car chase, we shot VistaVision backgrounds for every setup on second unit. Essentially, we repeated the second-unit camera shots but without the actor. On a stage at Universal Studios, this background film would be projected onto a movie screen while filming the real actor. This method of filming was called "process." Relying on my editorial and effects experience, I knew what backgrounds were needed for each of the first-unit shots. Editorial catalogued the shots and arranged them on a film rack on the stage. I knew from the continuity script which background to provide for each shot; a medium shot required a different background from a close-up. Bill Hansard ran the process stage. Just like we nicknamed the motion-capture dolly system the Tondreau, we called these shots "Hansard" shots, or at least Bob and I did.

I felt the pressure as we tried to move as quickly as possible through the shots on the stage while making sure that the right background was running during the shot. I had the storyboards as my guide, and since I had been there during the shooting of the backgrounds, I had a handle on it. I decided to set up three rolling corkboards and pinned up all the storyboards of the sequence so everyone could keep track of what we were shooting. After we completed a shot or sequence, I had Bob Z. step up to the board and cross off the storyboards that were done. I attached a red Sharpie on a long string for the purpose. This ritual was a morale booster to the crew.

THE LEGACY of my recent tenure at ILM stuck with me throughout the show, and really, throughout my career. I knew that a good part of the reason I was brought onto the movie was because I had a handle on visual effects. Most people in production were intimidated by the process, and because of the high cost of visual effects, they were skeptical about the truth behind the numbers. I quickly learned that once I left the magic kingdom of ILM, I would have to fight to bring their costs down. Very few big companies were in the visual-effects game at the time, so they had you over a barrel when it came to their charges. Every time an effects shot was scheduled on a given day, I was not only required to be on set, but I also was responsible for the day running smoothly, almost as if I were still at ILM. This was never clearer than when we were doing a shot that required the new toy, the Tondreau.

The Tondreau could be movie magic at its finest or a complete disaster. Live-action motion control opened up new world of possibilities to filmmakers. But it had its pitfalls, as we would discover. Doing a Tondreau shot was always a nail biter.

The Tondreau was put to the test on the first shot on the first day of principal photography. Christopher Lloyd was the actor. The back lot at Universal was freezing, as cold as I remembered it from my night shoots as an electrician. It wasn't the cold that bothered Christopher Lloyd that night, though. Chris had to replicate a character he had created four years earlier on *Back to the Future*. That sent his head spinning. I don't think he has any idea how he creates what he does, or, if he does, it is damn hard to dig down and find it. That was just for starters. After recreating his original performance, Chris then had to rush into the scene as his present-day character from the new film and interact with his earlier self. That's a lot to swallow for any actor, and, for Chris, it was an oversize mouthful. It put him under a lot of pressure. When it came time to shoot, Chris was hiding out in his motor home. He tried to calm himself with some liquor. Then he needed a cup of coffee or two before making his way to the set. When he arrived, he looked at Bob, tried to shake off the willies, and with a smile said, "OK, ready." Sometimes, you focus so much on the technology, you forget the affect it has on the actors. Some actors don't have a problem with special effects. Throw them a blue-screen environment with nothing around to hold onto, and they are fine. Others have a meltdown. After midnight, in the early hours of the morning, we had the shot. We all huddled around the video monitor and marveled at history in the making.

Then came the night the system crashed. The company had returned to the Hollywood United Methodist Church, the same location used on *Back to the Future*, to recreate the Enchantment Under the Sea dance. Rick Carter and his art department had done an impeccable job of matching the set from the first film. Not only did the design have to be perfect, but the set dressing, the costumes, the casting of the extras, and the dance choreography had to match exactly. Dean Cundey had to get his lighting to match as well. I found myself researching and printing loads of reference material for the art department and the wardrobe department. I enjoyed immersing myself in each department and helping them try to recreate the work that had been done four years earlier. Rick and Joanna were not on the first film, so they had to rely on the reference photos to bring them up to speed.

Michael J. Fox had to jump back up on stage and perform "Johnny B. Goode," just like he had done on the first film. For Michael, playing himself twice in one scene came easier than it did to Christopher Lloyd. Michael and Chris are completely different actors. Michael could be holding the script and learning the lines of a long scene during blocking or a rehearsal, then do the scene perfectly when the cameras rolled. He could be in the middle of sharing a joke with the crew, then shoot a take of a newly memorized scene, then return to finish the joke while the camera was getting set for take two.

Michael was not the problem that night. It was the Tondreau. It crashed when our hero was spying on himself playing guitar on stage. At first, everyone took advantage of the unforeseen breather brought on by a technical glitch. They started making small talk, laughing and joking, assuming everything would return to normal quickly. After some time had passed, the crew became more fidgety, the chitchat more nervous. The technicians from ILM tried and tried to get the Tondreau going again, to no avail. Discussions started to get serious. How long is it going to take to be up and running again? What if we can't get it up and running again? Walking away from the shot and coming back was not an option anyone wanted to consider. If we shut down and came back at a later date, we would have to start all over again. Redo everything we had done that night. Not only that, but we would also need to keep the set in place, pay the location fees to hold the location (assuming it was not booked and would be available to us), keep the extras on hold, and adjust the schedule to make room on another day to film the scene again. It would have been a nightmare. More time passed, and still, the boys from ILM could not fix their own technology. I felt their pain. I had been there. The clock was ticking with thousands of dollars going down the drain. Then Ian Kelly stepped in.

Bob and I were well aware of Ian's extraordinary work as an engineer during *Roger Rabbit*. We were so enamored with Ian that we convinced production to bring him over from England for the show. The producers had been scratching their heads a bit when Bob and I said we could not live without Ian, but they would not be scratching their heads any longer. Ian came up with a system to activate the Tondreau. On the spot he engineered a remote, handheld device with a "blooping" light that sent out a signal enabling the camera to "speak" to the Tondreau and follow its commands once again. Ian saved the system and the night of shooting. The blooping light was not an anomaly for that night. It became de rigueur for operating the Tondreau from that point forward.

By far the most challenging scene we did with the Tondreau took place in the dining room of Marty McFly's house in the future.

Back to the Future II

Michael J. Fox played himself as an older man as well as his own son and daughter, all in the same scene. For each scene using the motion-control system, the actor and director decide which character's performance to record first. Usually, it is the character who is the driving force in the scene, while the others react or respond. This character drives the camera and the dolly, whose motion is then set in stone. It cannot and does not change after that. After that performance is baked into the system, the set is taped off like a police line. No one can enter the forbidden area for fear that the dolly or camera might be bumped, which would cause each added performance not to line up properly. It is a very delicate process. This gets multiplied again when you add a third performance into the mix. One after the next, Michael performed as all three characters, changing his makeup, hair, and wardrobe in between.

During these changeovers, everyone on the crew was on standby. This scene was shot late into the night. With time to kill in between the changing of the characters, I sometimes would walk down to Amblin and go into the kitchen and eat a snack. I knew everyone there, and actually had my office there, so the compound was not off-limits to me. On my return, as I entered the stage, I felt a rumble and shake. When you live in Southern California, earthquakes are unmistakable. At first, we all looked around to be sure nothing was falling down around us. Then everyone reacted in the same way. What about the shot? Would it be okay or had the earthquake jogged the system enough that it might not line up and would need to be redone? Hours of work might be lost. Ken Ralston decided to chance it. The shot came out great in the end, but we all had to wonder about the odds of an earthquake hitting in the middle of a Tondreau shot. But that didn't stop us. Biff interacting with Biff, Marty interacting with Marty, and Doc with Doc,

Steve Starkey

countless Tondreau shots were stacking up throughout the show.

Nights and days started blending into one another. A mountain of effects shots started piling up at ILM and into the editing room. During filming, Bob spent as much free time as he could in the editing room, looking at cut sequences and also evaluating VFX shots. Sequences had to be locked in their final cut so the VFX shots could begin. So many VFX shots and so little time. Artie Schmidt and Harry Keramidas were busy in the editing room trying to keep up: Artie was mostly doing the dialogue scenes with Harry focusing on the action sequences. As production headed toward the end of shooting, I started to visit the editing room more often. It was like a truck had dumped a ton of unwieldy footage into the cutting room, and it all needed to be sorted out. I would come into their quiet space, away from the demanding chaos of set, envying the time I spent there, out of the fray, away from the moment-to-moment pressures of each shooting day.

"What do we edit next?" was always the question. "What does ILM need now?" I was the keeper of a very unrealistic schedule to complete the show. But I did not have to do it alone. I was so fortunate to have Suella Kennedy, who had worked as my production coordinator on *Roger Rabbit*, now working as the visual-effects producer on *BTF II*. I sometimes felt that with her running the show at ILM, it was not any different than how we had worked together on *Roger*, since I spent so much time in the editing room at Amblin in LA on that show. We worked hand in hand to lay out a realistic schedule to keep the beast fed at ILM. When principal photography finally ended on August 1, we were looking down the barrel of a quickly approaching release date: November 22, 1989. Only three and a half months. I am not sure what I was thinking when I agreed we could get it done. I don't think I had much choice in the matter. This was the kind of show that the studio was willing to throw money at. The release date was driving the train. With everything I had done on *BTF II*, it became clearer what an associate producer does on a show like this. Everything I knew how to do, many things that I had no idea how to do, and everything the producers did not want or have time to do. At this stage in the game, I was too busy to give it much thought. We had *Part II* of the trilogy to finish and the next sequel, *Part III*, to shoot!

CHAPTER 15

Back to the Future III

NORMALLY, when you wrap principal photography on a film, the director can look forward to pulling back into the quiet of the editing room and start to focus his or her attention on putting the film together. No more demands from the set, where question after question needs to be answered for shooting to move forward. Bob would say he felt like he was getting nibbled to death by ducks. Is this costume OK? How about the hair? Do you like the color of paint on the walls? What time do we set the wristwatch to? Do you like the framing of the shot? Endless questions. The editing room is just the director, the editor, and the film. That's a normal show. On the sequels, Bob would constantly be torn between the two shows and their looming deadlines. *BTF II* had a release date, and *BTF III* had a start date for shooting. No sooner had I corralled Bob into the editing room to review a scene or give notes on a visual-effects shot for *BTF II*, than he would be pulled away by production to keep the preparations moving forward on *BTF III*.

The preparations on *BTF III* hinged on where we would shoot the Western town. It was quickly determined that the town square on the Universal back lot would not do. We all knew that working at Universal would have had its benefits. First, the interior sets could be built and shot on sound stages. Secondly, we would be close at hand to finish the final work on *Back to the Future II*, now on an accelerated completion schedule. But those considerations did not carry the necessary weight to sway the filmmakers. This was their chance to shoot a real Western. They wanted the art department and the location scout to look beyond the walls of the studio. What worked on the Universal back lot for the Hill Valley Town Square in 1985, the altered town square in 1985, and the future, would not work for the early days of Hill Valley in 1885. Bob Z. and Bob G. thought it was too limited, and the vistas beyond the town would be nonexistent. They wanted a town whose buildings could work as both interior and exterior sets and be designed for the scenes as written. Only constructing the town in a remote setting would fulfill their vision. Bob would then have the freedom to have the actors come and go as he wished, utilizing real backgrounds. Ironically, as the years went on, you would never even consider asking Bob to shoot on a location when he could alternately shoot in the comfort and control of a sound stage.

Paul Pav, our location manager, hit the road to find a Western town or a setting for one, and, if possible, one that had a railroad that could tie into the location. We knew, or at least I did, no town would suffice. We would be building a town. Paul first looked locally but quickly discovered that the appetites of the filmmakers were larger than the Disney Ranch and whatever else could be found nearby. He had to move the search outside of LA. It did not take long for Paul and Rick Carter, the production designer, to find a possible setting for us to build in Jamestown, California, just outside of Sonora. By some miracle, Jamestown also had a railroad that ran for a few miles into wide-open Sierra Nevada foothill country. Before we took a ride on the train, Rick assured us that if we liked what we saw, we could get permits to build and shoot there. With that in mind, we headed out on the train and took in the scenery.

Then we saw it, or Bob did. The setting for our town, in a cozy valley, just off the tracks. We stopped the train, jumped off, and dragged ourselves through the brush into the open valley. From the canyon, gazing at the distant hills beyond, you couldn't see any signs of civilization. No roads or telephone poles.

As it turned out, Rick and Paul had secretly hoped that the filmmakers would take to the area. They had walked the various valleys that were near the train tracks, and this was their leading candidate. Bob picked his way through the site, discussing scenes and framing shots as we followed close behind. As he was growing more and more excited about building in this location, basic production requirements needed to be considered. Both Rick and Paul had to switch hats and answer the questions production presented to them: Was it close enough to the highway for easy access? In this case, it was. Was the road so close that it presented problems for recording sound? The highway was faintly audible but not enough to be a problem. Were there enough hotels nearby to accommodate the crew? They had canvased the town of Sonora and discovered that there were plenty of accommodations nearby. Rick and Paul had done their homework. It was quickly settled. We would build the town here. Now we just had to build it in time to start principal photography at the end of August.

With the *BTF II* train building up steam in the editing room, I had to keep Bob away from the prep of *Part III* long enough to keep *Part II* on track. He loved editing and equally loved the notion of shooting a Western, but there were just not enough hours in the day for both pleasures. Since I was always with him while he was doing his post-production work, I was able to be a fly on the wall during his prep meetings and could help when I saw that it was needed. I knew my priority was to keep *BTF II* on course for completion, but I jumped at the chance to be immersed in the prep of the next film as well. Bob kept getting dragged into meeting after meeting. In addition to the demands of the art department, period costume designs required review. Guns and horses and storyboards for the action sequences had to be buttoned down. There was additional casting to be done, along with approving the extras. The cameraman needed attention so he could prepare for his lighting. In other words, not much time for editing.

After only a short month of prep and editing in LA, the company moved to Jamestown. Actually, it was a big relief. After the arduous shoot on *BFT II*, getting out of town felt great. Liv and I loved the outdoors, and we still had a bit of summer and early fall weather to enjoy. We had our hearts set on finding a house rental on nearby Lake Tulloch, which was a short drive to location. The two Bobs and Neil had found rentals on the lake, but our house was the strangest by far. It had the shape of an octagon, which made it stand out among the other homes and cottages that circled the lake. I had felt a bit guilty asking production to find me a place by the lake, but we really wanted to have a special experience and enjoy the water whenever I had any time off. It turned out that my free time was limited, since we shot six days a week. Also, the workdays were extended by having to keep tabs on *BTF II*. Liv's daughter, Inge, visited us at the lake, which gave us quite a bit of time alone with her in a new environment. Inge also loved the outdoors, so we were able to enjoy swimming, hiking, and biking with one another. Inge seemed to be having the time of her life. I introduced her to all my friends on the cast and crew, and even to George Lucas, who had come up for a visit with his young daughter. Inge charmed them all.

Back to the Future III

ALTHOUGH HE WAS a city boy from Chicago, Bob Z. felt right at home shooting a Western. What's not to like? You leave the city and the studio behind and can breathe fresh air. Other than any film or TV show about World War II, Bob was fondest of Westerns. Classic themes and iconic motifs and styles filled his mind as he shot. Whether consciously or subconsciously, you could see the classic influences in his work as he set the shot for each scene. Just like he had done on the previous films, Bob established his entrance into Hill Valley on a large scale. The camera started tight, following our hero in those familiar Nike tennis shoes walking along the railroad tracks, then reached into the sky to reveal the Hill Valley of yesteryear. Extras in period costumes filled the streets, while horses and buggies went by. Marty gawked at the people and storefronts from his hometown of the past. What had been a café in the first film and the future, in the past was the local saloon. He dared to enter. Talk about a fish out of water. All heads turned on the newcomer. All eyes went to the Nike shoes.

Some of the faces at the bar were veterans of Western films: Harry Carey Jr., Dub Taylor, and Pat Buttram (who had voiced a toon bullet in *Roger Rabbit*). As Marty sidled up to the bar, the patrons looked him up and down. They didn't hold back on their questions to the newcomer, who tried to explain his shoes. "They're Nikes. We use them for running." "Runnin?" "Yeah, we run for fun." "For fun? What kind of fun is that?" Product placement at its best. A good joke and the Nike tennis shoe on prominent display in front of the camera. I had no problem getting my crew jackets and baseball caps.

I was relieved that there were far fewer effects shots in *Part III*. My presence on set was needed less, even though I enjoyed it immensely. As we drifted into night work, I loved the fact we were in a natural environment. It sure beat the back lot. I was thinking that these were the kind of movies I wanted to make. As soon as the stunt team and horse wranglers were no longer needed on the first unit, we were free to mount up a full-scale second unit on the train sequence. I headed back to old familiar territory. We rounded up all the second-unit boys from *Part II*. Max Kleven, the director; Bruce Moriarty, the first assistant director; and Don Burgess, the cameraman, all returned. They were all in their element. Max lived in horse country near Newhall, California; Bruce had been raised with horses in Canada and owned some horses in Florida. Don was a city boy, yet he was comfortable shooting anything outdoors. This time around we were filming a big action sequence around a thundering train. Overseeing the second unit is overstating my role, since all the players had much more experience than I did. But, hey, I was the associate producer, and I was there to learn. Having been through the experience on *BTF II*, I felt much more confident this time around. Also the gang seemed to have such an affinity for the outdoors and working around horses that I felt I could think more about how we were setting up for each shot rather than focusing on the fact the stuntmen were doing death-defying stunts.

THEN THE PEACE and serenity of the shoot suddenly came to an end. Both films seemed to converge on one another. *BTF II* was calling for attention while the relentless demands of shooting were pulling in the other direction. I had laid out a very tight schedule to make the delivery date. The dialogue predubs were about to begin, and I needed to record ADR lines with the actors. Since Michael J. Fox was shooting every day, we chartered a plane to Burbank to record his ADR. It turned out that Michael was an ace at ADR. He could record more lines in an hour than most actors could record in a morning. He would watch and listen to what he did on the set one time through, then produce a beautiful rerecording of the line. At this juncture, it was decided that Bob Gale and Artie would remain in LA to oversee *BTF II* sound. Harry Keramidas, our second editor, would remain in Jamestown with the cut of *BTF II*, to review the effects shots with Bob and cut them into the picture, making any necessary adjustments. I returned to Sonora, but that was short-lived. The holiday was over. We were barreling down toward completion.

Returning to Jamestown the day after ADR, the first unit started work on the train sequence. Unlike *BTF II*, where the principal actors did their portion of the action-car sequence on the stage, this time around, all the pieces or tie-in shots we needed with the real actors, or as Max Kleven called them, the "realies," would be shot on a side road by the speeding train. The shots would be very similar to the second-unit shots, only designed to be tighter in order to see the actors' faces. While doing the second-unit shots, we had worked out how to set the camera. Also, we had worked out the protocols or countdown to be ready to safely say, "Action!" For that reason, when first unit started shooting, the crew became a blend of the first and second units. Max Kleven, the stunt coordinator, and even Bruce Moriarty stuck around to help the first unit set up the shots and do them safely.

In the excitement of trying to get a difficult shot, safety was my primary concern. In the heat of battle, I felt that the question of safety had to be asked over and over again. I think I became an annoyance as I kept asking Max or the stuntmen if the setup was safe for Michael, Chris Lloyd, and Mary Steenburgen (Doc's love interest) to perform. The cast was game, but certainly not very experienced in the world of stunts. I continually reminded them not to be fearful of stepping forward if they had a concern with a shot. With an actor on horseback riding next to a moving train, it would not take much for things to go wrong and for someone to get hurt. I found myself pacing on the sidelines in constant fear. There is no doubt that the first unit brought a different presence and pressure to the set than we had on second unit, which I think heightened my anxiety.

The next weekend, work circled back to *BTF II*. We flew down to conduct a preview of the film. What could we learn? More importantly, what could we change with the time remaining? As it turned out, the biggest disappointment the audience had with the film was the ending. I suppose, if they had watched a film of the original 150-page script that Bob Gale turned in a year or so ago, they would have been thrilled, although the movie would have been three-plus hours long! I think the audience was disappointed that they would have to wait six months for *BTF III*. But that ship had sailed, and as far as we were concerned, so had the film. We were now rapidly heading toward completion. In fact, we had only 3½ weeks before the premiere!

BACK IN SONORA, every day was filled with shooting on *BTF III*, followed by a review of ILM shots and any last editorial changes on *BTF II*. At the same time, the sound mix was beginning in LA, and Bob Z. was needed on the dubbing stage. The only way to be in both places on the same day was to charter a plane. After a long day of shooting, with our ears filled with sunbaked dirt, we went to the local airstrip and headed to the Burbank airport. From there, we went straight to the mix stage to clear out the dirt and fill our ears with sound. Plopping down in a seat in the Hitchcock Theater on the Universal lot, I felt more like going to sleep than listening to a playback of the sound mix for the film. There would be no sleeping on the mix stage, though. *BTF II* was a really loud film. It appeared to be even louder when the sounds were not mixed properly. It is very difficult to second-guess the director's choices for how to mix the dialogue, music, and effects and create the desired balance. I had found that to be true on all the *Amazing Stories* shows that I mixed. When in doubt, the mixers tend to turn up the volume on all the tracks, making the competing sounds inaudible. After a long day of shooting, the sound was almost unbearable. It attacked your senses. Back to the beginning we went. Bob would explain his philosophy of the upcoming scenes, and then foot by foot, scene by scene, we inched our way through the mix. It quickly became apparent that Bob would have to be there for the entire mix. Every day. After a long night of mixing, we would head to the Universal Sheraton, get some sleep, then fly back to set early in the morning. God forbid that there were any flight restrictions, or the set would have been without their director. Both ends of the flight needed Bob. He seemed to have boundless energy for both jobs. Shooting and mixing. He would often prepare for his upcoming shooting day on the early morning flights north, so there was little small talk. In fact, I often fell asleep.

As the week progressed, I stayed behind in LA, running around town doing my work, then caught up with Bob on the mixing stage the next night. Just like on *Roger*, when I traveled back and forth from LA to Marin, I went where I thought my supervision was needed most. With Bob Z. it was the same. Bob would ask me to prioritize what he needed to accomplish each day in order to finish *BTF II*. He relied on me to tell him the most important things on the agenda, since he had so little time to spare while shooting. I knew when we signed on for the back-to-back movie idea, that we would have this conflict. But living through it was more trying than I thought. Night after night, back and forth, back and forth.

YOU KNOW you are getting toward the end when the main title and end credits need to be finalized. There is no reason this should be put off to the very end, but I have often found that to be the case. There are so many legal requirements surrounding the credits. As the weeks went by, I would receive draft after draft of updated credits, while credit administration and business affairs at the studio pored over the contracts. Whether it was for companies that we had product placement ties with, music publishing, or whatever, it seemed that only the deadline could finally put a stop to the endless tinkering. Pacific Title and Optical Company was the go-to place for title work. I had first worked at Pacific Title during my days in the editing room on the *Star Wars* films, then on *Roger Rabbit*. I knew the gang and felt comfortable working with them and making decisions. They were preparing to shoot their first pass at the titles.

In those days the titles were prepared on a long scroll, which was photographed by the optical camera as it rolled by the lens. Before the shooting of the credits begins, type is selected and set, then the speed of the roll is figured out. Once the timing is set, it doesn't change, since the music is scored to a very specific length. I carefully reviewed the credits on paper over and over again. Having an error in the end credits was simply terrible. All the crew members, when viewing the film with their friends and family, would sit through the intolerably long credits, waiting for their name to show up. If it was misspelled, I felt awful. If the name was not there, it would be a disaster. I relied on many others to review the credits with me. Joan Bradshaw, the production manager, looked over the credits for the crew. The heads of every department reviewed the names. Different divisions at the studio took a look. Changes were made. That was the purpose of the first pass: try to make your final corrections and get everything right. The names that appear in the credits are not necessarily at the producer's discretion. In other words, you cannot give a credit to whomever you wish. In fact, it is a negotiation with the studio. Do they allow drivers? How many electricians? How many on the visual-effects crew? Each studio has their rules. Cast credits are always done in advance. A lot of horse trading goes on. When Title Administration at the studio gives their blessing, you are approved to go.

I remember my first on-screen credit was as an assistant editor on *The Empire Strikes Back*. I felt really proud, almost nervous waiting for my name to appear. I never received credit in my two years as an electrician. Nor did I on *More American Graffiti*. After *Return of the Jedi*, my second film as an assistant editor, the producer, Howard Kazanjian, gave me a gift. He cut the frame from the 70mm print that had my name in the end credits and had it set in a small block of clear resin, so my credit frame was displayed inside. I was so touched. I knew how important a crew member's credit could be.

I came to the mixing stage with the roll of credits to review. I waited for a break. I thought this would be the last thing that the two Bobs and Neil would want to look at. But timing is everything. In the entry hallway leading onto the dubbing stage, I unrolled the entire credit roll, 10 or 12 feet long, and they looked at every credit, reading them aloud, and making subtle changes or asking questions. I got what I needed. I was now ready to go. Even under the pressure of finishing our work on all fronts, *BTF II* did not seem compromised. The effects were done, the sound was done. It was time to let the lab take over. The baby was about to be born.

With the mix in the bag, Bob Z. flew back to wrap filming at the Jamestown location. I found myself at the lab, just like on *Roger*, stepping in for Dean Cundey, who was still shooting. Ken Ralston and I timed the film, and I stayed on to approve all the elements needed to get the film into release-print production. I knew the guys well and stayed around day and night to meet their deadlines. I was amazed at how many prints of the film could be made in a short amount of time. They never wanted to tell the customer the volume of printing they were capable of. I think they kept it a secret so the customer wouldn't dally and push them to their limit. The lab was up against the wall and cranked out the prints in a hurry. I longed to be on the set and not worrying about finishing *BTF II*. How nice it would have been to just be filming *BTF III* with no other pressures. After *Roger* and *BTF II*, I was beginning to think this was how movies get made: under extreme pressure, without enough money, and always out of time. With that in mind, following the wrap of the Jamestown portion of the film, the company returned to Burbank for the world premiere of *Back to the Future II* at the Cineplex Odeon at Universal City.

At least we had Thanksgiving weekend off while *BTF II* hit the theaters. We were buoyed by the fact the film was doing good business. The following Monday we were off to shoot in Monument Valley. What is a real Western, after all, without the iconic landscape of Monument Valley, made so indelible by director John Ford? A few weeks earlier, while still shooting in Sonora, we had made a short trip to Monument Valley. On that first trip, the second unit had prepared the shots where Marty McFly is chased by Native Americans in his DeLorean. It turned out to be more difficult than

Back to the Future III

planned. We all arrived at the location at the crack of dawn and wondered what was going on. Dave Beanes, our unit manager and Paul Pav, our location manager, were negotiating with the Native Americans, who were extras on the film. They were not happy with their pay and were ready to walk or ride off. At least those who could. Many of the Native Americans were not good riders. Paul thought that his job was tough enough simply getting permission to shoot in historic Monument Valley. Now he had to deal with the unhappy extras. They were offered a small bump in their pay, and we were good to go again.

On our second trip, after the release of *BTF II*, we spent a glorious week shooting and simply appreciating the Monument Valley setting. I was even able to take a guided tour of the sacred sites in the park's surrounding canyons. This trip felt like a reward for the struggle of getting the first sequel out. We were all required to stay in Kayenta, Arizona, the closest town, since Goulding's Lodge, which overlooked the park, was closed. It was during our stay in Kayenta that I first I discovered that I was not an electrician anymore.

TWICE ON *BTF III*, I realized things were different. Despite the fact I had not done any work as a studio electrician since 1978, I always considered myself part of the crew. Even in the editing room on *Roger*, I always felt like one of the team. I never took the job as an associate producer to mean that I could not roll up my sleeves and be part of the gang. It turned out I couldn't have it both ways.

The first time this hit me was during the shoot in Monument Valley. After a long day of slogging through the dirt and trying to keep warm, we all headed back to the hotel, about 25 miles away in Kayenta, Arizona. The town was part of the Navajo Nation, where it was illegal to serve alcohol. I was able to purchase a good amount of beer for the crew, which I allowed them to drink in their hotel room only. Coming back from dinner, I heard a high level of partying going on in one of the rooms. It is not uncommon for one of the crew members to convert their room into a "grip lounge," where the crew, mostly guys, would drink and relax. You don't want to try to sleep next door to the grip lounge. I wandered down the hall to say a quick hello.

Before knocking on the door, I was excited by what I could hear: Everyone was having fun and letting off some steam. I knocked and entered the room. Slowly, but not that slowly, the lively conversations became quieter. Some stopped entirely. Michael J. Fox was there, but he was always ready to have a beer with the guys, so he fit right in. But with me, it was a bit different. It was like I was putting people on alert. I felt very self-conscious, knowing what was going on before I entered and knowing I had spoiled the spontaneity of the party. I stuck around for a short while. It was fine, and folks were welcoming, but I knew that things were different when I was in there. Even though I got along well with the crew, they could not quite be themselves with me around. It was a real slap in the face. Since when was I not welcome to the party, a guy who had always hung out and had a beer and played a few rounds of cards with anyone? Not that night. Hanging out with the boss changes things, no matter who you are. Now I was a producer, albeit an associate producer, and even though I did not see myself as different, some folks could not get past that. This was a new reality I had to begrudgingly accept. For better or for worse, I had to leave my past behind me.

Soon after we returned from Monument Valley, I was reminded of my place once again. We were on location at the Malibu Ranch. We were shooting a scene where Marty McFly, having narrowly escaped a grizzly bear, scrambles up and over the top of a hill and trips and rolls down the other side toward the camera. The cameraman called for a light to be brought up the hillside to add some fill light to the scene. Electric cable needed to be pulled across the open scrub-filled dirt to feed juice to the light. Seeing only a few electricians around, I jumped in and started to lend a hand. A couple of the guys waved me off, even though I knew what I was doing. I wasn't really thinking, just pitching in to help. That was the wrong thing to do.

First and foremost, it reflected badly on the electrical department, because it pointed to the fact that the guys were not around where they were needed. That really did not dawn on me when I impulsively reached in to help. Back in the day, that is, my days as an electrician, when the cameraman or gaffer was lighting the set, I always hung around the camera, since that was where the most pressing work was going on. There were probably numerous good reasons, like preparing for the next shot, why the electricians were busy elsewhere, but to have a producer point that out was not a good thing. And that's what my impulsive desire to help inadvertently did. That was definitely not my intention. It did not even cross my mind until the cable I had my hands on was jerked away by one of my former mates. They clearly told me that they could handle it. When I said I didn't mind, I used to be a juicer, it got a laugh, but the sentiment remained the same: Lay off. So I did. After they finished lighting, I joked around with the guys a bit, and there were clearly no bad feelings. But a line was revealed that I could not cross. You do what you do, and we'll do what we do. I stood back and waited around the camera for the next order to be barked at me that clearly did not have to do with lighting.

When we finally wrapped principal photography on *Part III*,

Steve Starkey

post production seemed like a breeze. We only had one show to work on. What a relief! Finish cutting. Check music and sound. Watch the visual-effects shots as they came into the editing room. Screen the film for family and friends. Recut. Record the music with laughs and no pressure. What a joy it was. I was even able to take a trip up to ILM to witness Ken Ralston and the crew crash a large-scale miniature train into a ravine. Ken had so many cameras shooting the shot, he even put me on as an operator. After shooting and finishing these two films back-to-back, it felt like we could do anything. The journey on the two sequels to *BTF* added up to about the same amount of time I spent on *Roger Rabbit*: a year and a half. I put everything I knew to the test and had passed. When the one sheets came out—the posters advertising the film—Bob Z. and Bob G. had a surprise for me. While the billing block is usually reserved for the most prominent players on the film, they had fabricated a poster with my name included. This was the first time I saw my name in big, bold print along with the other producers on the film. I felt honored and grateful that they had tipped their hats to my contributions on the film.

Strangely, though, here I was, an associate producer with three films under my belt working with Bob Zemeckis, and I was about to be unemployed. Now what? I decided to go in and meet with Bob. I wanted to thank him for having me along for the ride. He announced that he was planning to take a year off. He wondered out loud to me whether this was a problem. He was curious about what I would do. His taking a break was not a problem for me. I was happy to know that he considered me part of the team and was letting me in on his immediate plans. After all, we had just worked together for three years, almost every day. We parted ways with great experiences behind us and promised to keep in touch.

Back to the Future III

Before taking off, I also stopped in to see Kathy and Frank at Amblin. I was not interested in looking around Hollywood for work. I liked working with Bob and the Amblin family. I felt confident there would be plenty of work around the place, but now was time for a break without thinking about the future. As it turned out, our paths would cross sooner than I thought.

CHAPTER 16

Jurassic Park

THERE IS NOTHING like going on an extended holiday when you have a job prospect waiting for you on the return. One less thing to worry about. That was not the case with me after the *Back to the Future* sequels. I was unemployed. Somehow I thought my prospects were good, even though Bob Zemeckis had told me he was taking a year off. I felt that something would turn up. With that in mind, Liv and I took a vacation to Galiano Island, part of the Gulf Island chain in British Columbia, Canada. Kathy Kennedy's twin sister, Connie, had just opened an inn on the Island, so it was a perfect opportunity for a visit. We were happily surprised to be joined by Kathy and Frank Marshall.

Soon after our arrival, Kathy asked if I wanted to read galleys of a book called *Jurassic Park*, by Michael Crichton. Kathy was never on vacation from work. She was careful not to presume the same was true for me. I took the book and read it quickly. It was gripping and a page-turner. I told her that I could see the movie in the book. She said if all went well, Steven Spielberg was considering directing the film. She and Frank had already hired a small group of artists to do conceptual artwork, based on the images described in the book. Michael Crichton was taking a crack at the screenplay. Kathy said there were a few other projects starting up as well and suggested that when I finished my summer holiday, I should come to Amblin and check in with her and Frank. She felt sure there would be a job for me on one project or another at the company.

We already had plans to go to Telluride, both for the film festival and to visit Liv's sister Miki over the Labor Day weekend. When I mentioned my plans to end the summer at the film festival, Frank and Kathy decided to join us there. It would be their first time in Telluride. I loved the Telluride Film Festival. No awards, just great films to watch. Word of mouth told you which films to see. Coincidentally, one of the curators of the festival was Tom Luddy, whom I knew from my Berkeley days, when he was director of the Pacific Film Archive. Tom brought the same breadth of knowledge and love of movies to the festival that he had brought to the film archive. The only problem was that it was hard to tear yourself away from hiking and fishing to go inside and watch a film. I had to stay on in Telluride so I could get in my days in the great outdoors!

IN SEPTEMBER, when my summer vacation came to an end, I flew down from Marin County to meet Frank and Kathy and see what projects were starting up at Amblin. Kathy took me to a meeting on a project called *Hook*, a sequel of sorts to *Peter Pan*, to be directed by Spielberg. The project was currently in preproduction. The production meeting was about Tinker Bell. Could they shoot live action, as was done on the film *Darby O'Gill and the Little People?* Would it be best to shoot the actress against a blue screen then composite her into the live action? As the meeting went on, I found myself losing interest in their Tinker Bell problem. After the meeting, I told Kathy that I wasn't sure about *Hook*. She then took me over to visit the art department that was in the middle of doing conceptual artwork on *Jurassic Park*. As I said, I had read and liked the book, so I was already intrigued. I wandered through the art department and was amazed by the paintings that production designer Rick Carter and his team of artists had done. I told Kathy and Frank that this project looked like a lot more fun to me. What did they want me to do?

They wanted me to put together a budget and a production plan based on the first-draft screenplay by Michael Crichton, which closely followed the book. Now this was the challenge I was looking for. I had not mounted a movie from the ground up before. "When do you need it?" "If you are ready, we would like you to start right away." I was well rested and ready. I met with Rick and began to familiarize myself with his illustrations and the look of the show. He was well under way preparing renderings of key scenes from the book, mostly of the dinosaurs in their natural settings. I started to live and breathe dinosaurs along with Rick and his artists.

Rick and I knew each other well from working together on *Amazing Stories* and the two sequels to *Back to the Future*. We had a lot in common; we were both children of the sixties, in love with the Beatles, and graduates of UC Berkeley. That spin on life tightened our bond with one another. We started by breaking down the script together, trying to figure out what needed to be done on location and what we would have to shoot on stage. When the dinosaurs were in the scene, you really wanted to shoot as much as possible on stage, in order to better manage the large-scale puppets. But you always try to mix it up, blending stage and location work, so it feels like you are in a real place. This sleight of hand keeps the audience suspending their disbelief. It certainly would come into play with the dinosaurs.

While completely absorbed in the design of the movie, I couldn't lose sight of the dinosaurs. They were the real driving force behind what I needed to figure out in order to shoot the film. What method would we use to bring the dinosaurs to life? Would they be full-scale mechanical puppets, stop motion, or a new form of visual effects? I really needed to get to the bottom of it. Rick told me that there were plans, apparently at Steven's request, to have the brilliant team at Disney Imagineering build a full-scale animatronic T-Rex. I shook my head in disbelief. Really? It may be great for a theme park, but for a movie? It seemed so impractical. We would have to have one huge sound stage to accommodate that beast. I wondered how the hell it would work. I imagined that Steven wanted to have the giant T-Rex in the same frame as his actors, bringing a profound sense of awe and terror to the scenes. I must admit, that would be something to see on film. But there had to be another option. For the moment, since I hadn't explored any other alternatives, the folks at Disney Imagineering continued to move forward, and I turned my focus to all the other dinosaurs in the story.

I started my dinosaur exploration by going to the major creature shops in town. I knew that some of the dinosaurs would be full-size puppets. I quickly narrowed the field down to Rob Bottin and Stan Winston. I knew of Rob's work from *Total Recall* and *RoboCop*. Stan had done great work on *Aliens*, *Predator*, and *The Terminator*. I visited both creature shops and asked them to prepare a breakdown and budget for doing the film. Their breakdown would not only include which dinosaurs they would be building full scale, but how much articulation each creature would have, and what the on-set puppeteering manpower involved, including a fix-it or maintenance crew in case of a breakdown. Next I contacted Michael Lantieri, who had done such wonderful work on the *BTF* films. In addition to handling the myriad physical effects, he would supplement and support the puppeteering of the creatures in whatever way was necessary. He could also consult with me on who to hire to build the puppets.

I next went to Northern California to consult with Dennis Muren at ILM and Phil Tippett. I knew them both from my assistant editing days on the *Star Wars* films and my work at ILM on both *Roger Rabbit* and *BTF*. Techniques were evolving quickly, but I had to commit to a plan and budget accordingly. Dennis was to Steven what Ken Ralston was to Bob Z.: He was Steven's go-to visual-effects wizard. After Steven had tipped him off about *Jurassic Park*, Dennis had been experimenting on some groundbreaking techniques that might unlock how the dinosaurs could be pulled off, but it was in a research-and-development phase. I then met with Phil, the stop-motion guru. This was right up Phil's alley. His stop-motion work on the *Star Wars* films was brilliant, and he knew what he could do effectively. I knew I would use Phil, so I asked him to break out which shots he could or should do, and which shots should be puppeteered with full-scale creatures.

After talking it over with Dennis, Phil, and Michael, I decided to go with Stan Winston to build the full-scale dinosaurs. They would appear lifelike on screen, with all the mechanics for articulating the puppets built into the creatures. Michael would be in charge of on-set physical and mechanical effects. Phil would do all the stop-motion animation. Dennis would be in charge of blending all the techniques together as well as overseeing all the visual effects on the show. I now had my group of experts who could guide me in putting a plan into place.

All this research and figuring out of groundbreaking new imagery was in my wheelhouse. After mixing cartoons with live action, flying cars, and Tondreau shots, I was used to this. I knew how to methodically figure out the unknown. But now I was about to enter foreign territory. I had to figure out a shooting schedule and prepare a budget.

I had never scheduled or budgeted a show from scratch. I really was not familiar with Movie Magic, the budgeting-and-scheduling program that was in use throughout the industry. But I would learn. I started by carefully scheduling the days that involved the logistics of shooting with the dinosaurs. No one really knew how much time we would need to get through a day with dinosaurs, so my best guess from my recent experiences on effects shows would have to do. The other days were fairly straightforward. When I needed help, I knew a lot of people to call. Amblin had a great accounting staff, headed by Bonnie Radford. She assigned one of her accountants to work with me, but she was always willing to pitch in and keep us on track. Department by department, we built up a crew and budget, backing into my prep and shooting schedules.

Amblin had templates for many of their shows and, more specifically, for Spielberg-directed shows. We could plug in numbers that corresponded to his usual crew. In production, how much prep do you give the production coordinator and assistant directors? The accountants knew. How many costumers should I have in the wardrobe department? What kind of allowance should I give for prop purchases? They knew. Electric and grip crew and rigging, I knew. I knew camera as well. That is how we went through the budget. We shared information and plowed through it.

Post production was relatively straightforward. Steven always used the same editor, Michael Kahn. Michael cut quickly. His crew was minimal. John Williams would be the composer. We had many films to draw on for that budget information. I felt like I came up with a good, honest approach. Though this was my first time building a plan from scratch, it was starting to make some sense. Another unknown was the prep for the creatures. I would have to rely on

Stan Winston for that. There would be a preprep period with mostly Stan's crew before official prep began. He said it would take him about six months of lead time. In addition to Stan, a minimal art department and I would be the only people working for the first six months. We would also start casting. Then prep would begin, with departments and their crew coming on week after week as needed.

WHEN I COMPLETED the budget and overall plan, Rick Carter and I presented my work to Frank, Kathy, and Steven in the conference room at Amblin. Steven flipped to the last page of the budget and saw the number: $88 million. Steven looked up and said there was no way he was going to do the film for $88 million. He glanced at the total shooting days. Wow! He became a bit alarmed and wondered out loud how the budget had gotten so high. Then he perused it more carefully, stopping at the big line items. He noticed that $2 million had been put in for the construction of a full-scale T-Rex, not to mention the time and manpower for it on the set.

"Who put that in?" I didn't respond. I figured that he knew that had been the plan, but he asked anyway. Who was going to be the first to speak? Kathy didn't say a word. Rick was silent. Finally, I said, "I don't know. If you don't want it, we'll take it out." "Take it out. Whatever it takes, I want the number to be no more than $59 million." Steven was on a roll, and he was serious. I didn't have any idea of a target number going in; I just budgeted the script. Sometimes you must hang it out there to find out what the filmmaker, or in this case, Steven really wanted. The group started poking holes in the budget, but most of the suggestions would only trim it a bit here and there. The cuts would not get close to where Steven wanted it to be. I said the only way to really hit the number was to cut down the script. Steven said fine, cut down the script. Back in whatever scenes and creatures I can afford for $59 million. Not a penny more. Steven got up and left the room, onto his next meeting. I looked around the room. I knew what I had to do. A lot of cutting.

I was about to enter foreign territory. Tampering with a screenplay. Scripts were sacred to me. They were the Bible. That's what gave you guidance and provided all the answers. I was about to throw it up in the air, paste it back together, and back it into a number. What a crazy business. I retreated to my office in the Movies While You Wait Building, as it was called, in the Amblin complex. I was staring at the wall when Rick Carter joined me. "Another insurmountable opportunity." "Rick, you're right. Here is the good news. Steven cut out the $2 million T-Rex, so we are moving in the right direction." In all seriousness, we knew what needed to be done. Big set pieces had to go. Creatures needed to go. Scenes needed to be cut. Trims would not get us there. I remember a few times seeing 3x5 cards pinned up on a corkboard in a writer's office. We even had them for continuity in the editing room on the *Star Wars* films. I decided the best way to start the process was to write out each scene on a 3x5 card and pin them up on the wall next to my desk. Rick was already bubbling with ideas, but I wanted to be methodical. Just focusing on the cards allowed me to see the patterns and repetitions of the scenes. All these scenes made for good reading in the book, but the movie needed to be streamlined, budget cutting or not.

Each scene was scrutinized. Did the group taking their initial tour of the island really need to go to the river valley where they gaze at creatures who do not do anything or ever return to the story? The scene was eye candy. There would be plenty of dinosaurs to gawk at. If we cut the scene entirely, a set piece would be eliminated, thereby cutting the art department budget, which included a big construction cost. Creatures would be cut, so the Stan Winston budget would go down, along with some overlap with Phil Tippett and ILM. Shooting days would be lost. Stage costs would go down. The savings would be in the millions, not the hundreds of thousands. These were the kinds of cuts we needed to make. Every scene was put under the microscope. How many times do we need to be scared by the velociraptors? Maybe we didn't need as many velociraptors. On and on it went. While cutting scenes, I had to make sure the story still flowed logically and made good sense. I could not make cuts that left the screenplay confusing. Big set pieces needed to stay; spectacle was important, but less would be more.

At this stage, I was offered more help. Lata Ryan, a wonderful production coordinator from my *Back to the Future* days, started to work alongside me. She had worked under Joan Bradshaw and had learned a tremendous amount about production. She was a great sounding board and full of good ideas. She often made better assumptions about the reality of the shooting days than I did. She was also more facile on Movie Magic than I was and could relieve me of that burden. Colin Wilson had shown up on Amblin's doorstep from England. I knew him as an assistant editor in London on *Roger Rabbit*. He had acquired a massive amount of experience on big visual-effects shows. He wanted to spread his wings and move into production. He took quite a bit of the visual-effects workload off me as we moved ahead on the new budget.

I contacted Disney Imagineering and told them that their full-scale T-Rex was not going to be built. While disappointed, they understood. I contacted Dennis Muren, Phil Tippett, and Stan Winston to tell them that big cuts were under way. As we removed scenes and creatures, I would sit with the accountant to try to keep a running tally of how I was doing. All the numbers were coming down. I paid a visit to Stan Winston and told him what we were up against. I needed to save money at his shop, but not just by cutting out the puppets he was building. The overall costs in his first budget needed to come down. His initial budget was $15 million. I wanted it to be closer to $9 million. Surprisingly, despite the fact I had not cut enough of his workload to cut $6 million from his budget, he said it wouldn't be a problem. Really? I was surprised. "How do we make up the difference? I still need most of what you were planning to build." He then said to me frankly, "Steve, I can make an entire film for $9 million. If that is all you have to spend, I will make it work. We will back our work into your number, and you will not see the difference in quality." That was what I needed to hear. That was the approach I needed to take on the show. It gave me more confidence to move forward and make drastic cuts. Make the show great but back the show into the money I had to spend.

I did not just need to make dollar-for-dollar cuts, but the overall approach had to be simplified. Don't just cut the number of costumes, make the costumes for less money. I scheduled fewer shooting days and not just because we had cut scenes. The company would have to move more quickly on the scenes that remained. This overall approach was cutting money. I really had no idea if the plan would work, but I had no choice. ILM was more stubborn about budget reductions, but I simply told them they had less money to work with. The same with Phil Tippett. They complained that the workload was still enormous. I responded that if we can't do it for less, Steven won't make the movie. I believed that to be true. And they all started to believe it.

Finally, I had the number. Just what Steven wanted. Strangely, since I had the first-pass budget in place, reducing it and simplifying it was much easier and faster than the first go-round. I decided to write out the new story line, much like a treatment. I knew the story inside and out, having stared at my 3x5 cards every day for weeks. I planned to include my "pitch" of the new story in a packet with the budget and shooting schedule. We set the meeting.

The same group was present. Steven sat at the head of the table. I presented him with the treatment and the budget. The treatment was three typed pages long. He picked it up and started to read. He read the whole thing out loud, word for word. I wanted to crawl under the table. I had thought this was just going to be a discussion where I covered the highlights of the story and budget. Then everyone would go their separate ways, study the treatment, review the budget, and get back to me. That was not the case. He finished reading and set the treatment down then he picked up the budget. "What's the number?" "$59 million." He set the budget down and said, "I'll make it." That was it. Steven gave the green light to move forward on *Jurassic Park*. I couldn't believe it. Just like that, he was going to make the movie.

Before I could sit back and absorb what had just happened, Steven asked how long it would be before prep could begin in earnest. I told him that Stan Winston would need approximately six months to start building the creatures before prep would begin on the film. This time frame fit perfectly into Steven's moviemaking schedule. He would finish *Hook* then go right into *Jurassic Park*. But what would I be doing in the meantime? As it turned out, Frank had the answer to that.

CHAPTER 17

Noises Off

FRANK MARSHALL AND KATHY KENNEDY presented me with a plan. They thought it would be great if I would stay on and oversee the preprep on *Jurassic Park* since I knew the show inside and out. Mostly this would involve keeping tabs on Stan Winston and the early work at ILM. In addition, I could start contacting the crew and give them a heads-up about when the show would begin official prep. Since my work would not take up much time at all, Frank proposed that I join him as co-producer on a little movie that he was producing, until *Jurassic* kicked in full time. I jumped at the chance to work with Frank. The picture was called *Noises Off*, and it was based on the very successful stage play written by Michael Frayn. I knew nothing about the play, but as it turned out, a local production was running at a small theater in Glendale. The carefully crafted timing of the miscues and missteps in this very English farce were remarkable and done to a wonderful comedic effect. I had no idea how it would be made into a movie. That would be left up to the director of the film, Peter Bogdanovich.

Some know Peter Bogdanovich because of his classic film, *The Last Picture Show*, or quite possibly, *What's Up, Doc?* or *Paper Moon*. Many others know Peter from his relationship with the model and actress Dorothy Stratten, who was murdered by her estranged boyfriend while carrying on an affair with Bogdanovich. Frank and

Peter had become friends over the years and were still trying to resurrect an unfinished film by Orson Welles called *The Other Side of the Wind*. I really wasn't sure what I was walking into: working with a talented, yet eccentric movie director or a man with a storied life. Frank told me that he could not simply hire me as the co-producer of the film. I would first have to interview with Peter to gain his approval. Peter did not trust anyone, not even a friend of Frank's. Frank warned me that when I met Peter, I would probably also be under the scrutiny of his young wife, L.B. Stratten, Dorothy's sister, who was 22 years old at the time and recently married to Peter. The meeting alone would almost be worth the experience.

I drove up into Bel Air, just above Sunset Boulevard near UCLA. A circular driveway led me to the front door of a single-story Spanish-style home. I understood that Peter had previously owned a mansion in Bel Air that he had been forced to sell. He still had this home in the less glamorous part of his old neighborhood. He was trying to resuscitate his career, and Frank appeared to be lending him a hand.

Peter greeted me at the door and ushered me into the library. He was dressed in a casual way but with a suit coat and a neckerchief. The house was cold. L.B. was cuddled up in a lounge chair but quietly rose to greet me as I entered the room. Peter acted a bit befuddled, as if he were in the middle of some important business that he needed to clear from his mind before settling down to speak with me. Letting out a big breath, he was ready. "Tell me about yourself." I told him that I had gone to school at UC Berkeley. He wanted more. I said that I received a degree in the Humanities, an interdisciplinary program overseen by two professors, Alain Renoir and Jim Larson. Alain's name caught Peter's attention. "I am good friends of the Renoir family and know Alain quite well."

I should not have been surprised. In addition to directing many films, Peter was a film historian and film scholar and, as a journalist, had interviewed and written articles and books about many filmmakers. He quite possibly knew or had interviewed Alain's father, Jean Renoir, the director of such classic French films as *Grand Illusion* and *The Rules of the Game*. We exchanged stories about Alain. I told him that Alain had warned me to steer clear of a career in film, assuring me that I would find fulfillment in studying the classics. He said he was terribly bored on the set of *The Rules of the Game*. That got a laugh from Peter. L.B. smiled but remained silent. Then we glossed over my career as an electrician, my editing-room experiences, and more recently my work at Amblin as an associate producer in both television and film. I think we could have spoken for hours, mostly about Peter's experiences, but he seemed satisfied, and we parted amiably.

I came back to Frank and filled him in. I think that Frank was as nervous about what I thought of Peter as he was of my gaining Peter's approval. It turned out that Peter enjoyed our meeting and gave me a very positive assessment. I attributed his reaction to the fact I knew Alain Renoir. My life for the next six months was set. Looking after *Jurassic Park* and working on *Noises Off*.

THE NUMBER I was given for the budget was minuscule compared to *Jurassic Park*. It had to be. Disney, the studio making the film, would have little appetite for extravagance on a film of this type. In many ways, this would be a very simple show. The whole play took place on the front and back of one theater set. I told Frank that I would love to bring on Joan Bradshaw, who had worked as the production manager on the *Back to the Future* films, to work alongside of me. He cleared my choice with Peter, and we set to work on our very modest budget. Everyone who worked on the show needed to have Peter's approval. Peter mentioned that he would like to have Norm Newberry come on as his production designer. Peter trusted Norm and respected his work since they had worked together on *Mask*. Having Norm was a godsend. He was able to figure out how to efficiently make use of only one set and fit it on a single soundstage. By occupying only one stage, the minuscule budget seemed within reach.

Peter wanted Lázló Kovács, also from *Mask*, to shoot the film, but he was not available. He would have been too expensive for our show in any case. We instead hired Tim Suhrstedt, who was well suited to the work at hand. Maybe Peter approved of him because he had worked with Orson Welles on a small TV show. Or possibly because of his recent work on *Mystic Pizza*. I don't know. Mike Fenton, Amblin's go-to casting director, put together a wonderful cast. Once they nailed down Michael Caine and Carol Burnett, the remainder of the cast quickly fell into place. This cast was memorable for the fact they all worked and got along so well with one another. This was key to having a smooth production since they worked together every day. They were also friendly with the production staff.

I recall going to baseball games with Christopher Reeve and Michael Caine (Caine was a big baseball fan) and playing tennis with Chris Reeve. Chris brought along his tennis coach who stood on the court as we played a few sets. I still got the better of him. We also had dinners with Chris, Julie Hagerty, and Mark Linn-Baker a few times. Carol Burnett even asked me if I was single. Not for her but for her daughter, who must have been around my age. All in all, it was good fun.

When rehearsals began, Peter closed the set. No one was allowed in. This went on for three weeks. We just sat around and waited nervously. Eventually he let the script supervisor watch the rehearsals. Then his director of photography. Followed by Jerry Ketcham, his first assistant director. Finally, he let us all see if our production plan was going to work. Peter called Frank and me into a meeting and said he was having trouble blocking the scenes. He could not figure out how to film the carefully timed action in the front of the stage and backstage at the same time, while keeping up the breakneck intensity and farcical humor. He wanted help. He wondered if we could bring in the original Broadway stage director, Michael Blakemore, to help him block the play for the camera. Michael was flattered and happy to come out and help on the film. From that point on, everything went smoothly. Shooting was quick. In fact, we did so many camera setups each day, that one day, as each camera setup was completed, we rang a bell and had a "model" parade onto the set, holding up a card displaying the shot number, which served to keep the crew motivated and having some fun. The actors all worked as if they were doing a play. They had the whole play and script in their heads, so they could do any part of the shooting at any time. That could only work with seasoned actors.

While dabbling on *Jurassic Park* and having fun on *Noises Off*, I got a call from Bob Zemeckis. He asked if I were available for lunch. His hiatus from *Back to the Future* was over.

CHAPTER 18

A Meeting with Bob

LIVING UP TO his word, Bob Zemeckis had taken a year off since *Back to the Future III*. Knowing Bob as I do today, I can't believe he was able to take that long a break. He needs to be creating every day of his life. He needs film to pulse through his veins. He must have been going crazy. I was excited to have lunch with him and catch up. It was an easy stroll from the stage down the hill to Bob's office, which was in a rather drab, gray complex of offices for writers and producers. He was across the street from our old *Amazing Stories* offices and next door to the Amblin editing suites. The interior was simple, not really reflecting Bob's personality at all. I sat at a small round table with Bob and caught him up on my working life. While consulting on the preprep of *Jurassic Park*, I told him I was co-producing *Noises Off* with Frank Marshall, who was producing the show. Peter Bogdanovich was directing, and we were shooting just up the hill on Stage 37.

The conversation switched to Bob. He told me he had found a script that he was thinking of directing, and he would like me to produce the film. I can't recall if I was speechless but, knowing me, not for long. I had worked for so long to get to this place, and then it happened just like that. How many are as lucky as I was at that moment? I guess, at some point, you have to be if you are to become a film producer. During our time working together, Bob described to me the difference between good luck and pure luck. Pure luck is when a lottery ticket falls from the sky, lands on your front porch, you pick it up, and it's the million-dollar winner. You didn't even take the initiative to go out and buy the ticket. That is pure luck.

That was not the case for me. I think I was fully prepared and ready to become a film producer, and then came that fortunate turn of events—an offer from Bob. After a lot of hard work, and with a little bit of good luck, everything fell into place. I received that little bit of help to take me to the next level. I had worked on three pictures with Bob as an associate producer, and very closely with him at that. He knew what I was capable of. And we got along famously. We even drank the same whiskey and enjoyed drinking it together. In my case, this opportunity did not fall from the sky. I got my break after completing a rather unusual film education with a bit of good luck.

Bob pushed the script for *Death Becomes Her* toward me. He said he would like me to read it and let him know if it was something I might be interested in. "Do I have to read it?" I asked. Was it even possible that I would read it and say no? Bob Zemeckis was asking me to produce a movie with him, and it wasn't a dream. I did not hesitate. I told him that of course I would do it. I guess I should not have been so indiscriminate and at least have said I would read it and get back to him, but it was too late for that. I am sure he knew there was not a chance I would turn him down.

But now I had to come clean. I said that I had a bit of a problem. I had been working on *Jurassic Park* with Steven Spielberg since its inception. I was still overseeing the preprep of the show, so I was not sure how I could gracefully extricate myself from the project. I had a tremendous amount of respect for Steven and did not want

A Meeting with Bob

to screw up my relationship with him. Bob was and is a very close friend of Steven's. He said not to worry about it, he had already told Steven that he was stealing me from him. That came as a bit of a shock. I suppose, in hindsight, I should have known that Bob would check in with Steven, Frank, and Kathy and reveal his intentions before speaking with me. This was all one big family, after all. I was still surprised, nonetheless.

I never really thought about the fact that here were these two giant filmmakers, and they both wanted me to work for them. All I was thinking about were the logistics of how this dream was going to happen without any hitches and any resentment on Steven's part. I told Bob that I really needed to speak to Steven and, of course, Frank and Kathy. There is also a little back story to my immediate decision to commit to work with Bob on the spot. As it turned out, just a few days before this meeting with Bob, there had been a production meeting for *Jurassic Park*. This was the first all-hands-on deck meeting where I thought I would bring everyone up to speed on the preprep of the movie. Kathy was there, along with producer Jerry Molen and the key department heads, or at least those who were involved up to that point. It was the launch of the official prep leading up to production.

I don't know what I was thinking, but what transpired was not it. As the meeting went on, I could see those senior to me were taking over the meeting, and those I had been supervising were now responding to a new set of producers. I felt kind of left out. Even a bit slighted. I felt as if all the work I had done was not being fully appreciated and was getting delivered on a silver platter for the big guys to handle, with me helping them out as they saw fit. Certainly not what I was expecting or hoping for. I had thought, wrongly, I guess, that I was going to be an equal of some sort. But the writing was on the wall. So I left the meeting a little down but still excited about the project I had nurtured to this point and had gotten to the starting gate. I had given the project its first shape, and no one could take that away from me. Most importantly, I had gained the confidence I needed to move on to the next step. And the next step had arrived.

All this happens for a reason, as they say. It was in this context that I went to Steven with the news that Bob had offered me a producing position on his next film. I started by telling Steven that I was excited to have had the opportunity to take *Jurassic Park* to this crucial stage, but I could see that I would be one of many producing the show, and not at the level of the other producers. Working with Bob, I would be the only producer, along with him, and that this was the opportunity I was looking for. Grasping my train of thought, Steven said, "I understand completely. Take the job with Bob." Steven showed me so much consideration that day. He said that leaving his show was the right thing to do. I had been offered the opportunity of a lifetime. So that was it. I left his office with a sense of relief and excitement and more respect for Steven than I already had.

That was the end of a long, hard-traveled journey. I had made it. I was going to be the producer of a feature film, with Bob Zemeckis, no less. Suddenly, the seat felt hot. Up until that point, I had dreamed of producing a Hollywood film, but now that I was offered the opportunity, I did not know if I was ready to actually do it. Would I live up to the challenge of being in charge, without having those with more experience surrounding me? I had to brush aside these fears. There would be plenty of time to be terrified, but not now. That was coming. For now, I had to summon up my courage and enjoy the moment.

A Meeting with Bob

What I learned about producing is that having produced one film does not make you feel more prepared to take on the challenges of the next. Despite the fact that you may have gained some experience, each film has its own set of problems that makes it appear to be as difficult as the first. New insecurities arise on each outing with every new set of complications. These bouts with fear never leave you. Was it me, or does everyone have these same feelings? I don't know. All I do know is that I kept coming back, wanting to do it all over again. Why did I keep coming back? It started with being captivated by a new story filled with real human emotions, that had me travel inward, touching unknown regions of myself. Each story also satisfied my need to discover new places around the world. But ultimately, it gave me the opportunity to forge relationships with wonderful people, and, as a group, we were able to overcome "insurmountable opportunities" together.

Epilogue

OVER THE NEXT 28 years, I worked as a producer on the following films:

Death Becomes Her (1992)
Forrest Gump (1994)
Contact (1997)
What Lies Beneath (2000)
Cast Away (2000)
Matchstick Men (2003)
The Polar Express (2004)
The Prize Winner of Defiance, Ohio (2005)
Monster House (2006)
Beowulf (2007)
A Christmas Carol (2009)
Mars Needs Moms (2011)
Flight (2012)
The Walk (2015)
Allied (2016)
Welcome to Marwen (2018)

Acknowledgments

I learned that making a film required a village; no one person can do it alone. I had no idea that the same could be said about writing and publishing a book. Once again, just as in my filmmaking career, I was offered insights and encouragement by many friends who saw the opening chapters and told me they wanted to read more, and I wish to thank all of them: John Bell, Rick Carter, Marc Halpern, Derek Hogue, Leslie Johnson, Angel Maldonado, Lauren Miller, Dennis Muraoka, Dave Rochat, Mary Sue Tauke, Ben Waddell, and Pam Wilsey.

One person in particular, Tom Hanks, told me to make it better, as good as it can be. He made me feel that if I worked hard enough, I might wind up with something. He gave me the fortitude to rewrite and, then, rewrite again.

Peter Gethers convinced me that I had a voice and I could write with a sense of humor. I figured, if nothing else, maybe I would get a good laugh.

Others read the first draft and gave me the desire to keep going:

Jodie Ireland told me I had opened a window into a fascinating world she knew nothing about.

Michael Stinson said that his film students would be inspired by the book and that it would give them the encouragement to follow their dreams.

Henry and Karen Thorne took such joy in my stories that they made me feel the stories were worth telling.

Lis Wiehl found that the book would be appealing to those who want to break into the business, just like I did.

All of their support made me keep on, keepin' on.

I was fortunate to find an editor, Joan Tapper, who embraced my style and revealed to me a better way to write what I had intended to say!

Finally, I wish to thank the fine printer John Balkwill not only for the design of the book, but also for managing the production of the book and taking it to completion. He made everything look right.

Despite the fact that I have praised and expressed gratitude to many colleagues and filmmakers during my early days of working in film, I would feel neglectful if did not mention again my appreciation for the mentors who gifted me with their knowledge and kindness. When I pounded the streets of Los Angeles looking for a job, Ray Shackelford gave me hope and my first break as an electrician. Without that job, I would have left LA and pursued a different career. I am grateful to Jim Bloom, who gave me timely advice and opened the door to Lucasfilm. In the editing room on *Empire* and *Jedi*, I learned from Duwayne Dunham that my contribution to a film needed to be done to perfection and that my job would have an impact on the whole movie. George Lucas included me in all aspects of filmmaking, giving me confidence and respect and opening up a world of film I had not seen before. Thanks to Kathy Kennedy, Frank Marshall, and Steven Spielberg, the doors at Amblin were opened so wide that I couldn't help but step in and see what I would

Acknowledgments

find. Finally, I thank Robert Zemeckis, who gave me the chance to be a partner and producer.

I find it difficult to simply acknowledge my wife, Olivia Erschen, when she deserves much more. Her unwavering support of this book project was a constant source of encouragement. She committed hours of her time to guide me and improve upon everything I wrote. Only she does not know how lucky I am.

About the Author

Academy Award-winning producer Steve Starkey is a longtime collaborator with legendary filmmaker Robert Zemeckis. After producing *Death Becomes Her*, his first film with Zemeckis, Starkey went on to produce and win the Academy Award for Best Picture on the film *Forrest Gump*. Following the film *Contact*, Zemeckis and Starkey formed the company ImageMovers with agent Jack Rapke. The first of their distinctive films with the new company included *What Lies Beneath* and *Cast Away*. After producing *The Polar Express*, *Beowulf*, and *Monster House*, the first feature-length films using motion-capture, Zemeckis, Rapke, and Starkey launched a company at Disney, Imagemovers Digital, to make feature films using that technology. *A Christmas Carol* and *Mars Needs Moms* were made under their new banner. During this time, Starkey produced films for a number of other directors, including *Matchstick Men* with Ridley Scott and *The Prize Winner of Defiance, Ohio* with Jane Anderson. Returning to live-action filmmaking, Zemeckis and Starkey continued their collaboration on *Flight*, *The Walk*, *Allied*, and *Welcome to Marwen*.

www.ingramcontent.com/pod-product-compliance
Lightning Source LLC
Chambersburg PA
CBHW022031290426
44109CB00014B/823